Patricia Hynes' *Introducing Forced Migration* is an eclectic and extremely accessible exploration of this widely deployed but complex concept. Based on a rich variety of sources – summaries of 'key thinkers', key websites, extensive research and literature references, legal instruments, case studies – the book provides a comprehensive foundational understanding of forced migration, constituting a valuable resource for scholars, students and informed laypeople.

Roger Zetter, Professor Emeritus in Refugee Studies,
Refugee Studies Centre, University of Oxford, UK

The book is a first-rate introduction to the subject of forced migration. It not only clarifies different terms, concepts and approaches, but also provides concise discussion, backed by case studies, of the legal, social and political dimensions of the principal categories of forced migrants viz., refugees, internally displaced persons and trafficked persons. I would recommend the book to anyone wanting to understand one of the most important issues of our times.

B.S. Chimni, Distinguished Professor of International Law,
O.P. Jindal Global University, India

If you want a comprehensive resource on forced migration, *Introducing Forced Migration* is the textbook for you. Hynes offers critical definitions and policy perspectives that cover topics from the distinctions between refugees and asylum-seekers to human trafficking and displaced children. This book helpfully takes the reader through concepts and complexities of some of the most pressing migration concerns of today, including policy failures pertaining to the Rohingya and the Mediterranean 'crisis'.

Cathy Zimmerman, Professor Migration, Violence and Exploitation,
London School of Hygiene & Tropical Medicine, UK

This is a truly remarkable book that manages to introduce not only the complex issues of refugees, asylum seekers, internally displaced people, the trafficked and others under the heading of 'forced migration', but also brings in the key thinkers and writers on these subjects. It does so in a manner that is beautifully clear and accessible to students and a wider audience. The organisation of the material and the maps, graphs, photographs and other graphics are superb. Up to date, it is a brilliant introduction to one of the most pressing issues of the 21st century.

Tony Kushner, Professor, Parkes Institute, University of Southampton, UK, and author of *The Holocaust and Forced Migration*, 2017

With human stories and an appeal for social justice and human rights at its heart, this is a book that unravels complexities of definition, reveals misleading simplicity behind labels and counters popular and media-driven assumptions. It demonstrates how flawed international policy responses are based on little understanding. Essential reading for students, researchers, policy-makers and practitioners, the book critiques how the international community has responded. It signposts the need for political courage, vision and collaboration to create a context where hope can replace fear and diverse peoples can be protected from abuse, and their wellbeing enhanced in safer places.

Michael Preston-Shoot, Emeritus Professor of Social Work, University of Bedfordshire, UK

Introducing Forced Migration

At a time when global debates about the movement of people have never been more heated, this book provides readers with an accessible, student-friendly guide to the subject of forced migration.

Readers of this book will learn who forced migrants are, where they are and why international protection is critical in a world of increasingly restrictive legislation and policy. The book outlines key definitions, ideas, concepts, points for discussion, theories and case studies of the various forms of forced migration. In addition to this technical grounding, the book also signposts further reading and provides handy Key Thinker boxes to summarise the work of the field's most influential academics. Drawing on decades of experience both in the classroom and in the field, this book invites readers to question how labels and definitions are used in legal, policy and practice responses, and to engage in a richer understanding of the lives and realities of forced migrants on the ground.

Perfect for undergraduate and postgraduate teaching in courses related to migration and diaspora studies, *Introducing Forced Migration* will also be valuable to policy-makers, practitioners, journalists, volunteers and aid workers working with refugees, the internally displaced and those who have experienced trafficking.

Patricia Hynes is a Reader in Forced Migration in the School of Applied Social Studies, University of Bedfordshire, UK.

Rethinking Development

Rethinking Development offers accessible and thought-provoking overviews of contemporary topics in international development and aid. Providing original empirical and analytical insights, the books in this series push thinking in new directions by challenging current conceptualizations and developing new ones.

This is a dynamic and inspiring series for all those engaged with today's debates surrounding development issues, whether they be students, scholars, policy makers and practitioners internationally. These interdisciplinary books provide an invaluable resource for discussion in advanced undergraduate and postgraduate courses in development studies as well as in anthropology, economics, politics, geography, media studies and sociology.

Rural Development in Practice
Evolving Challenges and Opportunities
Willem van Eekelen

Using Evidence in Policy and Practice
Lessons from Africa
Edited by Ian Goldman and Mine Pabari

Southern-Led Development Finance
Solutions from the Global South
Edited by Diana Barrowclough, Kevin P. Gallagher and Richard Kozul-Wright

Introducing Forced Migration
Patricia Hynes

Mobile Technology and Social Transformations
Access to Knowledge in Global Contexts
Edited by Stefanie Felsberger and Ramesh Subramanian

For more information about this series, please visit: www.routledge.com/Rethinking-Development/book-series/RDVPT

Introducing Forced Migration

Patricia Hynes

Routledge
Taylor & Francis Group

LONDON AND NEW YORK

First published 2021
by Routledge
2 Park Square, Milton Park, Abingdon, Oxon OX14 4RN

and by Routledge
52 Vanderbilt Avenue, New York, NY 10017

Routledge is an imprint of the Taylor & Francis Group, an informa business

British Library Cataloguing-in-Publication Data
A catalogue record for this book is available from the British Library

Library of Congress Cataloging-in-Publication Data
Names: Hynes, Patricia, author.
Title: Introducing forced migration / Patricia Hynes.
Description: 1 Edition. | New York : Routledge, 2021. | Series:
    Rethinking development | Includes bibliographical references and index.
Identifiers: LCCN 2020045040 (print) | LCCN 2020045041 (ebook)
Subjects: LCSH: Forced migration. | Refugees—Social conditions. |
    Refugees—Legal status, laws, etc.
Classification: LCC HV640 .H8946 2021 (print) | LCC HV640 (ebook) |
    DDC 362.87—dc23
LC record available at https://lccn.loc.gov/2020045040
LC ebook record available at https://lccn.loc.gov/2020045041

ISBN: 978-1-138-05547-6 (hbk)
ISBN: 978-1-138-05548-3 (pbk)
ISBN: 978-1-315-16592-9 (ebk)

Typeset in Bembo
by Apex CoVantage, LLC

Dedicated to
Professor Barbara Harrell-Bond

Contents

Figures and maps

Figures

Maps

Tables

Boxes

Key thinkers

Key concepts

Box

Preface

The limitations of writing a book on forced migration are very apparent when looking at definitions of who is legally considered to be a refugee, asylum seeker, stateless person, internally displaced person, 'victim' or 'survivor' of human trafficking or a child 'on the move'. These legal, policy and practice-based categorisations and labels are rarely informed by those who have experienced the need to migrate with any degree of force or coercion. But they do have power, and responses are invariably based on their framings, with different international agencies providing support, assistance and protections. The distinction between 'voluntary' and 'forced' migration is difficult – some say impossible – to clarify in many cases. These labels also overlap, and myths and misrepresentations are abundant.

I recall realising the speed at which these categorisations can be switched upon driving out of a newly formed refugee camp in Thailand and seeing brokers talking with people who had arrived the previous day with only the clothes on their backs. The translator told us these are the men who recruit for maid positions in Bangkok. With Thailand not being a signatory of the 1951 Convention relating to the Status of Refugees, the 'refugee' label would never had applied, with a 'displaced persons fleeing fighting' categorisation in place in this instance. For those undocumented new arrivals recruited that day, it may have been that what is often referred to as 'human smuggling' was about to take place or, in a worse scenario, 'human trafficking'. Whatever the case, these closed camps with their restrictions on entry had not been a barrier, and more brokers were driving in as we left that isolated, insecure and muddy camp.

The initial chapters of this book provide an outline of different forms of forced migration as per their legal definitions, but at all times scholars in this area need to understand the flux and fluidity of the lived experiences of those forced to move and the agency involved in decisions to stay or go.

This book is the result of many years of practice, research and teaching around the topic of forced migration formed over hundreds of conversations with colleagues and friends. Disaggregating the statistics and headline news of the millions of people forced to migrate is part of this work. Dramatic headlines of 79.5 million people forcibly displaced worldwide need to be disaggregated to be understood and this book is an attempt to do that. From my work in refugee camps, urban centres with high refugee populations, border areas with people displaced within their own nationally bounded territories, people without citizenship, asylum seekers going through laborious and time-consuming refugee-status determination processes, people who have experienced exploitation and been trafficked internally, regionally or internationally, it need always be remembered that people's accounts and backstories are far more complex – and reveal much more – than any simple headline can capture. For many without the effective protection of a State, achieving social justice is a long, slow and grinding process.

What is often missing from these frameworks are the views and representations of those who have experienced the need to migrate. Thinking about border regimes, past paternalistic responses to forced migrants and what anti-racist and inclusive practices might look like are all part of this. The provision of basic items of food and shelter do not begin to address the causes or structural inequalities people experience during forced migration. There is more work to be done here.

Drafting a book on forced migration during a global pandemic has been full of contradictions. As some are asking whether this is the end of an age of migration and mobility, others are pointing out that the loss of employment will mean shifts towards the informal or illegal economy and resulting exploitation. For those living without the rights conferred by citizenship within societies and subsequently without protection from any state, basic survival can be a struggle and for many will lead to informal, precarious and potentially exploitative conditions. As some populations are being made immobile, self-isolating, socially distancing and having only essential contact with their families, others are trying to find the safety and sanitary conditions assumed by so many. Young Vietnamese men and women may well be stuck in basements, awaiting the next part of their journeys towards safer lives where they might ultimately be able to remit funds to their families. They might also, like many other nationalities, be contemplating stepping into refrigerated lorries or hanging under the chassis of lorries to make these next steps. People detained in Libyan detention centres after having made gruelling journeys across deserts await release and the possibility of a life with dignity. People making perilous journeys across seas towards Europe, Southeast Asia and/or Australia are being pushed back, away from the sanctuary and refuge enshrined within international law contrary to cornerstone principles of *non-refoulement*.

Now is the moment to ask the right questions in this area of scholarship: Will persecution decrease because of this pandemic? Will border restrictions increase, and what might this mean? Will people continuing to flee persecution need to circumvent borders? With declining family income, will more children need to take part in riskier forms of work or child labour? Will the 'age of migration' discussed in this book now be over, and are we about to move into an 'age of immobility'? This question is of course a generalisation and possibly too broad in terms of helping future scholarship. However, whilst states may consider COVID-19 a good motive for increasing their deterrence and hostile measures, for those needing to migrate, this simply increases the dangers and indignities of their journeys.

During the pandemic there has been no shortage of reports of the added impact on people. There were reports coming out of the Moria camp (on the Greek island of Lesbos before it burned down) that 18,000 people were living in a facility built for 3,000 and of parents not being able to wash their own children, let alone their hands on a regular basis. Reports have revealed the hidden harms of domestic violence and children witnessing abuse in confined accommodation during lockdowns from Cox's Bazar in Bangladesh to industrialised countries such as the UK. There are numerous reports from asylum seekers of being locked down in sometimes-shared accommodation in extended limbo while official decision-making processes that affect their lives slow down. Reports keep emerging from people who have experienced exploitation going through digital poverty and choosing between food or using the tiny data allowances they have to be online and have contact with others.

The pandemic has exposed inequalities and has been a wakeup call that social protections systems are needed to protect the less visible and insecure, in order to protect everybody. It is my hope that this book contributes to this discourse and that students reading this book and the suggested reading herein learn the facts about forced migration rather than rely on media reports, myths and misrepresentations that abound.

Acknowledgements

This book originated from teaching courses on forced migration and human rights within a range of contexts, most recently within my unit on the Complexities of Forced Migration, Human Displacement, Trafficking and Refuge. Over the past six years, students taking this class have honed and challenged my thinking on many occasions, and I would like to thank each and every one of them. Particular thanks go to those who had lived experience in these processes and were rightly demanding of why solutions were so sparse, difficult and seldom took the views of forced migrants themselves into account. These experts by experience and this student feedback have influenced the form and content of this book greatly, and it feels right that this invaluable input is captured for future scholars and students. A number of the points for discussion contained within this book are a direct result of their input, and for that I am thankful.

When teaching this unit and others within universities I quickly realised that an introductory and accessible text that covered key definitions and concepts of forced migration was missing. When Routledge proposed the possibility of writing such a book I was on the cusp of writing a research-informed book proposal based on my research and teaching across undergraduate and postgraduate levels, both introducing the topic and providing a basic understanding of forced migration, particularly the key definitions, statistics, changing patterns, ideas and key theories involved. It became clear that beyond this, the opportunity to signpost readers towards richer and thicker understandings of forced migration through further reading would be invaluable within an environment where the backstories of those forced to migrate are often absent and understanding of the causes as well as consequences involved are rarely connected in policy, practice, the public imagination or the media.

This book also has its roots in practice following close to a decade of working with people who had been forced to migrate from Burma, Laos, Viet Nam and Cambodia, living in camps in Thailand or residing within urban centres. I am very grateful to those who will remain necessarily anonymous who let me into their lives during this time and to those who remain good friends. This book is a tribute to you all, and I hope it captures the gap between the needs, aspirations and desires of those displaced and the policy 'solutions' devised *around* them rather than *with* them. Thank you all.

A key feature of this book is the work of key thinkers within the respective areas of forced migration. It has been incredibly useful to engage with academics around the Key Thinker Boxes, and I would like to thank the majority of the key thinkers included who have been extremely helpful in providing additional literature to me. I think these represent an exciting and new element to this text, and it is my hope I can find a way to continue this format so that the many people deserving of the Key Thinker position can be explored. Each one has been like writing a mini literature review, attempting to span early and contemporary scholarship, and it has been fascinating to reread the work of Professor Barbara Harrell-Bond and others to see the crossovers over time.

I am also grateful to Frankie Parrish and Rachel Natali at IDCM for the prompt replies regarding graphics for this book. Edgar Scrase at UNHCR and Giulia Serio at UNODC have been very helpful in confirming permissions for use of figures. I would also like to acknowledge funding from the Modern Slavery Innovation Fund where findings on human trafficking have been incorporated herein.

Many others from the University of Bedfordshire and beyond have supported me in perhaps unknowing ways by keeping my research and scholarly spirit alive and provided a balance in academic life generally. These include Brad Blitz, Ian Bridgeman, Helen Connolly, Nadine Finch, Jaya Ghosh, Philip Miles, Alex de Mont, Hemlata Naranbhai, Luljeta Nuzi, Lena Opfermann, Lorraine Radford, Chloe Setter, Jack Sheih, Angela Thurnham, Alison Tresidder and Cathy Zimmerman, amongst others. Also beyond the university, engagement within networks around human trafficking have brought me into contact with a range of professionals and academics who continue to inspire me, too numerous to repeat here. Thank you to Alketa Gaxha, Lola Gani-Yusuf, Valbona Lenja, Aye Olatunde and Hong Thi Tran for being so wonderful to work alongside during our recent research with IOM London into human trafficking from Albania, Viet Nam and Nigeria to the UK.

Special thanks go to Helena Hurd from Routledge, who invited me to write such an introductory text at a time when the pressures of the current higher education environment were personally arduous and challenging. Without Helena's patience, encouragement and understanding this book would never have been written, and I thank you for believing in this project over all this time. Matthew Shobbrook from Routledge has also been incredibly helpful and has kept me on track throughout. Thank you to Ko Aung for help with the cover design.

Finally, I wish to thank my family – Mark, Robbie and Jack – for allowing me enough time during evenings, weekends and then during a global pandemic to complete this book. Without you, and your support, this book would never have been written.

1 Introduction to the study of forced migration

Introduction

> One cold night in late February 1987 I stood on a gravelled road which was the border separating Iran from Afghanistan. It was around midnight. Deadly silent and pitch-dark. 'If I take a step,' I thought, 'I will be somewhere else. When my foot touches the ground on the other side of the road, I will not be the same person. If I take this step I will be an 'illegal' person and the world will never be the same again'.
>
> (Khosravi, 2007:321)

When Shahram Khosravi stepped across this border, he began a journey across international borders, through different national structures and a range of legal or socially constructed categorisations and labels given to people which rarely capture the complexities and nuances of the experience during migration (Crawley and Skleparis, 2017; Richmond, 1994; van Hear, 2012; Zetter, 2007). At an early stage of his journey he experienced being 'smuggled' from place to place by a 'middleman'. Such middlemen are often referred to as human smugglers, agents, brokers or facilitators. Later in his journey he met an 'undocumented' migrant who helped him escape the war in his own country and who Shahram could not consider to be a 'smuggler' due to his own precarious legal status. Others he encountered on his journey were being 'trafficked' for the purposes of exploitation into occupations not of their choosing and/or as a result of force or coercion. Being classed as 'irregular' or 'illegal', he was outside the protection of national laws and sought asylum in more than one country. After these various attempts, he became a 'refugee' and gained the protections of that legal status under the mandate of the United Nations High Commissioner for Refugees (UNHCR). Ultimately, after many years negotiating the actual journey and reinventions required of each label, he became a 'citizen' of Sweden.

In the space of a few years, in different locations and at different points in time, Shahram experienced the labels of being 'illegal', 'smuggled' by an 'undocumented' 'migrant', an 'asylum seeker', then a 'refugee' and ultimately a 'citizen'. Each of these labels offered forms of status that held with them different legal protections and entitlements (or lack of) rights.

There is considerable debate about whether these categorisations and labels constructed by policy makers or agencies with mandates to protect people who meet particular criteria are useful when thinking about migration – or, in the case of this book, forced migration. As we will see in in subsequent chapters, the labels of 'refugee', 'asylum-seeker' and 'trafficked person' lead to particular policy responses and outcomes. As Crawley and Skleparis suggest, the dangers of using these categories uncritically can lead to dynamic processes of migration being concealed:

> Taking the dominant categories as the basis of our analytical approach can limit our understanding of migration and make us potentially complicit in a political process which has, over recent years, stigmatised, vilified and undermined the rights of refugees of migrants.
>
> (Crawley and Skleparis, 2017:3)

Roger Zetter (2007) has also outlined the way in which rights and entitlements people depend upon and how they are labelled in the first instance are important. He argues that it is convenient for states to put people into neat bureaucratic categories – sometimes as 'political' refugees or 'economic' migrants – but that these categories invariably do not reflect the reality of people's lives. In relation to the label 'refugee', Zetter suggests that this and other categories are a source of bureaucratic 'fractioning of the [refugee] label' (2007:172–192) driven by the need to manage migration, particularly forced migration (see Key Thinker Box 2.4 in Chapter 2). As we see later in this book, there are often 'mixed flows' of migrants that are not easily categorised, reflecting the heterogeneous causes and drivers of displacement.

International migrants considered to have migrated following some form of persecution or force include internally displaced persons, refugees, asylum seekers, victims of trafficking, smuggled migrants, international migrants, internal migrants and various others. In practice, these categories overlap. People may gain refugee status, but following the logic of bureaucratic fractioning, 'temporary protection' may be offered, or forms of status that deny particular entitlements such as family reunion. 'Illegal migrants', 'overstayers', 'failed asylum seekers', 'trafficked migrant' and 'undocumented migrants' are just some of the labels now used to describe people forced to migrate. These definitions matter.

There is considerable power in definitions, and defining a population within such categories may or may not lead to appropriate responses to needs. Policy categories that inform humanitarian organisations should not be taken for granted as forms of knowledge. How forced migrants are labelled and the power of these definitions are considered throughout this book, as are the policy responses that follow on from such labels and definitions.

For some, migration is a defining characteristic of the post-Cold War period and beginning of the 21st century, and it has been asserted that we are living in an 'age of migration' (see Key Thinker Box 1.1 – Stephen Castles). For others we live in an 'age of mobility' with non-permanent migration accounting for much of the global movement of people (King, 2015; Skeldon, 2015). The forcible displacement of people is a part of this, with people fleeing persecution within and from their countries of origin. Bobbio (1996) has suggested we now also live in an 'age of rights', something which may be difficult to accept when thinking about the displaced. At the time of writing this book, immobility was a recurring theme during discussions about the impacts of a global pandemic.

Certainly, the subject of forced migration has arguably never been more topical. As this book is being written, people seeking sanctuary in Europe are dying en route in the Mediterranean and Aegean Seas (Crawley *et al.*, 2018; Crawley and Skleparis, 2017; IOM, 2016, 2017). During the summer of 2015, parallel narratives played out in the media of refugees in boats crossing the Mediterranean and the Andaman Seas. Those who made it to Europe were left facing fear of daily violence with rights and freedoms severely curtailed. The refugee 'crisis' in Europe took centre stage in media and policy discourses, and the 'crisis' narrative manifested itself into new border fences, increasing negative attitudes among European states towards those arriving. Behind these European headlines, refugees continue to flee persecution across the globe. In 2015 Rohingya refugees fled Burma in rickety boats across the Andaman Sea to seek refuge in Southeast Asian countries. Since 2017, some 670,000 Rohingya refugees have arrived in Bangladesh. Without the protection of a state, thousands of people such as the Rohingya live as 'stateless' persons.

Additionally, within the Americas, some 3.7 million Venezuelans were displaced during 2019, with the island of Aruba hosting the largest number of Venezuelans relative to its national population (1 in 6) (UNHCR, 2020). According to UNHCR statistics, this meant that there are now 4.5 million people from Venezuela across Latin America and the Caribbean displaced – made up of 93,300 refugees, 794,500 asylum seekers and 3.6 million 'Venezuelans displaced abroad'. Across Africa, following independence, 2.2 million people from South Sudan have been displaced, and there has also been renewed fighting and conflict within the Democratic Republic of the Congo and Central African Republic, leading to further displacement.

This introduction provides an overview of this sometimes arbitrary distinction between voluntary and forced migration and causes that are often perceived as either political or economic. The **difference between voluntary and forced migration is difficult** – many say impossible – to clarify. There is no single explanation of what distinguishes the causes and motivations for 'voluntary' migration from 'forced' migration, and a number of authors in this book highlight this in their work. Some argue that forced migration is one part of migration studies more broadly. Others consider forced migration as a distinct area of study in both its causes and consequences. The study of forced migration emerged in part out of 'refugee studies', which has its origins in the refugee studies programme set up by Professor Barbara Harrell-Bond at the University of Oxford in 1982, to address the gap of critical research in the field of refugee assistance (see Key Thinker Box 2.1 in Chapter 2).

This book has the title *Introducing Forced Migration*. However, a key caveat is that any attempt to bring together all writing, concepts and different perspectives on forced migration would fail. The topic of forced migration is not simplistic, rather it is multi-faceted and complex. This book is a starting point in understanding these complexities. This book seeks to unpack and explain the different forms of forced migration as they are socially and legally constructed. This book begins by looking at key questions about *who* forced migrants are, *where* the forcibly displaced are located, *why* people migrate and seek international protection, *how* people recreate their worlds in the face of increasingly restrictive legislation and policy and *what happens* to the forcibly displaced, including children. Migration of people across the globe is an enduring theme of human history, be it referred to as 'forced', 'voluntary' or a migration with 'mixed motivations'.

The main purpose of the book is to introduce the topic in an accessible and, hopefully, inspiring way. The key aims are twofold:

- Firstly, it seeks to provide a **basic understanding** of forced migration, particularly the key definitions, statistics, changing patterns, ideas and key theories involved
- Secondly, to provide opportunities and signpost readers towards **richer and thicker understandings** of forced migration by carrying out further reading, exploring the listed websites, reading the case studies that illustrate the lives of those who have been forcibly displaced and highlighting the realities of forced migration

Throughout the book, **summaries of key thinkers** who have shaped refugee studies and the study of forced migration are provided, although these by no means fully represent the breadth of authors engaged in the study of forced migration. Further key thinker summaries will be made available. There are also **flagged opportunities for further reflection, critical thinking and points for discussion** around the interdisciplinary study of forced migration. Some of the headings are framed as questions, and the subsequent text allows for exploration and consideration of the contested nature of terms and debates in forced migration.

Key Thinker Box 1.1   Stephen Castles – *The Age of Migration*

Stephen Castles is a Professor at the University of Sydney. Prior to this he was based at the University of Oxford, firstly as Director of the Refugee Studies Centre and then as Director of the International Migration Institute. His research and publications have been highly influential in the development of interdisciplinary research on migration studies for many years, none more so than a key text written by himself and co-authors – *The Age of Migration: International Populations Movements in the Modern World*, now in its fifth edition.

This book is widely considered to be a landmark study in migration studies, providing a foundation of knowledge by successfully framing and defining migration studies (Carling, 2015; Collyer, 2015; King, 2015; Skeldon, 2015). As King suggests, *The Age of Migration* does 'more than any other to ensure that the academic study of migration now occupies a central place in the social sciences' (King, 2015:2366). Simply put, it is considered to be the 'best and most successful introduction' (Skeldon, 2015:2356) to migration studies.

The Age of Migration was first published in 1993 and aimed to provide an accessible introduction to the study of global migration and consequences for society. Commencing with general trends and challenges of global migration the authors assert that it is possible to identify six key tendencies that may play a major role in future migration patterns:

1   The *globalisation of migration* will mean more countries will be affected by migratory movements and the diversity of areas of origin within countries is increasing
2   The *changing direction of dominant migration flows* relates to how, for centuries, Europeans moved to conquer, colonise and settle lands across the globe and the reversal of this pattern following World War II
3   The *differentiation of migration* relates to the different forms of migration, or immigration emerging over time which have been responded to by government policies in fragmented ways for labour migration, acceptance of refugees and distinct policies for other categories of migrants
4   The *proliferation of migration transition* when traditional emigration countries become immigration destinations
5   The *feminisation of migration* relates to the growing understanding that male-dominated movements of the past are now giving way to more women, including those fleeing persecution of those who experience trafficking
6   The *growing politicisation of migration* refers to how politicians now accord considerable priority to migration and how this growing salience of the issue of migration is a key reason for the argument that we now live in an 'age of migration'

Chapters 2 and 3 then provide an overview of the theories of *causes* and *impacts* of migration. Historical accounts of international migration prior to and post-1945 provide an exploration of colonialism, industrialisation, labour migration and issues surrounding migration within regions of the globe. Thereafter the political, economic and social meaning of migration and ethnic diversity is explored, including around migration and security post-9/11 in the US and subsequent attacks in Europe. The way that governments have tried to control migration through imposition of legal status – including for refugees, asylum seekers and people who have been smuggled or trafficked – is outlined and discussed, as are the political implications for growing ethnic diversity. The authors assert that migration is a normal and constant feature in human history.

A symposium on the fifth edition of *The Age of Migration* was published in a special issue of *Ethnic and Racial Studies* (2015, Vol. 38, No. 13), charting the developments and updates across each edition. Critiques and suggestions around areas for future development were provided, including how most people migrate within the borders of their own countries rather than from one country to another and the subsequent need to study 'internal' as well as international migration (King, 2015; Skeldon, 2015). Others suggested use of the term *'mobility'* rather than *'migration'* in the title to allow for non-permanent, or temporary, movements to be included in the analysis and tie the study of migration to new studies of 'mobilities' (King, 2015; Skeldon, 2015). Further emphasis on 'return migration' was also outlined so that a more detailed discussion of a 'migration-development nexus' could be explored (King, 2015). The lack of female scholars in the index of prominent experts was noted by another and how a more gendered analysis was lacking (Carling, 2015).

Other works by Stephen Castles are detailed in the bibliography at the end of this book, but alongside *The Age of Migration* two in particular are provided here and recommended as further reading.

International Migration at the Crossroads (2014) explores how agendas in the Global North since 9/11 around national security and avoidance of threat ignores how South to North migration is the result of growing global inequality and lack of human security in the Global South. It examines the significance of migration for human security and human development, linking this to processes of globalisation. Emerging forms of migration – the migration of women and forced migration – are drawn out, as are the issues of diversity and multiculturalism.

The Forces Driving Global Migration (2013) outlines how most destination countries favour entry of highly skilled migrants rather than lower-skilled migrants, asylum seekers or refugees. Which migrants are 'wanted' and which migrants are 'unwanted' are explored, focussing on who can cross borders to work safely with legal protection and who faces risks and exploitation as a result (2013:130). This is a theme that runs through social policy and throughout this book, with who is perceived to be 'deserving' and 'undeserving' during migration informing policy debates and having considerable impact on the lives of people.

Key references – Stephen Castles

Castles, S. (2013) The Forces Driving Global Migration, *Journal of Intercultural Studies*, 34(2), 122–140.

Castles, S. (2014) International Migration at a Crossroads, *Citizenship Studies*, 18(2), 190–207.

Castles, S., de Haas, H. and Miller, M.J. (2014) *The Age of Migration: International Populations Movements in the Modern World*, Palgrave Macmillan, London.

Legal instruments and definitions

Internationally, there are a range of legal instruments, Conventions, Protocols and Guiding Principles that serve to identify, define and disaggregate distinct populations of people who have been forcibly displaced. They include the:

- 1951 Convention relating to the Status of Refugees (known as the 1951 Refugee Convention)

  - The associated 1967 Protocol relating to the Status of Refugees (known as the 1967 Protocol)

- 1990 International Convention on the Protection of the Rights of All Migrants and Members of Their Families
- 1998 Guiding Principles on Internal Displacement

  - 2006 Protocol on the Protection and Assistance to Internally Displaced Persons (adopted by the Member States of the International Conference on the Great Lakes) (known as the 2006 Great Lakes IDP Protocol)
  - 2009 African Convention on Protection and Assistance for Internally Displaced Persons in Africa (known as the 2009 Kampala Convention)

- 2000 Protocol to Prevent, Suppress and Punish Trafficking in Persons, Especially Women and Children (known as the 2000 Palermo Protocol), which is a Protocol of the Convention against Transnational Organized Crime
- 2000 Protocol against the Smuggling of Migrants by Land, Sea and Air (known as the 2000 Smuggling Protocol)
- 1954 Convention relating to the Status of Stateless Persons (known as the 1954 Stateless Convention)
- 1961 Convention on the Reduction of Statelessness

Together with the instruments of the rights of migrant workers adopted by the International Labour Organization (ILO), these form the basis of the international normative and legal frameworks on international migration.

There are a range of additional Declarations, Covenants and Conventions relevant to this topic and highlighted throughout this book, which include:

- 1948 Universal Declaration of Human Rights★
- 1948 Convention on the Prevention and Punishment of the Crime of Genocide
- 1966 International Covenant on Civil and Political Rights★
- 1966 International Covenant on Economic, Social and Cultural Rights★
- 1966 International Convention on the Elimination of All Forms of Racial Discrimination
- 1979 Convention on the Elimination of All Forms of Discrimination against Women
- 1984 Convention against Torture and Other Cruel, Inhuman or Degrading Treatment or Punishment
- 1989 Convention on the Rights of the Child
                    ★ Together these make up the International Bill of Rights

It is also important to remember that individual countries will also have national law concerning refugees within their territories.

Important considerations and caveats when studying forced migration

As outlined earlier there are several key considerations when studying what is termed 'forced' or 'voluntary' migration.

Firstly, the **distinction between 'voluntary' and 'forced' migration** is fluid and is often arbitrarily drawn (see further reading from Crawley and Skleparis, 2017; King *et al.*, 2010; Richmond, 1994; van Hear, 2012; Zetter, 2007; Zolberg *et al.*, 1989).

Secondly, **categories and categorisations** of 'migrants', 'refugees' and others simplify the lived experiences of people and do not recognise that people may move between different categories throughout their lifetimes. For example an 'internally displaced' person may or may not become a 'refugee' at a later point.

Thirdly, **key terms** used within debates about forced migration are **contestable** and should be **critiqued**. Being critical of key terms is part of being a social scientist. For example, in recent years the phrase 'refugee crisis' or 'migration crisis' has been used by governments and politicians to describe migration from Syria, Afghanistan and other countries from which people are arriving on the shores of the Mediterranean. The term 'crisis' has been heavily criticised by a number of authors discussed in this book who argue that the 'crisis' is not a migration crisis, but rather a crisis of policy, political will and coordination by states to devise comprehensive solutions to address the protection needs of those arriving and not a 'refugee crisis'.

Another example would be the terms 'victim', and the binary alternative, 'survivor' found within debates on human trafficking. The term 'trafficking' itself remains contested, with confusion in practice between the use of the legal definition (the Palermo Protocol 2000) and 'human smuggling'. There is also considerable debate relating to the various forms of exploitation that constitute trafficking (Agustin, 2007; Anderson and O'Connell-Davidson, 2002; Gould, 2010; Palmary, 2010).

The term 'asylum seeker' has now been made mainstream and institutionalised into policy and practice but has been misused in the media, who have added on negative terms such as 'illegal', 'undeserving' or 'bogus' when describing people. There is no such thing as an 'illegal asylum seeker', but the **distinction between who is deserving and who is undeserving** within migration policies has become part of public imagination, mainly due to media accounts that confuse terminology.

Throughout this book these terms – *trafficked persons, trafficking, victims, survivors, modern slavery* and *refugee crisis* – and others are initially identified in inverted commas – but then omitted for ease of reading. When you see these terms flagged in this way, it is **an invitation to think about why they may be disputed and what the consequences of such labels might be**.

Fourthly, **different policy labels for people who are forced to migrate often overlap and may be experienced by the same person at different time periods**. As we saw at the start of this chapter, Shahram Khosravi experienced several policy labels at different times during his journey. Someone who has experienced 'human trafficking' may also be, in policy terms, a 'victim' of 'forced labour' and, simultaneously, an 'asylum seeker' (Khosravi, 2007, 2010).

Fifthly, in migration studies more broadly migration flows are often described from the 'South' to the 'North', with the word *South* acting as shorthand for developing, low or middle income countries and *North* industrialised and high-income countries. Equally, *East* and *West* sometimes refer to past tensions between the Soviet Union and the West. These **geographical markers do not adequately reflect the heterogeneity of nation–states** and also tend to ignore South to South migration.

Finally, the **compilation of statistics is invariably carried out using different definitions, approaches and methods**. As such, data can vary between agencies and governments, and it is very important to look at the methodology and methods used to consider why statistics have been compiled and why they are presented in the form provided. In other words, the framing of how data is collected and presented is important.

For example, the number of refugees across the globe has historically been recorded by UNHCR but does not include Palestinian refugees. The number of people who have been internally displaced within their own countries will be discussed in Chapter 3, and statistics of those who are considered to have been 'trafficked' across the globe in Chapter 4.

Measuring human trafficking poses considerable challenge as collecting data on people who are purposely less visible is fraught with methodological difficulties. Estimates of human trafficking require caution and should not be replicated uncritically. This topic has caused heated debates, and the actual number of people involved remains unknown.

Consequently, in any study relating to forced migration, there will be **limitations around the use of data**, and it is necessary to be aware of these limitations when using or presenting such data and statistics.

To help negotiate these complexities and caveats, chapters in this book look at the legal categories of who is a refugee, an asylum seeker, a stateless person or an internally displaced person (IDP) and who is a 'victim' of human trafficking before considering the 'mixed movements' (Zetter, 2019) of people and multiple drivers that often emanate from abuses of political, economic, social and cultural human rights.

Which organisations assist people who migrate?

Currently there are three key organisations who are mandated to assist people who migrate – UNHCR, UNRWA and IOM. The ILO has less of an operational role but holds a commitment to 'decent work' for migrants.

The **United Nations High Commissioner for Refugees (UNHCR)** was established in 1950 to provide international protection and to seek permanent solutions for refugees. Created after World War II, it was anticipated that the organisation would help millions of Europeans who had fled or lost their homes during the war. At this time, it was thought this would take three years and the organisation would then disband. However, it celebrated its 70th anniversary in 2020. It is the **only agency with a mandate to protect refugees** and is now known as the UN Refugee Agency. The cornerstone of its international protection mandate relates to safeguarding the rights and wellbeing of refugees and ensuring that nobody is returned to a country where they are in fear of persecution – a **principle known as** *non-refoulement* **– no return**. UNHCR has several categories of what they term 'Populations of Concern' (see Key Concept Box 1.1).

The **United Nations Relief and Works Agency for Palestine Refugees in the Near East (UNRWA)** was founded and began operations in 1950 following the 1948 Arab-Israeli conflict in 1948. It was established for the purposes of direct relief and works programmes specifically for Palestinian refugees which included education, health care, social services and camp infrastructure and improvements, including in times of conflict. Because there has not been a permanent solution to the Palestinian conflict, UNRWA's mandate has been repeatedly renewed since its establishment.

The **International Organization for Migration (IOM)** became a related agency to the United Nations in September 2016 following 65 years of existence and global operations outside the UN system and is **mandated to assist migrants**. Since 2016 it is now known as the UN Migration Agency and plays a key role in facilitation of migration worldwide. IOM considers that humane and orderly migration benefits migrants and society. As an intergovernmental organization,

IOM works with partners to meet operational challenges of migration, advance understanding of migration issues, encourage social and economic development through migration and uphold the human dignity and wellbeing of migrants (IOM, 2017). They also focus on the benefits of migration, both for individuals and families involved but also societal benefits. IOM assists those who are in situations of vulnerability and require humanitarian assistance as a result of weather events, conflict or persecution, or for those who have become stranded. They focus on migrants in need, rather than those who have the capacity and means to navigate migration processes themselves (IOM, 2017).

As such, operationally, the distinction between forced and voluntary migration becomes visible. This has now been reinforced within the global architecture for migration following a 2016 New York Declaration for Refugees and Migrants (New York Declaration) which outlined two distinct 'Compacts' – one for refugees and the other for migrants.

The **International Labour Organization (ILO)** has less of an operational role than UNHCR, UNRWA or IOM, and migration is one of around 40 different priorities for the organisation. However, it is important to remember ILO's commitment to 'decent work' for migrants and its aim in assisting nation-states to implement more effective policies on labour migration, including rights, employment and protection of migrant workers.

Key Concepts 1.1   UNHCR and 'Populations of Concern'

UNHCR has several categories of Populations of Concern. As outlined previously, these categories or labels are often disputed (for example see Key Thinker Box 2.4: Roger Zetter in Chapter 2). However, as the agency has a mandate to protect refugees, it considers the following categories:

Refugees include individuals recognised under the 1951 Convention relating to the Status of Refugees, its 1967 Protocol, the 1969 OAU Convention Governing the Specific Aspects of Refugee Problems in Africa, those recognised in accordance with the UNHCR Statute and individuals granted complementary forms of protection or those enjoying temporary protection. Since 2007, the refugee population also includes people in a refugee-like situation.

Asylum-seekers are individuals who have sought international protection and whose claims for refugee status have not yet been determined, irrespective of when they may have been lodged.

Internally displaced persons (IDPs) are people or groups of individuals who have been forced to leave their homes or places of habitual residence, in particular as a result of (or in order to avoid) the effects of armed conflict, situations of generalised violence, violations of human rights or natural or man-made disasters and who have not crossed an international border. For the purposes of UNHCR's statistics, this population only includes conflict-generated IDPs to whom the Office of the High Commission extends protection and/or assistance. Since 2007, the IDP population also includes people in an IDP-like situation.

Returned refugees are former refugees who have returned to their country of origin spontaneously or in an organised fashion but are yet to be fully integrated. Such return would normally only take place in conditions of safety and dignity.

Returned IDPs refer to those IDPs who were beneficiaries of UNHCR's protection and assistance activities and who returned to their areas of origin or habitual residence during the year.

Stateless persons are defined under international law as persons who are not considered as nationals by any State under the operation of its law. In other words, they do not possess the nationality of any State. UNHCR statistics refer to persons who fall under the agency's statelessness mandate because they are stateless according to this international definition, but data from some countries may also include persons with undetermined nationality.

Others of concern refers to individuals who do not necessarily fall directly into any of the groups listed but to whom UNHCR extends its protection and/or assistance services based on humanitarian or other special grounds.

Source: http://popstats.unhcr.org/en/overview

Who are international migrants?

Migration is normal. Throughout history people have migrated to improve their lives and gain better security for themselves and their families. Migration is also a part of processes of globalisation, development and social change.

In 2015, the total number of people living in a country other than their country of birth was equivalent to 3.3% of the population of the world – some 244 million people (UNDESA, 2016:1). In percentage terms, this figure has risen by only 1% since 1965 when 2.3% of the world's population lived outside their country of birth. **In other words, most people do not migrate –** nearly 97% of people worldwide did not live outside their country of birth during 2015 (see Figure 1.1).

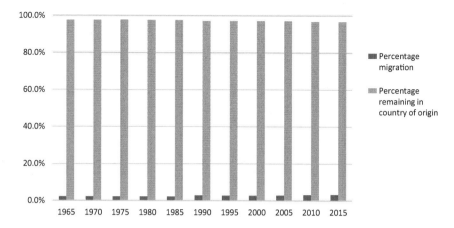

Figure 1.1 International Migration: 1965–2015
Source: UNDESA, various dates

Actual evidence about migration is often surprising and, even in a time of globalisation with increased access to transport and communications that facilitate migration, actual percentages of people on the move are perhaps unexpectedly low which means, as King *et al.* suggest: 'The rhetoric of migration exaggerates its scale' (2010:13).

For those who do migrate, currently most originate from middle-income countries (157 million in 2015), most are at working age and most migrate to countries that offer a higher standard of living. **It is not the poorest who migrate internationally**. Most move for work, and the majority of the world's migrants live in high-income countries. For example, in 2015, the largest number of international migrants – around 19% of international migrants (47 million) – lived and worked in the USA.

Who are forced migrants?

But what about people who do not choose to migrate and are in some way **forced** to leave their homes? In 2015, the number of people forcibly displaced worldwide as a result of persecution, conflict, generalised violence and/or human rights violations committed against them was 65.3 million people (UNHCR, 2016). This represented a rise of 5.8 million from the previous year where 59.5 million people had been forcibly displaced.

Of these 65.3 million people, some 86% were hosted in the world's 'low-income' or 'developing' countries (UNHCR, 2016:2–3). Policies of containment and deterrence to stop people reaching high-income countries will be considered in subsequent chapters. These policies have been described by many but, in Bauman's (2015) words, are designed and operationalised with 'callous unconcern and moral blindness'.

Of this 65.3 million figure:

- 21.3 million were refugees
- 40.8 million were internally displaced persons
- 3.2 million were asylum seekers
- Around half of refugees were children below the age of 18 years
- Included in these numbers are approximately 6.7 million people living in what have been called 'protracted refugee situations' (PRS) – this means they had been refugees for longer than five years, although some have been in these protracted situations for decades

Shown diagrammatically, the recorded statistics of people living in a country other than their country of birth and the total numbers of people migrating across the globe in 2015 are shown in Figure 1.2.

There are also increasing numbers of stateless people across the globe and, during the past two decades, the category of people experiencing human trafficking has emerged (UNODC, 2016).

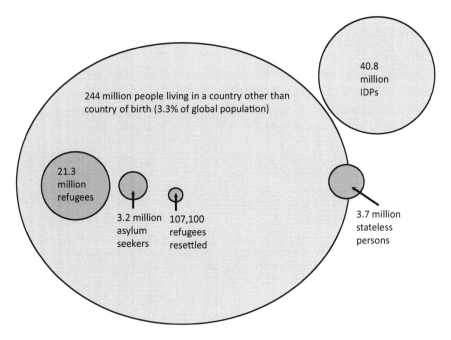

Figure 1.2 Global and Forced Migration: 2015

By the end of 2019 this figure had risen to 79.5 million people forcibly displaced worldwide, of which refugees made up 26 million people, IDPs 45.7 million, asylum seekers 4.2 million and 3.6 million people described under the term 'Venezuelans displaced abroad' (UNHCR, 2020). The figure for IDPs was subsequently updated to 50.8 million people (IDCM, 2020).

Points for discussion – critical thinking

Remember what we said about these categories and labels earlier in this chapter:

* Do you think some of these categories may be contestable?
* In what ways can they overlap in practice?
* What do they say about the life stage of people?
* How difficult would it be to get accurate statistics for these populations?
* Why do you think people who have experienced trafficking are not included in these 'Populations of Concern'?

Key theories of migration and forced migration

An important distinction to make when thinking about theory is between **macro, micro and meso approaches**. Macro level analysis relates to structural, overarching issues such as legal frameworks that seek to control migration, unequal political and economic contexts in a given country, the role of the state and aspects of historical relationships such as colonialism (Giddens and Sutton, 2017; O'Reilly, 2012). Micro-level approaches relate to individuals' motivations, resources, knowledge, understandings and what influences decisions to migrate. A mid-range theoretical approach at meso level considers linkages between people and societies at local or global level, looking at social networks (see details that follow).

There are a number of **binary positions** in migration studies that are not always helpful. For example literature may look at either international or internal migration or seek to distinguish between voluntary or forced migration without looking at what lies between these binary positions. Another distinction has been temporary or permanent migration, whereas recent studies are showing how migration across the life course is somewhere between. Studies often treat the binary points separately within the literature on migration as well as during data collection, analysis and within any subsequent policy responses.

There is no single theory of migration (Castles *et al.*, 2014; Kunz, 1973, 1981), nor are there single sociological explanations of conflict or ethnic relations (Richmond, 1994). King and Skeldon also resist attempting any 'grand theory' of migration which 'incorporates all types of migration, in all places and at all times' (2010:1619). Focussing on **one of the binaries within migration studies – international and internal migration** – King and Skeldon outline how the separation of these two 'migration traditions' results in a blurred 'boundary' between the distinct literatures, conceptualisations, methods and policy agendas (2010:1619–1621). They suggest that the term *migration* has become coterminous with international migration, rather than internal migration. As Castles *et al.* suggest, both forms of migration are driven by similar processes of social, economic and political change and internal migration is actually greater in scale than incidence of crossing international borders (2014:26). This is borne out in statistics around forced migration with the numbers of internally displaced persons (IDPs) much higher than those seeking asylum or gaining refugee status, as will be explored in subsequent chapters.

One of the earliest theories of migration related to internal migration. Ravenstein's 'laws of migration' saw migration as inseparable from economic development within countries (1885, cited in King and Skeldon, 2010; Castles *et al.*, 2014). Since then other theorists have put forward **'push' and 'pull' models of migration** that offer a simplistic framework, be these within or between countries. These push-pull models focus on factors that are positive and negative in sending and receiving areas/countries, asserting that people are pushed and pulled by particular economic or demographic factors. For example, people may be pushed to migrate because of a lack of employment and pulled due to the availability of employment in another part of the country or across a border. At first glance this model is compelling. However, this framework is considered deterministic – events being determined by external causes beyond the control of people – and does not take in the full range of reasons why people migrate or the ways in which people work with or resist such structures.

These **push–pull theories have been surpassed** in part by **approaches that embrace migration as a complex process and stress the role of migrants' agency** during migration. Studies describing how migrants overcome events and external causes such as social exclusion stress the creativity of people to overcome such structural constraints (Castles *et al.*, 2014). Studies on social networks – interpersonal ties that connect people – of migrants have also become important, emphasising how people can create conditions to enable migration through their individual and collective agency. People maintain and create social networks during migration through diaspora and language communities that have often been shaped by historical legacies of, for example, colonialism or geographical proximity. A shift in thinking around social networks has created an understanding of migrants as living within transnational social spaces (Castles, 2003:27; Boswell and Crisp, 2004:16; Castles, 2003:27; Vertovec, 1999, 2007).

For example, the theorist Emmanuel Marx (1990) pointed out the need to examine social networks within studies of refugees after drawing on a famous and seminal study by Thomas and Znaniecki (1918) on Polish immigrants in Chicago to chart the stages of resettlement and the establishment of formal associations. Marx combined 'network analysis' with the 'social worlds' of refugees, bearing in mind the social life of refugees because this embraced matters whose significance he could not appreciate, including the networks of social relationships held (1990:193). This idea around the social world of refugees is also not confined to a particular geography or territory – in fact, a territorial base can be dispensed with completely. In other words, social networks help to enable the process of migration to happen.

Calls to analyse forced migration as a 'social process in which human agency and social networks play a major part' continue (Castles, 2003:13). In terms of the distinction between voluntary and forced migration, **forced migration is often related to not having any choice** but to migrate, utilising such social networks. The reasons why people migrate are invariably complex, and separating social, economic or political reasons is extremely difficult.

In Key Thinker Box 1.2, Anthony Richmond outlines how a distinction between voluntary and involuntary migration is not useful, but is in fact 'misleading' and 'untenable' because of the degree to which 'all human behaviour is contained and enabled' (1998:20). This forced or involuntary element has been outlined by many others and should be a constant consideration for you as you learn about this topic.

Overall, migration studies has historically not always drawn on broader social science theory and concepts. Therefore, when studying forced migration, drawing on theories from the field of social science is advised. **Migration studies is necessarily an inter-disciplinary exercise**, so work from human geography, sociology, anthropology, political science, economics, psychology, history and other academic disciplines is key to offering explanations for causes, patterns and consequences of migration.

Key Thinker Box 1.2　Anthony Richmond – *Global Apartheid*

Anthony Richmond's (1994) seminal text – *Global Apartheid* – examines the impact of post-industrialism, postmodernism and globalisation in relation to 'international migration, racial conflict and ethnic nationalism'. Locating refugees within population movements following the collapse of the Soviet Union, he notes how Western European countries were – more than 20 years ago – taking 'severe measures to deter and exclude spontaneous arrivals of asylum seekers' (1994:xi). He wrote this at a time when there were 16.3 million refugees and asylum seekers around the world, plus 25 million IDPs.

Using the analogy of the South African hedge of bitter wild almonds planted by Dutch settlers in 1660 to keep populations separate, Richmond argued that 'new hedges are being built' in the form of 'increasingly repressive and restrictive measures to restrain the flows of migrant labourers and refugees from Africa, Asia, the Caribbean and Latin America' (1994:xiv). For Richmond, these new hedges were guards at airports, coastguard patrols, gunboats turning back ships holding asylum seekers and so-called 'illegal' immigrants, fingerprinting and other advanced technologies to excluded the 'unwanted'. The denial of voting rights and citizenship for those with different ethnic origin to majority groups are outlined as another mechanism of exclusion. He outlines how the predominantly 'white' and wealthy countries of North America, Europe and Australasia 'endeavour to protect themselves from what they believe are imminent threats to their territorial integrity and privileged lifestyles' (1994:xv). This central paradox, he suggests, creates conditions wherein people are labelled as 'illegal' and 'undesirable' rather than being considered useful workers or fleeing from oppressive regimes.

Influenced by the structuration theory of Anthony Giddens, Richmond highlights several key concepts necessary to understand international migration – power, conflict, agency, structuration, security, identity and communication – and goes on to explore each of these theoretically. He outlines how any sociological theory of international migration should explain the scale, direction and composition of population movements plus factors that determine the decision to move in the first instance, integration in receiving countries and eventual outcomes, including remigration and return movements. Two key conclusions are made. Firstly, that a clear distinction between the economic and socio-political determinants of population movements is inappropriate (1994:58). Secondly, that a distinction between voluntary and involuntary movements is 'untenable', partly because human behaviour is always constrained and enabled by the structuration process (1994:58).

Richmond considers that a better description would be a **continuum between 'proactive' and 'reactive' migration** (1994:59, 1988). The less choice a person has places them closer to the 'reactive' pole, so refugees who have little choice but to flee persecution are situated here. Other forms of international migration such as retiring to another country would therefore sit at the other end of this continuum, closer to the 'proactive' pole. In other words, the amount of control and choice a person has dictates whether they migrate reactively or proactively. This is important for displaced populations who may have few alternatives available at the point they migrate. Where people sit in terms of **motivations for migration being economic or socio-political** is also discussed. Refugees would be aligned with the socio-political pole, whereas retirees would be closer to the economic pole.

Although there is some reference in the book to what would be regarded as outdated terminology – for example, the 'Third World' – this book made a number of key points useful in contemporary debates. For example, Richmond argued that the new world order requires rethought so that short-term interests yield to policies promoting the long-term interest of all (including developing countries) (1994:205). Today's SDGs have this idea at their core. He also argued that the nation-state and state sovereignty could not be maintained in an era of international migration, that all boundaries and borders are permeable and could not therefore be defended with walls, armed guards, iron curtains or computer surveillance systems. These arguments continue today, be they in alternative language and terminology.

Key references – Anthony Richmond

Richmond, A.H. (1988) Sociological Theories of International Migration, *Current Sociology*, 36(2), 7–25.

(If interested in reading more about theories of migration, this early paper makes a clear distinction between *macro* and *micro* theories of international migration and provides details of several key theories, including Anthony Giddens' structuration theory.)

Richmond, A.H. (1994) *Global Apartheid: Refugees, Racism and the New World Order*, Oxford University Press, Oxford.

(As previously outlined with extensive empirical analysis and comparative studies)

The United Nations Sustainable Development Goals

In September 2015, representatives of more than 150 international Heads of State, Governments and other agencies met in the headquarters of the UN in New York to establish a new global development framework to replace earlier Millennium Development Goals set at the turn of the century. They established a set of **17 Sustainable Development Goals (SDGs)**, with 169 associated Targets to provide a measurable framework for efforts to achieve a global vision by 2030. Part of the vision of this framework would envisaged:

> a world of universal respect for human rights and human dignity, the rule of law, justice, equality and non-discrimination; of respect for race, ethnicity and cultural diversity; and of equal opportunity permitting the full realization of human potential and contributing to shared prosperity. A world which invests in its children and in which every child grows up free from violence and exploitation. A world in which every woman and girl enjoys full gender equality and all legal, social and economic barriers to their empowerment have been removed. A just, equitable, tolerant, open and

socially inclusive world in which the needs of the most vulnerable are met . . . a world in which every country enjoys sustained, inclusive and sustainable economic growth and decent work for all.

Details of the 17 SDGs can be found at: https://sustainabledevelopment. un.org/sdgs.

The SDGs and forced displacement

Within migration studies, there has been a slow recognition that migration and development are linked and that the gap between relief and development should be addressed. The term '**migration–development nexus**' describes how migration policy intersects with development policy as outlined by Carling: 'The migration–development nexus is the totality of mechanisms through which migration and development dynamics affect each other' (Carling, 2017:1).

As Carling (Ibid.) suggests, such a definition allows an understanding that there are complicated interdependencies between migration and development. For example, Carling suggests that **remittances** to the society of origin both signal the benefits of migration and sustain the livelihoods of those who remain. Carling suggests that thinking of these areas as a nexus allows for complex two-way relationships to be understood (Carling, 2017:2). However, Carling goes on to point out that migration studies now has a total of 36 different nexuses and, while there are connections between different areas of migration, these are not always well defined (Ibid.).

With the arrival of the SDGs, migration and human trafficking have, for the first time, been inserted into mainstream development policy. Several SDGs and associated Targets relate to forced displacement, migration more broadly, trafficking and causes of forcible migration. Those most closely aligned are:

Goal 5: Achieve gender equality and empower all women and girls

Target 5.2: Eliminate all forms of violence against all women and girls in the public and private spheres, including trafficking and sexual and other types of exploitation.

Target 5.3: Eliminate all harmful practices, such as child, early and forced marriage and female genital mutilation.

Goal 8: Promote sustained, inclusive and sustainable economic growth, full and productive employment and decent work for all

Target 8.7: Take immediate and effective measures to eradicate forced labour, end modern slavery and human trafficking and secure the prohibition and elimination of the worst forms of child labour, including recruitment and use of child soldiers, and by 2025 end child labour in all its forms.

Target 8.8: Protect labour rights and promote safe and secure working environments for all workers, including migrant workers, in particular women migrants, and those in precarious employment.

Goal 10: Reduce inequality within and among countries

Target 10.7: Facilitate orderly, safe, regular and responsible migration and mobility of people, including through the implementation of planned and well-managed migration policies.

Goal 16: Promote peaceful and inclusive societies for sustainable development, provide access to justice for all and build effective, accountable and inclusive institutions at all levels

Target 16.2: End abuse, exploitation, trafficking and all forms of violence against and torture of children.

It is intended that Target 16.2 will be measured, among other indicators, by assessing the numbers of victims of trafficking, disaggregated by age, sex and forms of exploitation. As outlined earlier, such quantification of trafficking poses a considerable challenge as collecting data on trafficking is fraught with methodological difficulties (see Chapter 4).

Points for discussion – connections between categorisations of the forcibly displaced

Carling has provided a three-page document on the 36 different migration nexuses. Please read this and think about how all these different areas are connected.

- Do you think there is a strong connection between development and migration?
- Why do you think providing connections or links between different topics has been so compelling for different authors in the area of migration studies?

Carling, J. (2017) *Thirty-six migration nexuses, and counting*, view at: https://jorgencarling.org/2017/07/31/thirty-six-migration-nexuses-and-counting/

Point for discussion – describing the forcibly displaced

People who are forced to migrate are often described in negative or polemic ways. Why do you think this might be the case?

Outline of the book

The initial chapters in this book provide an outline of different forms of forced migration and key legal definitions of who is a 'refugee', 'stateless person', 'internally displaced person' or 'victim of trafficking'.

In the next chapter – Chapter 2 – the topic of people who cross borders to seek protection from persecution is explored in greater depth. There is a discussion of the internationally recognised **legal definition of a refugee** according to the 1951 Convention relating to the Status of Refugees and the subsequent 1967 Protocol relating to the Status of Refugees and other definitions contained within regional mechanisms for protecting refugees. Thereafter available statistics for the number and locations of refugees are outlined. Why international protection for refugees is crucial and how 'durable solutions' have evolved over time are explored through the work of a number of key thinkers who have shaped the protection of refugees over time.

Chapter 3 goes on to reveal how forcible displacement occurring within national borders is statistically higher than for those who cross borders. This chapter therefore looks at those who have been internally displaced – **internally displaced persons (IDPs)** – and protection needs and gaps. The 1998 Guiding Principles on Internal Displacement are discussed as is their integration into regional protection mechanisms. Again, a focus on key thinkers are drawn upon as are maps and key concepts such as 'hosting' of IDPs.

Chapter 4 looks at who is a **'victim' of human trafficking** according to the 2000 Protocol to Prevent, Suppress and Punish Trafficking in Persons Especially Women and Children, otherwise known as the **Palermo Protocol**. In the context of tight control of borders across the globe, adults and children can also be 'smuggled' or 'trafficked' within and across borders. Problems with statistics and estimates of trafficking, the issue agency of those involved and other debates that are hotly debated in relation to trafficking are outlined. Key thinkers and key concepts plus case studies are utilised to illustrate these debates.

Chapter 5 is dedicated to looking at both **mixed migrations** (Zetter, 2019) and the **'root causes'** of human displacement, distinct patterns related to political events and associated human rights violations. The root causes of forced displacement have been debated for several decades, and understanding human rights is vitally important within the study of forced migration.

Chapter 6 considers how **children are affected by forcible displacement**, both within and across borders, and how **women and children** have been depicted in forced migration debates. The United Nations Convention on the Rights of the Child (UNCRC) defines children as being below the age of 18 years. This chapter looks into the descriptors and categorisations of children used to offer protection. It also considers how the causes and consequences of forcible migration can be gendered. Issues around sexual and gender-based violence during conflict and displacement are viewed through the use of case studies to ground the work of key thinkers.

In Chapter 7 **legislative and policy responses** to displaced persons are explored, including UNHCRs 'durable solutions' of resettlement, local integration and repatriation and regional case studies of policy responses towards refugees, asylum seekers, IDPs and people who have experienced human trafficking. This includes recent Global Compacts – one for refugees and another for migrants. Chapter 7 also introduces the **issue of ethics** in both working with people who have been displaced and conducting research with displaced populations. Scenarios are provided for students to work through – these are based on working and conducting research in humanitarian contexts. Suggested further reading around the need to move beyond standard 'Do no harm' ethical frameworks are provided. Examples of ethical guidance available in the field of forced migration are included.

Finally, Chapter 8 addresses contemporary issues in the past five years. Case studies of forced migration are included on what has been termed a 'refugee crisis' across Europe and the arrival of Rohingya refugees into Bangladesh. The case study of Rohingya refugees felling what many have termed a genocide in Myanmar allows consideration of statelessness and the way in which the rights of the displaced fall into cracks of international protections. Emerging and future trends in research in this area are discussed. Suggested further reading completes this book.

Further reading

Carling, J. (2017) *Thirty-six Migration Nexuses, and Counting*, view at: https://jorgencarling.org/2017/07/31/thirty-six-migration-nexuses-and-counting/

Castles, S., de Haas, H. and Miller, M.J. (2014) *The Age of Migration: International Populations Movements in the Modern World*, Palgrave Macmillan, London.

(In particular see Chapter 2 – sections on functionalist, neo-classical and historical-structural theories and Chapter 3 – section on the transformation of receiving societies.)

Crawley, H. and Skleparis, D. (2017) Refugees, Migrants, Neither, Both: Categorical Fetishism and the Politics of Bounding in Europe's 'Migration Crisis', *Journal of Ethnic and Migration Studies*, 44(1), 48–64.

Khosravi, S. (2007) The 'Illegal' Traveller: An Auto-ethnography of Borders, *Social Anthropology*, 15(3), 321–334.

Khosravi, S. (2010) *'Illegal' Traveller: An Auto-Ethnography of Borders*, Palgrave Macmillan, Basingstoke, Hampshire.

King, R. and Skeldon, R. (2010) 'Mind the Gap!' Integrating Approaches to Internal and International Migration, *Journal of Ethnic and Migration Studies*, 36(10), 1619–1646.

(In particular see Figure 1 on migration pathways that outline the range of options available to migrants, including return migration, and the interface between internal and international migration.)

O'Reilly, K. (2012) *International Migration & Social Theory*, Palgrave Macmillan, London and New York.

(This is about all forms of migration, not only 'forced migration' but there is a chapter specifically dedicated to refugee and forced migration that focusses on children)

Zetter, R. (2007) More Labels, Fewer Refugees: Remaking the Refugee Label in an Era of Globalization, *Journal of Refugee Studies*, 20(2), 172–192.

References

Agustin, L.M. (2007) *Sex at the Margins: Migration, Labour Markets and the Rescue Industry*, Zed Books, London and New York.

Anderson, B. and O'Connell-Davidson, J. (2002) *Trafficking – A Demand Led Problem?*, Save the Children, Sweden.

Bauman, Z. (2015) *The Migration Panic and Its (Mis)Uses*, view at: www.socialeurope.eu/2015/12/migration-panic-misuses

Bobbio, N. (1996) *The Age of Rights*, Polity Press, Cambridge.

Boswell, C. and Crisp, J. (2004) *Poverty, International Migration and Asylum*, Policy Brief No.8, United Nations University World Institute for Development Economics Research (WIDER), Helsinki.

Carling, J. (2015) A Landmark in the Landscape of Migration Studies, *Ethnic and Racial Studies*, 38(13), 2373–2376.

Castles, S. (2003) Towards a Sociology of Forced Migration and Social Transformation, *Sociology*, 37(13), 13–34.

Castles, S. (2013) The Forces Driving Global Migration, *Journal of Intercultural Studies*, 34(2), 122–140.

Castles, S. (2014) International Migration at a Crossroads, *Citizenship Studies*, 18(2), 190–207.

Collyer, M. (2015) Steel Wheels: The Age of Migration 5.0, *Ethnic and Racial Studies*, 38(13), 2362–2365.

Crawley, H., Duvell, F., Jones, K., McMahon, S. and Sigona, N. (2018) *Unravelling Europe's 'Migration Crisis': Journeys over Land and Sea*, Policy Press, Bristol.

Giddens, A. and Sutton, P.W. (2017) *Sociology* (8th ed.), Polity Press, Cambridge.

Gould, C. (2010) The Problem of Trafficking, in Palmary, I., Burman, E., Chantler, K. and Kiguwa, P. (Eds.), *Gender and Migration: Feminist Interventions,* Zed Books, London.

Internal Displacement Monitoring Centre (IDMC) (2020) *Global Report on Internal Displacement*, IDMC and Norwegian Refugee Council, Geneva, Switzerland.

International Organization for Migration (IOM) (2016) *Assessing the Risks of Migration along The Central and Eastern Mediterranean Routes: Iraq and Nigeria as Cast Study Countries*, IOM, Geneva.

International Organization for Migration (IOM) (2017) *Migrant Vulnerability to Human Trafficking and Exploitation: Evidence from the Central and Eastern Mediterranean Migration Routes*, IOM, Geneva.

King, R. (2015) Migration Comes of Age, *Ethnic and Racial Studies*, 38(13), 2366–2372.

King, R., Black, R., Collyer, M., Fielding, A. and Skeldon, R. (2010) *The Atlas of Human Migration: Global Patterns of People on the Move*, Earthscan, Brighton.

King, R. and Skeldon, R. (2010) 'Mind the Gap!' Integrating Approaches to Internal and International Migration, *Journal of Ethnic and Migration Studies*, 36(10), 1619–1646.

Kunz, E.F. (1973) The Refugee in Flight: Kinetic Models and Forms of Displacement, *International Migration Review*, 7, 125–146.

Kunz, E.F. (1981) Exile and Resettlement: Refugee Theory, *International Migration Review*, 15, 42–51.

Palmary, I. (2010) Sex, Choice and Exploitation: Reflections on Anti-Trafficking Discourse, in Palmary, I., Burman, E., Chantler, K. and Kiguwa, P. (Eds.), *Gender and Migration: Feminist Interventions*, Zed Books, London.

Ravenstein, E. (1885) The Laws of Migration, *Journal of the Statistical Society of London*, 48(2), 167–235.

Richmond, A.H. (1988) Sociological Theories of International Migration, *Current Sociology*, 36(2), 7–25.

Richmond, A.H. (1994) *Global Apartheid: Refugees, Racism and the New World Order*, Oxford University Press, Oxford.

Skeldon, R. (2015) What's in a Title? The Fifth Edition of The Age of Migration, *Ethnic and Racial Studies*, 38(13), 2356–2361.

Thomas, W. and Znaniecki, F. (1918) *The Polish Peasant in Europe and America*, Badger, Boston.

UNDESA (2016) *International Migration Report 2015*, United Nations Department of Economic and Social Affairs, Population Division, New York.

United Nations High Commission for Refugees (UNHCR) (2016) *Global Trends: Forced Displacement in 2015*, United Nations High Commission for Refugees, Geneva.

United Nations High Commission for Refugees (UNHCR) (2020) *Global Trends: Forced Displacement in 2019*, United Nations High Commission for Refugees, Geneva.

UNODC (2016) *Global Report on Trafficking in Persons 2016*, United Nations Office on Drugs and Crime, Vienna.

van Hear, N. (2012) Forcing the Issue: Migration Crisis and the Uneasy Dialogue between Refugee Research and Policy, *Journal of Refugee Studies*, 25(1), 2–24.

Vertovec, S. (1999) Conceiving and Researching Transnationalism, *Ethnic and Racial Studies*, 22(2), 447–462.

Vertovec, S. (2007) Super-diversity and Its Implications, *Ethnic and Racial Studies*, 42, 125–139.

Zetter, R. (2019) Theorizing the Refugee Humanitarian-Development Nexus: A Political-Economy Analysis, *Journal of Refugee Studies*, https://doi.org/10.1093/jrs/fez070

Zolberg, A., Suhrke, A. and Aguayo, S. (1989) *Escape from Violence*, Oxford University Press, Oxford.

2 Who is a 'refugee' and who is an 'asylum seeker'?

Introduction

> In the first place, we don't like to be called 'refugees'. We ourselves call each other 'newcomers' or 'immigrants'.
>
> Our optimism, indeed, is admirable, even if we say so ourselves. The story of our struggle has finally become known. We lost our home, which means the familiarity of daily life. We lost our occupation, which means the confidence that we are of some use in this world. We lost our language, which means the naturalness of reactions, the simplicity of gestures, the unaffected expression of feelings. We left our relatives in the Polish ghettos and our best friends have been killed in concentration camps, and that means the rupture of our private lives.
>
> Nevertheless, as soon as we were saved – and most of us had to be saved several times – we started our new lives and tried to follow as closely as possible all the good advice our saviors passed on to us.
>
> (Arendt, 1943)

This chapter poses the questions of who is a refugee and who is an asylum seeker, both under international law and in a broader sociological sense. Written towards the end of the World War II, and before the full horrors of the Holocaust had been revealed, Hannah Arendt's quotes illustrate how being a refugee involves loss and the struggle to regain dignity over time.

International laws to protect refugees were devised after World War II, at a time when protecting refugees from persecution was taken very seriously. This chapter details the forms of protection established to protect refugees. Both the 1951 Convention relating to the Status of Refugees and the subsequent 1967 Protocol relating to the Status of Refugees will be outlined – as will other definitions contained within regional mechanisms for protecting refugees. The right to seek asylum will also be explored.

Thereafter, the geography of the world's refugees are examined, including the 26 million refugees worldwide – 20.4 million under the mandate of UNHCR and 5.6 million Palestinian refugees under a separate mandate of UNRWA at the time of writing this chapter (UNHCR, 2020). Then, people who live in what have become known as protracted refugee situations (PRS) will be considered. A short outline of history of the 'durable solutions' of resettlement, local integration and repatriation available for refugees are then provided. How people seeking asylum move through a Refugee Status Determination process will illustrate the declining availability of legal routes to seek asylum and gain 'refugee' status.

Throughout, short summaries of the work of key thinkers and key concepts are provided, along with examples to bring to life these real-world dilemmas.

Who is a refugee?

The term *refugee* has extensive historical roots, and how it is used has evolved over time and across a broad range of academic disciplines and social policies. The term *refugee* has also been used across a range of academic disciplines such as sociology, anthropology, geography, history, psychology and international relations. The study of forced migration – also sometimes referred to as refugee studies – involves working across academic disciplines or using a multi-disciplinary approach. The founder of Refugee Studies was Professor Barbara Harrell-Bond who founded the first research centre on forced migration – the Refugee Studies Programme (now Refugee Studies Centre) at the University of Oxford in 1982 (see Key Thinker Box 2.1) utilizing a multi-disciplinary approach.

The term *refugee* was first used in 1573 in France during the late 17th century to describe how people fleeing persecution were granted asylum and assisted (Zolberg *et al.*, 1989:5). The first refugees were Huguenots fleeing France who arrived in England in 1685 after being persecuted on the basis of their religion. As will be seen later in this chapter, religion is now one of the five causes recognized within the 1951 Refugee Convention. In ordinary usage, the term *refugee* has been used to describe and signify somebody who is in flight, escaping oppression or persecution and is seeking freedom, safety and refuge. As Goodwin-Gill explains:

> Implicit in the ordinary meaning of the word 'refugee' lies an assumption that the person concerned is worthy of being, and ought to be, assisted, and, if necessary, protected from the causes and consequences of flight.
>
> (Goodwin-Gill, 1996:3)

In times of unlimited immigration the distinction between who is a refugee and who is migrating for different reasons is less important than it has become in the late 20th and beginning of the 21st century (Zolberg *et al.*, 1989). In the contemporary world, strict criteria are applied to make the distinction between refugees and other migrants. Today there is little agreement in public discourse around who is deserving of protection, asylum and support and who is undeserving (Sales, 2002). It is not coincidental that these debates have emerged alongside restrictive immigration policies. Disagreement about who is a refugee continue, but when life and liberty are at stake, accurate decision making is critical for those in need of protection from persecution.

Perceptions play an important role in this. As the anthropologist Lisa Malkki (see Key Thinker Box 2.2) suggests:

> Asylum states and international agencies dealing with refugees . . . tend to share the premise that refugees are necessarily 'a problem'. Not just 'ordinary people'.
>
> (Malkki, 1995:8)

Malkki highlights how **literature about refugees often locates this 'problem' within the bodies and minds of people classified as refugees rather than a broader understanding of the circumstances that have caused displacement** or the oppression and violence that produce refugees in the first instance. Locating the problem of displacement of individuals in this way results in descriptions being very polarized (Zetter, 2007; see Key Thinker Box 2.4). How refugees are seen and defined is important, and a range of often binary and opposite descriptions have been applied to describe them. As shown in Table 2.1, throughout history these have included:

Table 2.1 Positive and Negative Labels of Refugees and Asylum Seekers

Positive labels	Negative labels
Deserving	Undeserving
Assets	Burdens
Capable	Vulnerable
Survivors	Victims
Angels	Devils
Movers and shakers	Threats
Autonomous agents	Problems
Agents of development	Dependent
Agents of democracy	Terrorists
Genuine	Bogus
Champions of change	Powerless
A resource	A threat
Mobile	Mobile

Refugees are sometimes described as being capable, autonomous agents who are assets to the societies they inhabit. Equally they are also often referred to as vulnerable, powerless burdens on society who might pose a national threat to the countries they reach and within which they are able to find refuge. In many cases, mobility is often considered as being both positive (due to any enhancement in status involved and benefits to both the society they migrate to and their families in countries of origin due to remittances returned) or as overtly negative, requiring controlling measures, mechanisms to deter new arrivals and closure of borders. As can be seen, binary thinking outlined in other chapters dominates descriptions and perceptions of those forced to migrate.

For writers such as Turton (2003), the way in which refugees are portrayed and perceived becomes important when, for example, they need to access services. Someone perceived as being a 'vulnerable victim' might be able to access to services, resources, advice or assistance whereas someone perceived as being a 'capable survivor' might not gain similar access. Turton (2003) proposed that **refugees and asylum seekers should be considered as 'ordinary people' who have been through extraordinary circumstances**, bypassing such binary conceptions and the range of polar opposites outlined earlier.

With much less emphasis on individual causes and taking a far more structural stance, the political theorist Aristide Zolberg argued that **the creation of nation-states was in itself a 'refugee-generating process'** (1989:228) with **refugees being 'a by-product of social change'** (1989:262). According to Zolberg, persecution was directed against groups – religious, national or social groups – who had gained these characteristics simply by being born. For Zolberg, historical processes involved in transformation of empires into nation-states resulted in refugees who could be delineated into three sociological types:

1   The activist – dissenters whose actions contribute to the conflict that ultimately forces them to flee
2   The target – individuals who, through membership of a particular social group, are singled out for violent action
3   The victim – those who are randomly caught in the crossfire or are exposed to generalized violence

The first and second type are considered part of international refugee law, although the third type – the victim – only sees protection within regional mechanisms as outlined in later text.

Points for Discussion – Labelling

*   Can you think of any other terms that have been applied to refugees or asylum seekers?
*   Are they positive or negative?
*   Why do you think those labels exist?

Key Thinker Box 2.1   Barbara Harrell-Bond – *Imposing Aid*

Professor Barbara Harrell-Bond OBE founded the first research centre on forced migration – the Refugee Studies Programme (now Refugee Studies Centre at the University of Oxford in 1982.

Her 1986 seminal text – *Imposing Aid: Emergency Assistance to Refugees* – exposed the shortcomings of the aid regime and delivery of aid for refugees through voluntary, national and international agencies. Widely considered to be essential reading – and essential learning – this book provoked strong reactions at the time of publication. Harrell-Bond asked why there was 'no tradition of independent, critical research in the field of refugee assistance' (1986:xi), pointing out that agencies involved were aware of the same mistakes being repeated over and over again in setting up and implementing aid to refugees. The way in which refugees were viewed as a temporary phenomenon means aid was delivered under emergency relief and subsequent structures rather than adoption of a developmental approach.

Imposing Aid focused on an emergency assistance programme for Ugandan refugees in southern Sudan which aimed to promote economic independent for refugees. Harrell-Bond and her team initially observed the emergency programme. They then conducted a random sample of 10,675 refugees across 2,017 households who were then assisted by UNHCR and NGOs across 22 different settlements and 3 transit camps. As today, most refugees lived outside the official relief system, and interviews were also conducted with 3,814 refugee households who had selfsettled in the district and were not receiving official assistance. Some 200 children's drawings of 'refugee life' were collected, and more than 100 hours of refugee 'voices' recorded. At the time of the fieldwork for this study – March 1982 to September 1983 – participatory methods and attempts to capture the creative energies of participants of aid were not prevalent in the delivery of aid.

Key findings were that the assistance programme was based on **equity of distribution** of material support. Harrell-Bond argued that treating all refugees as equal actually exacerbated economic differences, with the more vulnerable groups becoming more impoverished by the lack of nuanced support mechanisms. Harrell-Bond also argued that the very **concept of 'refugee' was an artificial category** that suited donors and the aid industry more than the people in receipt of such aid. The convenience – for the delivery of aid – of hosting refugees in 'camps' where refugees are visible was part of this critique as was the prevailing approach of the time that refugees themselves were to blame for the failures of aid programmes and their own economic dependence on future aid. A reversal of this thinking – that the often utilised phrase 'dependency syndrome' was the fault of refugees themselves – was proposed by Harrell-Bond, who suggested that the actual fault lay in the way in which aid was managed and delivered by humanitarian agencies.

Subsequent work by Harrell-Bond has focussed on protests against UNHCR by refugees and details of the interactions between refugees and their 'helpers' within humanitarian aid structures. By continuing to carry out independent, critical research into the lives of refugees – and continually encouraging others to do the same – Harrell-Bond has shaped the study of forced migration (Harrell-Bond, 2002, 2008a, 2008b).

She also wrote about setting up refugee legal aid organisations in the 'South', not only working on this topic in theory but bridging into activism and practice on a regular basis. She co-founded or established several organisations and networks, promoting legal assistance for refugees around the world:

- International Research and Advisory Panel (IRAP), which became the International Association for the Study of Forced Migration (IASFM) – http://iasfm.org
- Refugee Law Project (RLP) from the School of Law, Makerere University, Uganda – www.refugeelawproject.org
- Africa and Middle East Refugee Assistance (AMERA), Egypt – www.amerainternational.org
- Southern Refugee Legal Aid Network – https://srlanetwork.wordpress.com
- Rights in Exile Programme, UK – www.refugeelegalaidinformation.org

A documentary in tribute to her life – 'A Life Not Ordinary' – can be found here: https://vimeo.com/273494590.

A special issue of Forced Migration Review in tribute to her life can be found here: www.fmreview.org/sites/fmr/files/FMRdownloads/en/ethics/Tribute-BarbaraHarrellBond.pdf

Key references – Barbara Harrell-Bond

Harrell-Bond, B. (1986) *Imposing Aid: Emergency Assistance to Refugees*, Oxford University Press, Oxford.

Harrell-Bond, B. (2002) Can Humanitarian Work with Refugees be Humane? *Human Rights Quarterly*, 24, 51–85.

Harrell-Bond, B. (2008a) Building the Infrastructure for the Observance of Refugee Rights in the Global South, *Refuge*, 25(2), 12–28.

Harrell-Bond, B. (2008b) Protests Against UNHCR to Achieve Rights: Some Reflections, in Grabska, K. and Mehta, L. (Eds.), *Forced Displacement: Why Rights Matter*, Palgrave Macmillan, Basingstoke.

Key Thinker Box 2.2   Lisa Malkki – *Purity and Exile*

Lisa Malkki is an anthropologist and Professor at Stanford University. She is widely cited in forced migration studies as a result of her one-year field research between October 1985 and October 1986 in Tanzania, which looked at how political violence and exile produce a sense of historical consciousness and national identity among people who have been displaced. The resulting 1995 seminal text – *Purity and Exile: Violence, Memory and National Cosmology among Hutu Refugees in Tanzania* – explored how Hutu refugees from Burundi, driven into exile in Tanzania after the 1972 massacre constructed their histories in both refugee camps and in urban settings. She found that a key aspect of living in refugee camps involved the creation of an elaborate 'mythico-history' of the Hutu people wherein history was involved in everyday thought and social action. For those living in more urban settings she found identities related more closely to practical circumstances, day-to-day life and the ability to lose the identity of 'refugee' and 'adopt strategies of invisibility' (1995:155). It also examined how essentialised categories of identity such as 'Hutu' and 'Tutsi' were produced in contexts of violence and exile and how 'processes of making and unmaking' identities evolved in both locations (1995:17).

This ethnography explores a number of key concepts that continue to be explored within refugee or forced migration studies, including how refugees occupy a liminal position in the world, citing Turner's 1967 explanation of being 'betwixt and between' during rites of passage. It also explored how refugees are often seen as threats to national security (see also Douglas, 1996). For Malkki, states and international agencies framing refugees as a 'problem' relates to the political oppression or violence that created their displacement rather than being embodied within those classified as refugees. Refugees, she argued, thus become 'idealized and generalized as a type of person' (1995:9) rather than as 'ordinary people' experiencing displacement.

Other and subsequent work by Malkki has explored the history of 'the refugee', 'refugee studies' and the refugee camp as a device of power and control as well as the tendency to regard movement across borders with a focus on loss rather than transformation (1995a, 1995b). She has also focussed on how refugees are often depoliticised and dehistoricised by international organisations within the humanitarian sector (1996).

These publications and her more recent work can be viewed at: https://profiles.stanford.edu/liisa-malkki?tab=publications.

Key references – Lisa Malkki

Douglas, M. (1996) *Purity and Danger: An Analysis of the Concepts of Pollution and Taboo*, Routledge, London.

Malkki, L. (1995a) Refugees and Exile: From 'Refugee Studies' to the National Order of Things, *Annual Review of Anthropology*, 24, 495–523.

Malkki, L. (1995b) *Purity and Exile: Violence, Memory and National Cosmology among Hutu Refugees in Tanzania*, University of Chicago Press, Chicago and London.

Malkki, L. (1996) Speechless Emissaries: Refugees, Humanitarianism and Dehistoricization, *Cultural Anthropology*, 11(3), 377–404.

Turner, V. (1967) *The Forest of Symbols: Aspects of Ndembu Ritual*, Cornell University Press, Ithaca, NY.

Who is a refugee under international law?

Under international law, the term *refugee* has a distinct meaning and is operationalized through refugee status determination (RSD) procedures to decide who is and who is not a refugee. These RSD procedures tend to be implemented either by States or UNHCR.

In international law a 'refugee' according to the **1951 Convention relating to the Status of Refugees** (hereafter the 1951 Refugee Convention) is a person who:

> owing to a well-founded fear of being persecuted for reasons of race, religion, nationality, membership of a particular social group or political opinion, is outside the country of his nationality and is unable or, owing to such fear, is unwilling to avail himself of the protection of that country; or who, having a nationality and being outside the country of his former habitual residence . . . is unable or, owing to such fear, is unwilling to return to it.

The signing of this Convention occurred at a point in time when protection from persecution was taken very seriously. Prior to the drawing up of the 1951 Refugee Convention, particular groups had been persecuted during World War II – Jews, gypsies, communists and homosexuals – and this Convention was initially restricted to events that occurred in Europe before 1 January 1951. A subsequent **1967 Protocol relating to the Status of Refugees** (hereafter the 1951 Refugee Protocol) removed the time limitation of the 1951 Convention so that events after 1951 could be included and, at the same time, made the 1951 Convention universal in its application, with a reach beyond Europe.

Both the 1951 Refugee Convention and the 1967 Refugee Protocol were applied to individuals, requiring a case-by-case examination of their claims (Goodwin-Gill, 1996:8). To be a refugee, four key characteristics were involved. Firstly, the person had to be outside their country of origin. Secondly, they were in a position where they are unable or unwilling to avail themselves of the protection of that country, or to return there. Thirdly, such inability or unwillingness is due to a well-founded fear of persecution. Finally, the persecution feared is based on reasons of 'race', religion, nationality, membership of a social group or political opinion.

For example, Rohingya Muslims fleeing contemporary Burma would clearly be categorised as having a well-founded fear of persecution based on their religion in signatory countries. Another example could be membership of a particular social group (PSG) wherein persecution stems from not being loyal to the government. There have been a number of cases involving such PSGs being seen as an obstacle to governments. For example, the Vietnamese bourgeoisie in the late 1970s was seen as an obstacle to economic and social restricting of the country. In terms of persecution on the basis of political opinion, members of the Karen National Union (KNU) who had until recently been in opposition to the central Burmese government and even those living in KNU areas were considered to be subject to persecution on the basis of imputed political opinions.

Points for discussion – the 1951 Refugee Convention

- Can you think of other examples beyond the existing five basis of 'race', religion, nationality, membership of a particular social group or political opinion?
- What do you think is missing?

When the 1951 Convention and 1967 Protocol were written, there was much less awareness of the forms of persecution that can be based specifically on gender. Such gender-based persecution is often hard to prove and, without this being a basis of the 1951 Refugee Convention, some countries such as South Africa have now adopted a sixth basis of persecution – sexual and gender-based violence.

Nor does the 1951 Convention or 1967 Protocol make provision for any of the below:

- Generalised violence
- Mass killing
- Social and economic persecution
- The effects of war
- Victims of 'natural' disasters
- The fear of hunger

At the same time the United Nations High Commissioner for Refugees (UNHCR) was established by the General Assembly to provide international protection for refugees and seek permanent solutions to their plight. Their work was to be 'non-political' and 'humanitarian', concentrating on groups of refugees. However, there is a contradiction that endures up to today – the work of UNHCR relates to groups and categories of refugees, whereas the legal refugee definition is individualistic (Goodwin-Gill, 1996:8).

Points for discussion – global responsibility for refugees

- Is it right that rich countries such as the UK and Germany – who have both ratified the 1951 Refugee Convention – be allowed to limit the number of refugees they receive?

- Why should countries that are considered low- or middle-income host the majority of refugees?
- Why do you think this happens?

Regional mechanisms

There are also regional mechanisms for protecting refugees which incorporate the definition of a refugee under the 1951 Convention and the 1967 Protocol. The Organisation of African Unity (OAU) has a legal definition under the **1969 Convention Governing the Specific Aspects of Refugee Problems in Africa** (hereafter the 1969 OAU Convention), which has a two-part definition. The first part is as per the 1951 Refugee Convention. However, there is a second part which reads:

> The term refugee shall also apply to every person who, owing to external aggression, occupation, foreign domination or events seriously disturbing public order in either part or the whole of his country of origin or nationality, is compelled to leave his place of habitual residence in order to seek refuge in another place outside his country of origin or nationality.

This definition was adopted on 10 September 1969 and entered into force on 20 June 1974. It has been signed or ratified by most of the member states of the African Union (AU). The definition is wider than the 1951 Convention, as it adapted that definition to the realities of the developing world. It also recognised that persecution could occur as a result of the actions of non-state agents. The 1969 OAU Convention therefore added in causes of persecution not recognised within its European counterpart. Additional aspects include flight from:

- External aggression
- Foreign domination
- Events seriously disturbing the public order

Group determination of persecution was also included in this and it was recognised that wars of national literation might also involve non-state agents.

Points for discussion – 1969 Organisation for African Unity Convention

- What was happening across African prior to the adoption of the 1969 OAU Convention?
- How might this have influenced the writing of this Convention?

In South America, the 1984 Cartagena Declaration took this definition a step further and broadened the refugee definition again. Although not a formally binding treaty, it recognised the 1951 Refugee Convention definition and added additional elements:

> To reiterate that, in view of the experience gained from the massive flows of refugees in the Central American area, it is necessary to consider enlarging the concept of a refugee, bearing in mind, as far as appropriate and in the light of the situation prevailing in the region, the precedent of the OAU Convention (article 1, paragraph 2) and the doctrine employed in the reports of the Inter-American Commission on Human Rights.

Hence the definition or concept of a refugee to be recommended for use in the region is one which, in addition to containing the elements of the 1951 Convention and the 1967 Protocol, includes among refugees persons who have fled their country because their lives, safety or freedom have been threatened by 'generalized violence, foreign aggression, internal conflicts, massive violation of human rights or other circumstances which have seriously disturbed public order'.

Again, group determination of persecution was also included in this and additional aspects included flight from:

- Refugees from generalised violence
- Refugees as a result of foreign aggression
- Internal conflicts
- Massive violations of human rights
- Circumstances which have seriously disturbed the public order

This expanded definition has since been used in contexts of mass influx within South America.

Point for discussion – 1984 Cartagena declaration

- What was happening in South America prior to the 1984 Cartagena Declaration being signed?

Who is an asylum seeker, and who has the right to seek asylum from persecution?

An asylum seeker is a person making a claim for asylum under the 1951 Refugee Convention and 1967 Refugee Protocol. Article 14(2) of the UDHR outlines how: 'Everyone has the right to seek and to enjoy in other countries asylum from persecution'.

This right to asylum is one of the most important obligations in international law. It protects people around the world who are at risk of persecution by their own State. There is an ongoing need for countries to provide a safe place for people to live when applying for asylum. This safe place should include non-discrimination (Article 3 of the 1951 Refugee Convention), freedom to practice their religion and the religious education of their children (Article 4), access to courts (Article 16), the right to wage-earning employment (Article 17), housing (Article 21), public education (Article 22), public relief (Article 23) and freedom of movement (Article 26) amongst other Articles of the 1951 Refugee Convention.

A key principle enshrined in the 1951 Convention is the principle of *non-refoulement*, a cornerstone of international law (Article 33). This Article means that States cannot return anyone to their country of origin where their life or freedom could be threatened as a result of their race, religion, nationality, membership of a particular social group or political opinion. Therefore, if someone seeking asylum is likely to be tortured or subject to cruel, inhumane or degrading treatment on their return, this is against international law. There is similar wording about *non-refoulement* in, for example the UDHR, the UN Convention on Torture and in domestic human rights Acts.

However, even though Article 14 of the UDHR outlines how everyone has the right to seek asylum, there is **no automatic right to be granted asylum** within the UDHR, the 1951 Refugee Convention or other international Conventions. In other words, whilst international law recognizes the right to asylum, States do not always provide it in the spirit of the original conception of asylum, and many take policy measures to avoid allowing this right to be fulfilled.

This means that the interpretation of the law is vital. A process of **refugee status determination (RSD)** is required which, in countries such as the UK, is carried out by the State. For refugees inside and outside refugee camps in the low- and middle-income countries, this process is often carried out by UNHCR.

To move through being an asylum seeker to gaining the status of being a refugee is rarely easy and often lengthy, complex and frustrating.

Point for discussion – the principle of non-refoulement

•   Why do you think the principal of *non-refoulement* is so important in international law?

Globally, how many people are refugees?

Statistics relating to refugees and other populations forcibly displaced are regularly provided by UNHCR in yearly 'global trends' reports.

Since UNHCR was established in 1950 and the 1951 Refugee Convention and 1967 Refugee Protocol compiled, recorded numbers of refugees have risen. As can be seen on Figure 2.1, by the end of 1951 there were 2.12 million refugees recorded. By the time the 1967 Refugee Protocol was drawn up, there were some 2.36 million refugees and 'returnees' (returned refugees or IDPs) known to UNHCR. When the Berlin Wall fell in 1989 there were 14.94 million refugees and 'returnees' and by the turn of the century, some 21.87 million refugees, asylum seekers, IDPs, returnees and other persons of concern were recorded as populations of concern by UNHCR. A decade later – the end of 2010 – there were 43.7 million forcibly displaced people (UNHCR, 2011).

As outlined in Chapter 1, by the end of 2015, of the 65.3 million people forcibly displaced worldwide, 21.3 million were refugees or people in what UNHCR term 'persons in refugee-like situations'. Of these, 16.1 million were under UNHCR's mandate of protection, and 5.2 million Palestinian refugees were registered by the United Nations Relief and Works Agency for Palestine Refugees in the Near East (UNRWA) (UNHCR, 2016). By the end of 2019 this number had risen to 26 million refugees worldwide with 20.4 million under UNHCR's mandate and 5.6 million under UNRWA's.

As can be seen in Figure 2.1, this incremental rise in those displaced globally are recorded by UNHCR.

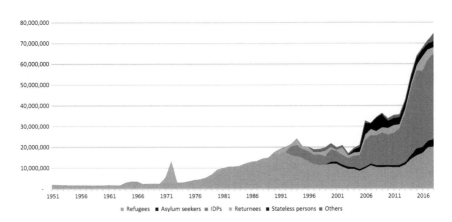

Figure 2.1 UNHCR Statistics: 1951–2018

An interactive webpage of Figure 2.1 can be found at: http://popstats.unhcr.org/en/overview.

In the period between 2010 and 2018, UNHCR recorded an increasing number of people displaced worldwide of which the number of refugees and asylum seekers also increased – see Figure 2.2:

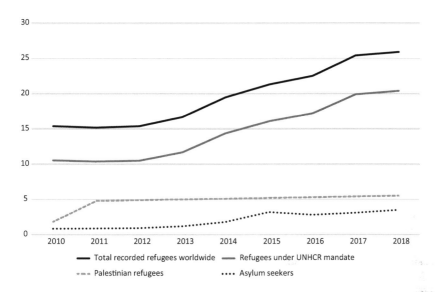

Figure 2.2 Recorded Displacement of Refugees and Asylum Seekers: 2010–2018

Figure 2.2 illustrates how the additional of Palestinian refugees adds to the total number of refugees worldwide. Table 2.2 provides an additional consideration around how these figures sit within the total recorded displacement worldwide. As can be seen, by 2018 the total number of refugees recorded worldwide makes up less than one third of the total recorded displacement figure that is often recounted in the media when reporting on refugee movements.

Table 2.2 Total Recorded Displacement Worldwide – Refugees and Asylum Seekers: 2010–2018

	Total recorded displacement worldwide	Total recorded refugees worldwide	Refugees under UNHCR mandate	Palestinian refugees	Asylum seekers
2010	43.7m	15.4m	10.55m	1.82m	0.837m
2011	42.5m	15.2m	10.4m	4.8m	0.895m
2012	35.8m	15.4m	10.5m	4.9m	0.937m
2013	51.2m	16.7m	11.7m	5.0m	1.2m
2014	59.5m	19.5m	14.4m	5.1m	1.8m
2015	65.3m	21.3m	16.1m	5.2m	3.2m
2016	65.6m	22.5m	17.2m	5.3m	2.8m
2017	68.5m	25.4m	19.9m	5.4m	3.1m
2018	70.8m	25.9m	20.4m	5.5m	3.5m

Source: UNHCR Global Trends, various dates

Palestinian refugees

As outlined in Chapter 1, the **United Nations Relief and Works Agency for Palestine Refugees in the Near East (UNRWA)** was established in 1950, as a temporary agency, to provide humanitarian relief to more than 700,000 refugees and displaced persons who had been forced to flee their homes in Palestine as a result of the 1948 Arab-Israeli conflict in 1948.

Initially established to carry our relief programmes, over time its operations have evolved to include a range of services and improvements to camp infrastructure in Jordan, Lebanon, Syria and the occupied Palestinian territory. It contributes to the welfare of the initial and subsequent generations of Palestinian refugees who are defined as 'Persons whose normal place of residence was Palestine during the period 1 June 1946 to 15 May 1948, and who lost both home and means of livelihood as a result of the 1948 conflict'.

According to UNHCR there are now 5.5 million Palestinians refugees who are considered to be the longest example of a protracted refugee situation (PRS) (see the link that follows).

You can find a useful timeline of events relating to Palestinian refugees here: www.unrwa.org/who-we-are

Point for discussion – Palestinian refugees

• If UNRWA was set up as a temporary agency in 1950, why is it still working with Palestinian refugees after nearly 70 years?

Where do refugees come from?

The countries of origin of refugees forced to flee persecution change over time. For example, some 250,000 refugees from Belgium arrived in the UK between 1914 and 1918 (Kushner and Knox, 1999). Between the 1940s to the early 1950s, some 300,000 Polish displaced persons arrived in the UK and around 20,000 Hungarian refugees fled communism post-1956 (Ibid., 1999). Since then there have been significant refugee situations across Africa after independence movements, Southeast Asia following the end of the Vietnam/American War and within South America.

In recent years refugees fleeing the conflict in the Syrian Arab Republic have become the highest recorded number of refugees worldwide. In 2014, refugees from the Syrian Arab overtook Afghanistan, which had previously seen the highest numbers of refugees for several years prior to this. As can be seen in Table 2.3, following violence in Rakhine State, Burma, refugees from Myanmar now also feature in the 'top 5' countries of origin (excluding Palestinian refugees).

Table 2.3 Countries of Origin of Key Refugee Movements: 2013–2018

2013	2014	2015	2016	2017	2018
Afghanistan (2.56m)	Syria (3.88m)	Syria (4.9m)	Syria (5.5m)	Syria (6.3m)	Syria (6.7m)
Syria (2.47m)	Afghanistan (2.59m)	Afghanistan (2.7m)	Afghanistan (2.5m)	Afghanistan (2.6m)	Afghanistan (2.7m)
Somalia (1.12m)	Somalia (1.11m)	Somalia (1.1m)	South Sudan (1.4m)	South Sudan (2.4m)	South Sudan (2.3m)
				Myanmar (1.2m)	Myanmar (1.1m)
				Somalia (0.98m)	Somalia (0.9m)

Source: UNHCR Global Trends, various dates

Where are the world's refugees hosted?

Although there is a strong perception that most refugees travel to high-income countries, in reality most refugees are hosted in low- or middle-income countries. In 2018 for example, only 16% of refugees were hosted in high-income countries, and approximately one-third of the global refugee population were hosted in least-developed countries (some 6.7 million people).

By the end of 2018, **Turkey had hosted the largest number of refugees worldwide for five consecutive years** (see Table 2.4). Most of these refugees were from Syria, with smaller numbers from Iraq, Iran and Afghanistan. Turkey protects Syrians under the country's Temporary Protection Regulation that does not involve individual refugee status determination (RSD) processes. Syrian refugees are also hosted in Lebanon, Jordan, Iraq and Egypt.

In practice, Turkey hosted around 18% of UNHCR-mandated refugees during 2018, whereas the rest of Europe hosted less than this proportion (UNHCR, 2019).

Up to the end of 2013, Pakistan had hosted the most refugees for several years, with 1.6 million refugees living in the country, and it continued to host large numbers of refugees up to the end of 2018. Uganda hosts refugees mainly from the Democratic Republic of the Congo and South Sudan. Sudan also hosts refugees from South Sudan. Germany hosted 1.1m refugees by the end of 2018, again mainly from Syria and smaller numbers from Iraq, Afghanistan and a range of other countries.

Bangladesh continues to host refugees from Myanmar, many of whom are recorded as stateless from Rakhine State, having had their citizenship rights systematically eroded over the past few decades by the Myanmar military government. Refugees from Myanmar have also been hosted by Malaysia, Thailand, India and China for the past few decades.

Figure 2.3 outlines both countries of origin and countries with newly registered refugees and asylum seekers during 2018. As can be seen, Venezuela now has refugees entering Peru and, to a lesser extent, the USA.

Table 2.4 Countries that Host Refugees: 2010–2018

2010	2011	2012	2013	2014	2015	2016	2017	2018
Pakistan (1.9m)	Pakistan (1.7m)	Pakistan (1.6m)	Pakistan (1.6m)	Turkey (1.59m)	Turkey (2.5m)	Turkey (2.9m)	Turkey (3.5m)	Turkey (3.7m)
Iran (1.1m)	Iran (887,000)	Iran (868,200)	Iran (857,400)	Pakistan (1.51m)	Pakistan (1.6m)	Pakistan (1.4m)	Pakistan (1.4m)	Pakistan (1.4m)
Syria (1m)	Syria (755,400)	Germany (589,700)	Lebanon (856,500)	Lebanon (1.15m)	Lebanon (1.1m)	Lebanon (1m)	Uganda (1.4m)	Uganda (1.2m)
		Kenya (565,000)	Jordan (641,900)	Iran (982,200)	Iran (979,400)	Iran (979,400)	Lebanon (998,900)	Sudan (1.1m)
			Turkey (609,900)	Ethiopia (659,500)	Ethiopia (736,100)	Uganda (940,800)	Iran (979,400)	Germany (1.1m)
				Jordan (654,100)	Jordan (664,100)	Ethiopia (791,600)	Germany (970,400)	Bangladesh (906,600)
							Bangladesh (932,200)	
							Sudan (906,600)	

Source: UNHCR Global Trends, various dates

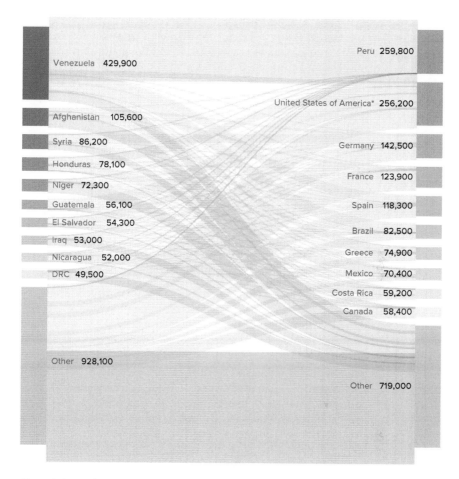

Figure 2.3 Newly Registered Refugees and Asylum Seekers in 2018
Source: UNHCR, 2019

Statelessness

It has been estimated that there are between 10 and 12 million people who are stateless across the globe (Blitz, 2011; UNHCR, 2018). However, data captured by governments and communicated to UNHCR was limited to 3.9 million stateless individuals in 78 countries by the end of 2018.

Statelessness in a legal sense refers to people who are not considered nationals of any State. The 1954 Convention relating to the Status of Stateless Persons (hereafter the 1954 Stateless Convention) was initially designed as a framework to meet the protection needs of those who had been left stateless after WWII. Initially it was designed as a Protocol to the 1951 Refugee Convention, but later it became a stand-alone instrument. Both refugees and stateless persons experience an absence of international protection, but the plight of those who experience statelessness has been neglected, arguably for the past four decades. This Convention defined a stateless person as 'a persons who is not considered a national by any State under the operation of its law'.

The 1954 Stateless Convention was similar to the 1951 Refugee Convention, but there were two key differences:

1   There is no protection from *refoulement*
2   There is no protection against penalisation for illegal entry or stay

However, if a stateless person is also a refugee, he or she enjoys protection from *refoulement*.

Following this Convention, the 1961 Convention on the Reduction of Statelessness (the 1961 Statelessness Convention) emerged. This framework, designed to ensure no future cases of statelessness after WWII, called upon signatories to prevent as well as reduce the number of people who experienced statelessness. The 1961 Statelessness Convention recognises that the underlying cause of statelessness relates to sovereign States being free to set up their own terms for membership. When these terms exclude particular populations, the result can be statelessness.

It is useful when thinking about statelessness to consider the work of Hannah Arendt, particularly her 1951 work on *The Origins of Totalitarianism*. Arendt argued that those who were excluded by the State experienced a situation wherein they **lost the right to have rights** and, because of this, also lose their homes, State protection and, less tangibly, a place in the world.

This legal anomaly often prevents people from accessing fundamental civil, political, economic, cultural and social rights.

Authors such as Brad Blitz have argued that Arendt's concept of statelessness – and the loss of the right to have rights – can include those in statelessness-like situations. Blitz looks at the example of refused asylum seekers in the UK who 'endure an existence not unlike stateless people' (Blitz, 2011) because they have lost their entitlement to protection by the country in which they sought asylum and may be unable to return to their countries of origin. Unable to work and unable to access the entitlements afforded to citizens of the UK, Blitz suggests that the numbers of stateless persons in the UK remains unknown.

There are a few key examples of stateless persons in the world today. These include the Bidoon in Kuwait who were not given Kuwaiti nationality at the time of independence when the British ended the protectorate in 1961. Stateless people from Haiti who live in the Dominican Republic, Romani people in Europe and people in detention in Ukraine have also been cited as examples of statelessness. A recent example relates to the Rohingya population from Rakhine State in Myanmar, made stateless due to the restrictive provisions and application of the Myanmar Citizenship Law, which confers citizenship on the basis of ethnicity. As a result of their statelessness, the Rohingya in Myanmar suffer entrenched discrimination, marginalisation and denial of a wide range of human rights (see Chapter 8 for further details).

For children, statelessness can occur as a result of inter-generational exclusion, gender discrimination or a lack of birth registration amongst other reasons (ISI, 2017). Not having a nationality often means services, social welfare, education and health facilities are denied (Bhabha, 2017). For children displaced across international borders because of armed conflict or political oppression, basic services are likely to be offered by charities or the voluntary sector, if at all (Boyden and Hart, 2007).

Protracted refugee situations

It is not well-known that a large proportion of refugees have lived in exile for several decades awaiting a 'durable solution' to their displacement. When refugees have been in exile for more than five years it is referred to by UNHCR as a **protracted refugee situation (PRS)** and defined as where '25,000 or more people of the same nationality have been in exile for five consecutive years or more in a host country' (UNHCR, 2016:20).

By the end of 2018, some 15.9 million refugees were considered by UNHCR to be in protracted situations. This represented 78% of all refugees, with no protracted refugee situations resolved during 2018 (UNHCR, 2019).

Figure 2.4 provides an overview of key protracted refugee situations under UNHCR's mandate. The first example relates to Afghan refugees in Pakistan and Iran. Refugees from the Democratic Republic of the Congo can be seen to have been hosted by Uganda, Burundi, Tanzania, Rwanda and South Africa. If the example of refugees from Myanmar is considered, the following chart highlights how refugees have been hosted in Bangladesh, Malaysia and Thailand for more than three decades. Likewise Somalians have been hosted in Ethiopia, Kenya, South Africa and for Yemen close to four decades.

Not all PRS are included in this chart. For example, the full extent of Palestinian refugees who have been displaced for nearly 70 years requires further thought, with only those in Egypt highlighted in this chart. In 2018 there were 5.5 million Palestinian refugees registered with the UNRWA and only a small proportion are represented below. UNHCR's definition does not include those who do not live in refugee camps and stay in urban settings around the world (Loescher and Milner, 2005).

The causes of such protracted displacement tend to arise out of coming from countries where conflict and persecution has been ongoing for decades and where policies to contain refugees – known as **containment policies** – mean that States consider protection should be provided in regions of origin rather than in the global North (Hyndman and Giles, 2017). UNHCR's initial operations of long-term 'care and maintenance' programmes in refugees

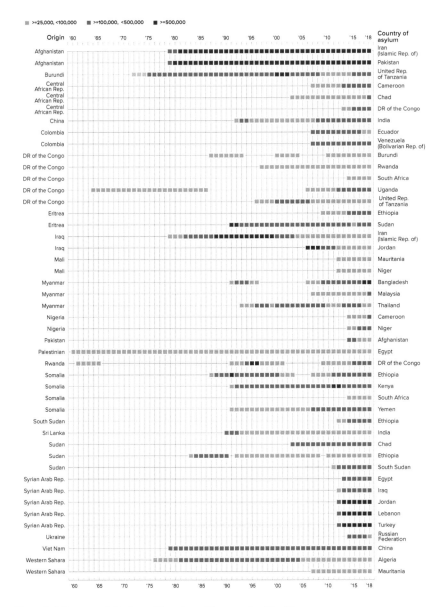

Figure 2.4 Protracted Refugee Situations Characterized by Size

Source: UNHCR, 2019

camps provides low levels of assistance, also taking little account of the evolving needs of refugees in these situations (Crisp, 2002; Hyndman and Giles, 2017). It is increasingly recognized that there needs to be a shift from these care and maintenance programmes towards 'self-reliance' for refugees. However, few alternative solutions have been offered beyond an expectation that host States allow for local integration (see discussion of 'durable solutions' that follows). The expectation that refugees become self-reliant also often ignores structural contexts in countries of asylum that work against this in practice, including refugees not having access to a full range of rights. Solution-focused responses are generally lacking.

The consequences of PRS for refugees are many and include sexual violence, physical violence, human rights violations, lack of access to education, bans on employment and an overall lack of focus on the abilities of individuals contained within them. As can be seen in Figure 2.5, protracted situations can be in isolated environments, far from towns or cities in host countries.

Figure 2.5 Isolated Protracted Refugee Situations

Source: Hynes, 2020

Figure 2.6 Protracted Refugee Situations in Insecure Setting
Source: Hynes, 2020

They might also be located in dangerous areas. Figure 2.6 shows the location of a protracted refugee situation next to the Salween River between Thailand and Myanmar, circa 1999 which at the time was heavily militarised on the Myanmar side.

An alternative definition of PRS – populations of 10,000 or more restricted to camps or segregated settlements in situations for the last five years or more – was proposed by the US Committee for Refugees and Immigrants (USCRI, various dates). This definition drew attention to the situation of refugees who had lived in camps, or in the term used by USCRI, had been 'warehoused' for five years or more, calling for a rights-based approach to refugees that recognizes both their human rights as well as their refugee rights.

Points for discussion – protracted refugee situations

- What strikes you as important or of note in the earlier chart?
- Why do you think 78% of all refugees are living in protracted refugee situations?
- Which description do you think best describes this – *protracted refugee situations* or *warehousing*?

Key Thinker Box 2.3   Jeff Crisp – @JFCrisp

Between 2006 and 2013, Jeff Crisp was the Head of Policy Development and Evaluation at UNHCR, where he combined first-hand experience of humanitarian operations throughout the world with editing UNHCR's Evaluation and Policy Working Paper Series. Until February 2017, this 'New Issues in Refugee Research' series brought together some 284 contributions from UNHCR staff, consultants and associates as well as researchers wishing to publish preliminary results of research. See all working papers at: www.unhcr.org/uk/search?comid=4a1d3be46&cid=49aea93a6a&scid=49aea93a3b

These important and freely available working papers included some of Crisp's own papers on, for example, insecurity and violence in Kenyan refugee camps (1999a), the politics of counting refugees (1999b), the international refugee regime (2003), the durable solution of local integration (2004) and the role of UNHCR in protracted refugee situations, amongst others (Slaughter and Crisp, 2009).

Jeff Crisp's publications span a broad range of topics relating to refugee, migration and humanitarian issues. For example, debates about the use of refugee camps in contexts of displacement during the 1970s, 1980s and late 1990s were informed by Crisp's work. This debate was broadly between those who were against the use of refugee camps and those who considered them a necessity. In an article for the *Forced Migration Review*, Crisp and Jacobsen (1998) challenged assumptions that self-settlements were a better option for refugees than those in organised settlements or refugee camps. They pointed out that camps could offer a safer and more secure option and that refugees often organise themselves into camp-like settlements before official agencies arrive. This was the case for refugees along the Thailand-Burma border for various organisations and self-identified, ethnically based populations. When discussing the occurrence of violence in large refugee camps – Kakuma and Dadaab – in Kenya, Crisp (1999a) concluded that the insecurity affecting refugees is deeply rooted in the structures devised to manage refugees in these camps, the political economy of the Kenyan state and the circumstances of the refugees themselves.

Nearly 20 years ago, when discussing the often controversial topic of refugee statistics, Crisp (1999b) outlined how scholars often relied on the then two main agencies for refugees for statistics – UNHCR and the then United States Committee for Refugees (USCR) – even though these two sets of statistics were often different from each other. As Crisp outlined (1999b), refugee statistics are related to categories and labels assigned (for a discussion on 'labelling' of refugees, see also Key Thinker Box 2.4 Roger Zetter). By way of example, Crisp provided the eight different labels in a 1996 plan of action to address displacement in the former Soviet Union: *refugees, persons in refugee-like situations, internally displaced people, involuntarily relocating persons, repatriates, formerly deported peoples, illegal migrants* and *ecological migrants.* Crisp also pointed to the way in which industrialised states are selective in their presentation of statistics, often to justify restrictive social policies by highlighting increases in the numbers of people making applications.

This politics of numbers remains as pertinent today as illuminated by Crisp's account (Crisp and Long, 2016), There is a similar story with contemporary statistics on human trafficking or 'modern slavery', with UNODC mandated to provide reports on human trafficking globally and organisations such as IOM collaborating with NGOs and producing different numbers.

By 2002, Crisp was writing about the issue of three million refugees living in protracted refugee situations (PRS) in Africa at the end of 2001 under long-term 'care-and-maintenance' programmes that did not either promote self-reliance amongst refugees or allow for positive interactions between refugees and local populations. This 'care-and-maintenance' approach was modelled on a relief rather than developmental approach, entailing the establishment of large, visible and internationally funded refugee camps (Crisp, 2002).

In a 2004 paper, the contradictions between economic cases to liberalise restrictions on migration and political pressures for policies to deter, obstruct or limit the arrival of migrants were presented with options presented to respond to such challenges. Boswell and Crisp (2004) outlined how the absence of legal routes for migration had led, at that time, to expansion of human trafficking and smuggling networks and the dangers of exploitation therein.

Now an Associate Fellow at Chatham House and a Research Associate at the Refugee Studies Centre at the University of Oxford, Crisp regularly contributes to debates around voluntary repatriation (Crisp and Long, 2016), the evolution of UNHCR's urban refugee policy (2017) and a range of other critical issues within the topic of forced migration.

He also regularly Tweets @JFCrisp.

Key references – Jeff Crisp

Boswell, C. and Crisp, J. (2004) *Poverty, International Migration and Asylum*, Policy Brief No.8, United Nations University World Institute for Development Economics Research (WIDER), Helsinki.

Crisp, J. (1999a) *A State of Insecurity: The Political Economy of Violence in Refugee-populated Areas of Kenya*, Working Paper No.16, Evaluation and Policy Analysis Unit, United Nations High Commission for Refugees (UNHCR), Geneva.

Crisp, J. (1999b) *"Who Has Counted the Refugees?": UNHCR and the Politics of Numbers*, Working Paper No.12, Evaluation and Policy Analysis Unit, United Nations High Commission for Refugees (UNHCR), Geneva.

Crisp, J. (2002) *No Solutions in Sight: The Problem of Protracted Refugee Situations in Africa*, Working Paper No.68, The Center for Comparative Immigration Studies, University of California-San Diego, La Jolla, California.

Crisp, J. (2003) *A New Asylum Paradigm? Globalization, Migration and the Uncertain Future of the International Refugee Regime*, Working Paper No.100, Evaluation and Policy Analysis Unit, United Nations High Commission for Refugees (UNHCR), Geneva.

Crisp, J. (2004) *The Local Integration and Local Settlement of Refugees: A Conceptual and Historical Analysis*, Working Paper No.102, Evaluation and Policy Analysis Unit, United Nations High Commission for Refugees (UNHCR), Geneva.

Crisp, J. (2017) Finding Space for Protection: An Inside Account of the Evolution of UNHCR's Urban Refugee Policy, *Refuge*, 33(1), 87–95.

Crisp, J. and Jacobsen, K. (1998, December) Refugee Camps Reconsidered, *Forced Migration Review*, 3, 27–30.

Crisp, J. and Long, K. (2016) Safe and Voluntary Refugee Repatriation: From Principle to Practice, *Journal on Migration and Human Security*, 4(3), 141–147.

Slaughter, A. and Crisp, J. (2009) *A Surrogate State? The Role of UNHCR in Protracted Refugee Situations*, Working Paper No.168, Evaluation and Policy Analysis Unit, United Nations High Commission for Refugees (UNHCR), Geneva.

What solutions are available for people who flee persecution?

As noted earlier, the signing of the 1951 Refugee Convention occurred at a point in time when protection from persecution was taken very seriously and it was an attempt to ensure those displaced in Europe were provided legal status. Prior to this, particular groups had been persecuted during World War II, including Jews, gypsies, communists and homosexuals, who were systematically murdered during the Holocaust. The 1951 Refugee Convention was drafted alongside other human rights instruments, including the 1948 Universal Declaration of Human Rights when a 'never again' refrain was held in the minds of the drafters. The Convention became universal with the development of the 1967 Refugee Protocol, which removed the geographical limitation.

Since then, the 'never again' element has proven wrong (Kushner and Knox, 1999). Despite the 1948 Genocide Convention, genocide has occurred in Cambodia (1975–1979), Rwanda (1994), Bosnia (1995) and Darfur (2003–present) amongst others (see Chapter 5 on human rights and refugees). There has not always been an adequate response to these wherein refugees have been provided with protection as envisaged for Europe in 1951 and the world after 1967.

Solutions have continued to be illusive (Castles, 2004; Helton, 2002). As Barbara Harrell-Bond commented in the mid-1990s:

> 'The history of responses to refugees in the twentieth century has been one long series of attempts to circumvent the problem'.

(1995:2)

However, there are three key 'durable solutions' available for refugees. These are:

1 Resettlement in a third country
2 Local integration within a country of asylum
3 Voluntary repatriation to the country of origin

Between 1945 and 1985, the durable solution of **resettlement** was promoted in practice, although voluntary repatriation was in principle the preferred solution (Chimni, 1999; van Selm, 2014). For example, during this period, millions of refugees from Southeast Asia were resettled in largely western countries.

From 1985 to 1993, **voluntary repatriation** became the promoted solution, with emphasis on the 'voluntariness' of repatriation processes (Chimni, 1999). By 1993, the idea of 'safe return' was introduced in the context of more temporary protection offerings in Western Europe during wartime in the former Yugoslavia (Chimni, 1999). In 1996, 'imposed return' – involuntary repatriation – was announced by the then Director of International Protection of UNHCR, Dennis McNamara (Chimni, 1999; Crisp and Long, 2016). This meant that refugees could be sent back to their countries of origin 'to less than optimal conditions in their home country' and, importantly, against their will.

The 1990s were declared to be the **decade of repatriation**, although this was not necessarily based on empirical studies based on the complexities of such responses, with some commentators suggesting this to be based on the interests of host states (Chimni, 1998, 1999). For example, in the early 1990s, the 'voluntary repatriation' of some 350,000 Khmer refugees from refugee camps in Thailand to Cambodia took place despite key pre-conditions around peace, removal of landmines and security for repatriation not being met.

Echoing the earlier statement by Barbara Harrell-Bond, B.S. Chimni has argued:

> 'that it is the absence of burden sharing in the post-Cold War era which explains the growing acceptance of involuntary repatriation as a solution to the global refugee problem'.
>
> (Chimni, 1999:1)

Chimni does not accept that temporary aid upon return and development aid to the country of origin is enough to sustain repatriation in itself. Rather, he suggests that:

> unless there is a clear recognition of the role external economic factors play in creating the conditions which lead to refugee flows, and steps proposed to address them, the humanitarian aid community may . . . be seen as an instrument of an exploitative international system which is periodically mobilized to address its worst consequences.
>
> (Chimni, 1999:1)

Other sometimes less-than-voluntary forms of return include the Assisted Voluntary Return (AVR) programmes where people return to their countries of origin following failed asylum claims (Hammond, 2014). IOM tends to facilitate these returns which, to date, have been under-examined in the literature available on 'voluntary' returns.

Alongside this, the use of temporary solutions, the terminology and practice of temporariness has also been increasing. For example, in the UK some forms of humanitarian protection are now time bound to five years.

Local integration has sometimes been referred to as the 'forgotten solution' (Jacobsen, 2001) but refers to circumstances wherein refugees become integrated into the country that has hosted them during exile. It includes the receipt of citizenship of the country of asylum following a formal process of application (Hovil, 2014). Local integration often also refers to informal processes wherein refugees become integrate themselves through local agreements, employment or other forms of relationships within countries of asylum.

It has been suggested that there is now a **hierarchy of solutions** with voluntary repatriation considered an optimum solution by UNHCR with less focus generally on the options of resettlement and local integration (Crisp, 2004).

In rethinking the existing three durable solutions, authors have considered whether migration itself might offer a fourth solution (Long, 2014), the suggestion being that refugees could become migrants to offer another solution for those living within situations of PRS. A key critique of this line of thinking is that becoming a migrant, for employment purposes, does not lead to citizenship and could lead in some instances to exploitation of that particular vulnerability. Hammond (2014) has also outlined how many refugees opt not to return to their countries of origin but rather to 'establish themselves in multiple locations at the same time' with some family members simultaneously living in the country of asylum and some returning to countries of origin. Other suggestions have focussed on overtly economic rather than political solutions such as employing refugees in Special Economic Zones (Betts and Collier, 2017). Few solutions proposed have been based on asking refugees themselves about solutions that might be available to them (Hynes and Loughna, 2005) or focussing on their hopes, aspirations and capabilities.

In 2017 and in response to the so-called crisis in the Mediterranean, Francois Crepeau the then Special Rapporteur on the Human Rights of Migrants, **called for a longer-term strategy for human migration** at a global level, pointing out that the 'migration crisis' was driven by policy and that placing restrictions on mobility was a key part of the problem rather than the solution. Crepeau suggested that both the Sustainable Development Goals (SDGs) and two new Global Compacts on refugees and migrants were an opportune time to begin offering more regular, safe, accessible and affordable mobility options to people and as a consequence transform the way States manage migration.

The power of definition: labelling refugees, forced migrants and the forcibly displaced

The way in which refugees and others forced to migrate are discussed and labelled is an important consideration when thinking about responses and potential solutions. Refugees have been given a huge variety of labels over time, sometimes to enable States to avoid their protection responsibilities under the 1951 Refugee Convention. Labels such as *illegal migrants, persons in refugee-like situations* and *economic migrants* regularly appear in media reports across the globe, highlighting both the lack of awareness of refugee protection rights but also the ways in which policies frame refugees in problematic ways.

For example, in the late 1990s, refugees arriving from Burma into Thailand became labelled *'Displaced Persons Fleeing Fighting'* (DPPF) rather than a previous term *'Displaced Persons'* (DPs). These changes in terminology occurred at the same time as a clamp-down on new arrivals into Thailand, which saw several thousand people denied access into Thailand. UNHCR's terminology in public statements and press releases reflected this transition with the earlier use of *refugee* being replaced by the term *displaced persons*.

At the same time, refugee camps along the Thailand–Burma border acquired a new label of being *'Temporary Shelters'* (TS). These temporary shelters involved changes to the regulations around conditions. There were new restrictions imposed on the materials to be used to build houses, reinforcing the temporary nature of the camps. Bamboo thatch was no longer allowed for rooves, bamboo sleeping platforms were no longer allowed and refugees slept under blue plastic sheeting under a new allocation of space for each house well below international standards. The temporary shelters were set up in rows rather than in the previous 'village style' of former camps. Restrictions on the building of schools were imposed and fences constructed around some of the camps.

For a country such as Thailand that was not party to the 1951 Refugee Convention, these changes were indicative of a growing intolerance towards refugees on their territory. Making life more difficult for arrivals echoed the tactics used in previous refugee situations with Vietnamese, Lao and Khmer refugees who, in the words of McNamara (1990), were subject to a policy known as 'humane deterrence', denoting the restrictive treatment of newcomers by receiving governments in order to deter further potential asylum seekers.

Alongside this, a new category – the 'Border Case' – became utilised by UNHCR from around the mid-1990s. It meant that those who applied for protection following a risky journey to Bangkok and were recognised as 'Persons of Concern' had to return to border camps if they were unable to prove the risk of 'secondary persecution' at the border. Border cases were denied assistance from UNHCR and advised to go back to the border areas, where UNHCR was severely restricted in the exercise of its protection mandate.

This type of labelling, ordering, categorisation and classification of refugees is found in numerous locations. As Janmyr and Mourad (2018) suggest, individuals fleeing the Syrian conflict to Lebanon are given various legal, bureaucratic and social labels by state and non-state actors. These include *registered refugee, labourer, displaced* and *foreigner*, each of which consequently governs their presence within Lebanon. The authors go on to explore how further categorisation – around 'vulnerability' – dictates eligibility for resettlement procedures. To be vulnerable enough involves being 'a survivor of violence or torture, women and girls at risk, and those with medical needs or disabilities' (Ibid., 2018:7).

Roger Zetter is a key thinker around this issue of labelling (see Key Thinker Box 2.4).

Key Thinker Box 2.4   Roger Zetter – Labelling 'Refugees'

Roger Zetter is an Emeritus Professor of Refugee Studies following his retirement as the fourth Director of the Refugee Studies Centre at the University of Oxford in 2011. He was also the founding editor of the *Journal of Refugee Studies*, which has been at the heart of refugee studies and forced migration studies since 1988. Zetter's initial research was on Greek-Cypriot refugees, particularly some 180,000 people who were negotiating new identities as refugees in the south following the Turkish occupation of northern Cyprus in 1974. This experience led to continued questioning of institutional and bureaucratic power and the labelling of refugees and other categories of forcibly displaced people across all stages of the refugee and displacement cycle. Zetter has contributed two seminal contributions to refugee studies on the topic of labelling.

The first of these (Zetter, 1991) is one of the most widely cited and influential papers in refugee studies. Written at a time when refugees were mainly contained in regions of origin within the global South, this paper examined how and with what consequences people become labelled as refugees within public policy and practice. The paper looks at how identity is **formed, transformed and politicized** and how processes of labelling relied on 'convenient images' of refugees as objects of public policy. The conceptual tools of bureaucratic labelling, such as **stereotyping, control**, the **designation** of labels in often rapid and traumatic circumstances and political power relationships are outlined, using empirical data from Cyprus and other secondary research data. Zetter suggests the label of *refugee* conveys a complex set of values and judgements beyond legal definitions. He also suggests that institutions (mis)conceive refugees through 'apparently normal, routine, apolitical, conventional procedures of programme design and delivery' (1991:46), whereas refugees themselves conceive their identities in very different terms to those imposed by such labelling processes but may nonetheless manipulate the labels imposed on them.

The second paper on labelling (Zetter, 2007) revisits this earlier conceptualisation of refugee labelling. Zetter suggests that refugee labelling continues to offer vital insights into the impacts of bureaucratic power but that the 'convenient images' of refugees have changed (2007:174) and have been replaced with a **'fractioning' of the label of *refugee*.** It is suggested that this fractioning, driven by global processes and increasingly complex patterns of migration, results in a whole new range of bureaucratic categories, designed to prevent access to the 'refugee' label. For example, discussions of 'genuine' refugees emerge, and the 'asylum seeker' label becomes mainstream in legislation and policy along with the withdrawal of rights associated with being a refugee; forms of temporary protection becomes the norm. This new range of categories also incorporates deterrent measures, and new procedures transform the label into increasingly discriminatory outcomes such as detention or compulsory dispersal. The resulting reduced eligibility to the full rights of a refugee, argues Zetter, force individuals into illegality such as 'illegal' employment due to state restrictions on the right to work (Zetter, 2014). State policies thus criminalise refugees for seeking asylum, and a discourse of 'clandestine', 'illegal' and/or 'bogus' asylum seekers emerge. As in the 1991 paper, the formation, transformation and politicisation of the 'refugee' label frame this conceptualisation.

Continuing the theme of labelling and changing vocabulary, Zetter (2018) considers how **the term *forced migrant* and the use of *forced displacement* is increasingly replacing the 'refugee' in debate**. Zetter suggests that *forced migrant* and *forced displacement* offer an opportunity to capture the complexities of root causes, drivers, process and consequences of migration. However, this wider conceptualisation reduces focus on protection as a fundamental right of the refugee. Zetter outlines how international agencies are broadening the scope of their involvement with forcibly displaced people, and there is a need to conceptualise forced displacement across a range of scenarios which include escape from armed conflict and human rights violations, environmental degradation and climate change, natural disasters and development-induced displacement. The blurred distinctions between different categories of people and multiple drivers that produce 'mixed movements' of people are discussed, as is the increasing use and largely negative connotations of the term *irregular migrants* as distinct from regular (or voluntary) migrants within global debates.

Beyond this focus on labelling, Zetter has also written on a broader range of issues relating to refugees: protracted displacement, refugee communities, social capital, climate change and population displacement, and dispersal policies for asylum seekers. Benezer and Zetter (2014) has also written on refugee journeys as a uniquely defining feature of the process of exile, pointing out the lacuna in refugee studies and how an understanding of the formative experience of the journey would better inform our appreciation of refugee identity and policy responses.

Of particular interest for students of development studies, Zetter's recent work (2019) uses the development lens to consider recent development-led responses to large-scale, protracted refugee crises. He focusses on the **humanitarian-development nexus**, a term that is increasingly used by policy makers, and some scholars with little critical engagement, to describe an approach that brings refugees into development processes based on neo-liberal globalisation processes. Zetter provides theoretical reflection on this 'development turn' in refugee studies and policy, arguing that the shift from the welfare model of refugee assistance towards privatised development assistance does little to engage with the underlying determinants of forced migration or hegemonic policy interests. Whilst, ostensibly, developmental strategies support refugee agency, resilience and self-sufficiency, the underlying dynamics, he explains, reflect 'core-periphery' development theories popular from the 1970s onwards. At the periphery, the main refugee hosting states are subordinated to the interests of global capital at the core – donor states and refugee and development institutions and actors – which, at the same time, reinforce refugee containment policies of the 'global North'.

Key references – Roger Zetter

Benezer, G. and Zetter, R. (2014) Searching for Directions, Conceptual and Methodological Challenges in Researching Refugee Journeys, *Journal of Refugee Studies*, 28(1), 297–318.

Zetter, R. (1991) Labelling Refugees: Forming and Transforming a Bureaucratic Identity, *Journal of Refugee Studies*, 4(1), 40–62.

Zetter, R. (2007) More Labels, Fewer Refugees: Remaking the Refugee Label in an Era of Globalization, *Journal of Refugee Studies*, 20(2), 172–192.

Zetter, R. (2014) Creating Identities, Diminishing Protection and the Securitisation of Asylum in Europe, Chapter 2, pp. 22–35, in Kneebone, S., Stevens, D. and Baldassar, L. (Eds.), *Refugee Protection and the Role of Law: Conflicting Identities*, Routledge, London.

Zetter, R. (2018) Conceptualising Forced Displacement: Praxis, Scholarship and Empirics, in Bloch, A. and Dona, G. (Eds.), *Forced Migration: Current Issues and Debates*, Routledge, London.

Zetter, R. (2019) Theorising the Humanitarian-Development Nexus: A Political Economy Analysis, *Journal of Refugee Studies*, fez070, https://doi.org/10.1093/jrs/fez070

Further reading

Bhabha, J. (2017) The Importance of Nationality for Children, in *The World's Stateless Children*, Institute on Statelessness and Inclusion, The Netherlands.

Blitz, B. (2011) Stateless by Any Other Name: Refused Asylum-Seekers in the United Kingdom, *Journal of Ethnic and Migration Studies*, 37(4), 657–673.

Boyden, J. and Hart, J. (2007) The Statelessness of the World's Children, *Children & Society*, 21, 237–248.

Castles, S. (2004) Why Migration Policies Fail, *Ethnic and Racial Studies*, 27(2), 205–227.

Chimni, B.S. (1998) The Geopolitics of Refugee Studies: A View from the South, *Journal of Refugee Studies*, 11(4), 350–374.

Chimni, B.S. (1999) *From Resettlement to Involuntary Repatriation: Towards a Critical History of Durable Solutions to Refugee Problems*, Working Paper No.2, New Issues in Refugee Research, UNHCR, Geneva.

Harrell-Bond, B. (1995) *Refugees and the International System: The Evolution of Solutions*, Refugee Studies Programme, University of Oxford, viewed on 5 August 2019 at: www.rsc.ox.ac.uk/files/files-1/rr-refugees-international-system-1995.pdf

Hyndman, J. and Giles, W. (2017) *Refugees in Extended Exile: Living on the Edge*, Routledge, London and New York.

Loescher, G. and Milner, J. (2005) The Long Road Home: Protracted Refugee Situations in Africa, *Survival*, 47(2), 153–174.

Slaughter, A. and Crisp, J. (2009) *A Surrogate State? The Role of UNHCR in Protracted Refugee Situations*, Working Paper No.168, Evaluation and Policy Analysis Unit, United Nations High Commission for Refugees (UNHCR), Geneva.

UNHCR (various dates) *Global Trends*, United Nations High Commissioner for Refugees, Geneva.

References

Arendt, H. (1943) We Refugees, in Robinson, M. (Ed.), *Altogether Elsewhere*, Faber and Faber, Boston and London.

Arendt, H. (1951) *The Origins of Totalitarianism*, Penguin Books, London.

Betts, A. and Collier, P. (2017) *Refuge: Transforming a Broken Refugee System*, Penguin Random House UK, Milton Keynes.

Goodwin-Gill, G.S. (1996) *The Refugee in International Law*, Clarendon Press, Oxford.

Hammond, L. (2014) 'Voluntary' Repatriation and Reintegration, in Fiddian-Qasmiyeh, E., Loescher, G., Long, K. and Sigona, N. (Eds.), *The Oxford Handbook of Refugee and Forced Migration Studies*, Oxford University Press, Oxford.

Helton, A.C. (2002) *The Price of Indifference: Refugees and Humanitarian Action in the New Century*, Oxford University Press, Oxford.

Hovil, L. (2014) Local Integration, in Fiddian-Qasmiyeh, E., Loescher, G., Long, K. and Sigona, N. (Eds.), *The Oxford Handbook of Refugee and Forced Migration Studies*, Oxford University Press, Oxford.

Hynes, P. and Loughna, S. (2005) *Did Anybody Ask the Refugee? Rethinking Durable Solutions*, at 9th International Conference of the International Association for the Study of Forced Migration (IASFM), Sao Paulo, Brazil.

Institute on Statelessness and Inclusion (2017) *The World's Stateless Children*, ISI, The Netherlands.

Jacobsen, K. (2001) *The Forgotten Solution: Local Integration for Refugees in Developing Countries*, New Issues in Refugee Research, UNHCR Working Paper No. 45, UNHCR, Geneva.

Janmyr, M. and Mourad, L. (2018) Modes of Ordering: Labelling, Classification and Categorization in Lebanon's Refugee Response, *Journal of Refugee Studies*, 31(4), 544–565.

Kushner, T. and Knox, K. (1999) *Refugees in an Age of Genocide*, Frank Cass, London and Portland, OR.

Long, K. (2014) Rethinking 'Durable' Solutions, in Fiddian-Qasmiyeh, E., Loescher, G., Long, K. and Sigona, N. (Eds.), *The Oxford Handbook of Refugee and Forced Migration Studies*, Oxford University Press, Oxford.

Marx, E. (1990) The Social World of Refugees: A Conceptual Framework, *Journal of Refugee Studies*, 3(3), 189–203.

McNamara, D. (1990) The Origins and Effects of 'Humane Deterrence' Policies in Southeast Asia, in Loescher, G. and Monahan, L. (Eds.), *Refugees and International Relations*, Clarendon Press, Oxford.

Sales, R. (2002) The Deserving and the Undeserving? Refugees, Asylum Seekers and Welfare in Britain, *Critical Social Policy*, 22(3), 72. Sage Publications, London, Thousand Oaks and New Delhi.

Turton, D. (2003) *Refugees, Forced Resettlers and 'Other Forced Migrants': Towards a Unitary Study of Forced Migration*, New Issues in Refugee Research, Working Paper No. 94, Evaluation and Policy Analysis Unit, UNHCR, Geneva, Switzerland.

United Nations High Commission for Refugees (UNHCR) (2011) *UNHCR Global Trends 2011: A Year of Crisis*, UNHCR, Geneva.

United Nations High Commission for Refugees (UNHCR) (2016) *UNHCR Global Trends 2015*, UNHCR, Geneva.

United Nations High Commission for Refugees (UNHCR) (2018) *Global Trends: Forced Displacement in 2017*, UNHCR, Geneva.

United Nations High Commission for Refugees (UNHCR) (2019) *Global Trends: Forced Displacement in 2018*, UNHCR, Geneva.

United Nations High Commission for Refugees (UNHCR) (2020) *Global Trends: Forced Displacement in 2019*, UNHCR, Geneva.

USCRI (various dates) *World Refugee Survey*, US Committee for Refugees and Immigrants, Washington, DC.

van Selm, J. (2014) Refugee Resettlement, in Fiddian-Qasmiyeh, E., Loescher, G., Long, K. and Sigona, N. (Eds.), *The Oxford Handbook of Refugee and Forced Migration Studies*, Oxford University Press, Oxford.

Zolberg, A.R., Suhrke, A. and Aguayo, S. (1989) *Escape from Violence: Conflict and the Refugee Crisis in the Developing World*, Oxford University Press, Oxford.

3 Who is an 'internally displaced person'?

Introduction

This chapter looks at another form of displacement – within countries of origin – for people who are displaced due to armed conflict, generalized violence, violations of human rights natural or human-made disasters. Unlike refugees, internally displaced persons (IDPs) do not have an international legal definition to confer special legal status. Instead, non-binding guidance is available – the 1998 Guiding Principles on Internal Displacement – and this is discussed later, as is its integration into the 2006 Great Lakes IDP Protocol and the 2009 African Convention on Protection and Assistance for Internally Displaced Persons (commonly referred to as the Kampala Convention).

This chapter therefore considers the **50.8 million internally displaced persons (IDPs) in the world as at the end of 2019** who are considered to be a category of concern for UNHCR. Causes of internal displacement, where IDPs are located in the world and global trends are outlined. Thereafter, examples of IDP situations are provided with elaboration of the needs and risks inherent in the experience of being internally displaced. Again, short summaries of the work of key thinkers, maps and key concepts are provided along with case studies and points for discussion.

Throughout, readers should be alert to protection of IDPs being primarily about national protection mechanisms. In other words, the domestic legislation of a State should mean that IDPs do not lose any rights because they have been displaced (Kalin, 2014:166). IDPs should enjoy all the relevant guarantees of human rights applicable to the wider population. However, in many cases, IDPs may be discriminated against and treated as second-class citizens in their own country (Ibid.). Readers should bear in mind limitations and challenges inherent in providing protection within a State – a sovereign State – without a legal or institutional base for the international community to provide protection or assistance. A short timeline of selected legislation including IDPs is provided in Figure 3.1.

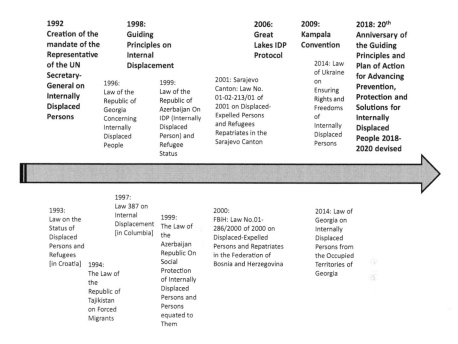

Figure 3.1 Selected Timeline of Law and Policy on IDPs

Sources: IDMC; Brookings Institution; Global Protection Cluster

Who is an Internally Displaced Persons (IDP)?

The Guiding Principles on Internal Displacement devised in 1998 (reprinted 2004) describe IDPs as:

> persons or groups of persons who have been forced or obliged to flee or to leave their homes or places of habitual residence, in particular as a result of or in order to avoid the effects of armed conflict, situations of generalized violence, violations of human rights or natural or human-made disasters, and who have not crossed an internationally recognized State border.

As can be seen, this definition outlines how IDPs are forced or obliged to flee their homes in a similar fashion to refugees but have not crossed an international border and therefore are unable to gain the protection of international law. Also, the causes of internal displacement are much broader than those included within the 1951 Refugee Convention. For IDPs, fleeing armed conflict, generalized violence, human rights violations as well as national or human-made disasters are recognized causes.

In the foreword to these Guiding Principles, Sergio Vieira de Mello, the then Under-Secretary-General for Humanitarian Affairs, noted that the humanitarian community had become increasingly aware of the crisis of internal displacement which, at that time, affected over 20 million people worldwide. With increasing awareness and better data collection, by the end of 2019, this figure had risen to 50.8 million people. The Guiding Principles focused awareness raising and mobilization of support within the humanitarian community. It was also hoped that they would assist governments in providing for the security and well-being of their displaced populations.

In the introductory notes of these Guiding Principles, Francis M. Deng (see Key Thinker Box 3.1) outlined the monumental task of ensuring protection for people forcibly uprooted but who remained within the borders of their own countries. He outlined how the Guiding Principles had been developed over several years following a mandate given to him in 1992 by the Commission on Human Rights and resolutions of the UN General Assembly. This mandate began with studying:

1   The causes and consequences of internal displacement
2   The status of IDPs in international law
3   The extent to which needs are addressed
4   Ways to improve protection and assistance to IDPs

The resulting 1998 Guiding Principles resulted in 30 distinct principles:

- Principles 1–4: General principles
- Principles 5–9: Principles relating to protection from displacement
- Principles 10–23: Principles relating to protection during displacement (civil, political, economic, social and cultural rights)
- Principles 24–26: Principles relating to humanitarian assistance (only once the relevant State has accepted an offer to provide assistance)
- Principles 28–30: Principles relating to return, resettlement and reintegration (the right to choose whether to return, integrate locally or settle in another area of the country)

Reading these Guiding Principles is a very good start to understanding the challenges involved in protecting IDPs – view at: www.internal-displacement. org/internal-displacement/guiding-principles-on-internal-displacement

Additionally, considering the development of law and policy on IDPs before and after these 1998 Guiding Principles is useful (see Figure 3.1).

Point for discussion – refugee or IDP?

- What are the key distinctions between being a refugee or an IDP in terms of the causes of displacement and international protection available?

Key Thinker Box 3.1   Francis M. Deng – IDP Guiding Principles

Contributions to understanding **internally displaced persons** by Francis M. Deng include a range of journal articles, books, reports and editorials (Cohen and Deng, 1998a, 1998b; Deng, 1993, 1994, 2010). In his and Roberta Cohen's (1998a) work containing cases studies of ten countries affected by internally displacement – Burundi, Rwanda, Liberia, Sudan, the former Yugoslavia, Caucasus, Tajikistan, Sri Lanka, Columbia and Peru – Cohen and Deng began to map out the coerced displacement of people within the borders of their own countries as a result of armed conflicts, internal strife and systematic violations of human rights. This mapping of country specific conditions has since been carried out by the Norwegian Refugee Council and the Internal Displacement Monitoring Centre (IDMC) (see earlier text).

Cohen and Deng's additional book in the same year (1998b) analysed the causes and consequences of displacement within borders, highlighting how those displaced internally suffered from an absence of legal or institutional bases for protection and assistance from the internal community. Strategies for preventing displacement and a legal framework tailored to the needs of those displaced internally were outlined.

Simultaneously, the 1998 Guiding Principles on Internal Displacement were published, with an introductory note by Deng in his role as the representative of the UN Secretary-General on Internally Displaced Persons (see earlier section, Who is an IDP?).

A 2010 contribution – *Protecting the Dispossessed: A Challenge for the International Community* – detailed the then 25 million people internally displaced, who had already exceeded the numbers of refugees worldwide and detailing the increased attention to IDPs worldwide. In a first-person narrative, Deng draws on interviews from governments, international organisations, individuals and country visits across the globe, arguing that **sovereignty entails responsibility** to ensure the safety and welfare of citizens and that the international community must uphold this standard and make violators accountable for their actions.

Francis M. Deng is now a Senior Fellow of the Brookings-LSE Project on Internal Displacement, and a full list of his contributions to this topic can be found at: www.brookings.edu/author/francis-m-deng/

Key references – Francis Deng

Cohen, R. and Deng, F.M. (1998a) *The Forsaken People: Case Studies of the Internally Displaced*, Brookings Institution Press, Washington, DC.

Cohen, R. and Deng, F.M. (1998b) *Masses in Flight: The Global Crisis of Internal Displacement*, Brookings Institution Press, Washington, DC.

Deng, F.M. (1993) *Protecting the Dispossessed: A Challenge for the International Community*, Brookings Institution Press, Washington, DC.

Deng, F.M. (1994) Internally Displaced Persons, *International Journal of Refugee Law*, 6(2).

Deng, F.M. (2010) *Protecting the Dispossessed: A Challenge for the International Community*, Brookings Institution Press, Washington, DC.

The Kampala Convention and the Great Lakes IDP Protocol

The definition provided within the 1998 Guiding Principles on Internal Displacement has become part of the legally binding 2009 African Convention on Protection and Assistance for Internally Displaced Persons in Africa (also known as the **Kampala Convention**). It has also become a part of the 2006 Protocol on the Protection and Assistance to Internally Displaced Persons, adopted by the Member States of the International Conference on the Great Lakes (also known as the **Great Lakes IDP Protocol**). The definition has also been incorporated into national laws and policies within Uganda, Nepal, Iraq and Sudan (Kalin, 2014:163). Both the Kampala Convention and the Great Lakes Protocol extend the definition of IDPs to include those displaced by development projects.

While the notion of an IDP in the Guiding Principles is not a legal definition that confers special legal status similar to refugee status, this inclusion of the definition into national laws and policies allows for human rights of those affected to be applicable in line with the rest of the population within the country.

This shift from soft to hard law is clear in the case of the 2009 Kampala Convention, which sets out standards for the protection of people from arbitrary displacement (Kalin, 2014:171). The Kampala Convention entered into force in December 2012 and, as of May 2019, has been ratified by 27 of the African Union's 55 Member States. This requires appropriate legislation to be enacted and the creation of frameworks for coordination of IDP assistance. As can be seen in Map 3.1, shaded States are now legally bound under this Convention. The lighter colour reflects those that have signed but are not yet legally bound, and the rest of the map shows States that are yet to sign or ratify the Convention.

A timeline of national and sub-national policies within Africa around internal displacement also provides a useful framework for considering the development of law and policy on IDPs within Africa (see Figure 3.2).

Where are people internally displaced?

According to the Internal Displacement Monitoring Centre (IDMC), which is part of the Norwegian Refugee Council, there were **50.8 million internally**

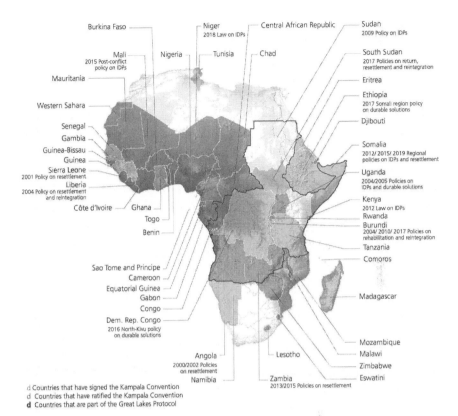

Map 3.1 Kampala Convention Ratifications: 2019

Source: Internal Displacement Monitoring Centre (IDMC)

displaced people recorded by the end of 2019 – 45.7 million as a result of conflict and violence, and 5.1 million as a result of disasters (IDMC, 2020). IDMC has published independent reports on internal displacement since 1998, and this most recent report means that the 79.5 million people forcibly displaced, as recorded by UNHCR by the end of 2019, has now grown. As has been the case for a number of years, the largest proportion of UNHCR's total figures were IDPs.

As of the end of 2019, there were 33.4 million new displacements associated with conflict and disasters across 148 countries and territories in 2019, the highest figure since 2012 (see Map 3.2).

Figure 3.2 Timeline of National and Sub-National Policies within Africa: 2000–2019
Source: Internal Displacement Monitoring Centre (IDMC)

As can be seen, 24.9 million people were displaced by disasters (darker circles) and 8.5 million by conflict (lighter circles) by the end of 2019.

Figures 3.3 and 3.4 highlight new internal displacement due to conflict and disasters during 2018. When looking at these graphs the relative size of population within each country should be considered. For example, Yemen's total population is around 29 million whereas Ethiopia, as the second most populated country in Africa after Nigeria, has a population of around 112 million.

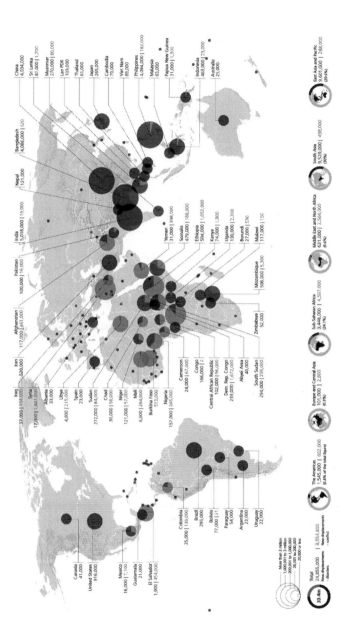

Map 3.2 New Displacement by Conflict and Disasters: 2019

Source: IDCM

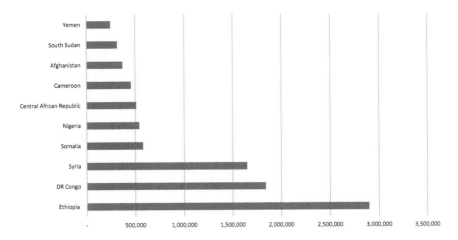

Figure 3.3 New Internal Displacement Due to Conflict: 2018

Source: IDMC, 2019

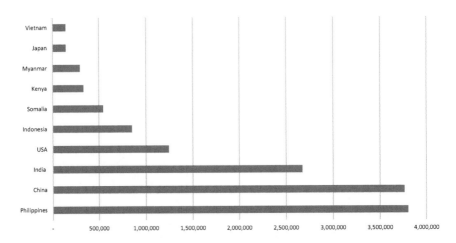

Figure 3.4 New Internal Displacement Due to Disasters: 2018

Source: IDMC, 2019

Case study: Yemen

There have been a number of key political events that have led to a rise in internal displacement in Yemen. The war that broke out in Yemen in 2015 was the result of ongoing conflict between the Yemeni Security Forced (YSF) and al-Houthi supporters (also known as the Houthi movement). By 2015, around 300,000 people had been displaced by the conflict (IDMC, 2019). There were several rounds of conflict between 2004 and 2010. In early 2011, the Arab Spring and protests eventually led to the resignation of the then president with a new president elected in early 2012. As is the case in a number of countries, the subsequent transitional government did not make sufficient reforms to improve the daily lives of its population. In July 2014 the government decided to remove fuel subsidies, and mass protests were the result. A coalition of Arab states, led by the Kingdom of Saudi Arabia, launched airstrikes against the Houthi movement in March 2015, and the president was then forced to leave the country.

This case study shows us just how important an understanding of the history of events within a county and an understanding of the local context is in thinking about internal displacement.

In an October 2019 report by the IDMC – *Yemen: Urban Displacement in a Rural Society* – the nature of rural to urban displacement is discussed. The country has had a predominantly rural population, and it is shown how war and displacement in Yemen are not primarily an urban phenomenon, despite media accounts that often highlight urban battles. The report documents how rural-to-rural displacement and urban-to-urban displacement are the predominant patterns of movement. As such, the usual assumption that displacement from rural to urban areas is not the case in Yemen. One of the reasons cited for this is that:

> The war has . . . rendered typical pull factors to cities, such as access to basic services and livelihood opportunities, all but irrelevant, meaning that rural to urban displacement is not as common as it might otherwise have been.
>
> (IDMC, 2019:5)

It explains how, despite the war, IDPs in urban areas still have better access to basic services such as water and electricity than those remaining in rural areas. Those living in rural areas are forced to travel long distances for health and education services.

The report also outlines how understanding trends prior to the war will be key in developing solutions to internal displacement. For example, they outline how the decline of rural life and spread of informal settlements outside urban centres affected access to water and electricity. With IDPs living in areas alongside the urban poor, sanitation has become a pressing issue.

The report also outlines how 80% of the population are now in need of protection and assistance in 'what has been described as the world's worst humanitarian crisis' (IDMC, 2019:6). It estimates at least 2.3 million of the country's population of around 29 million were internally displaced by the end of 2018 (IDMC, 2019:7).

Case study: the Philippines

As can be seen in Figure 3.3, the Philippines had the highest amount of new internal displacement during 2018. In this year, 3.8 million people experienced internal displacement due to disasters. The location of the Philippines within the 'typhoon belt' and 'ring of fire' makes it prone to weather-related and other disasters such as earthquakes, typhoons, floods, landslides and around 20 tropical storms each year (IDCM, 2019).

There is also internal displacement in the southern islands – Mindanao – due to four decades of internal conflict and instability. Following a visit to the country in 2015, the Special Rapporteur on the Human Rights of Internally Displaced Persons suggested that intensified efforts were required to achieve lasting peace.[1] In 2018, there were some 188,000 new displacements recorded due to conflict and violence (IDCM, 2019).

The IDMC webpage[2] for the Philippines makes clear that the causes of displacement relate to disasters as well as development projects that affect indigenous people (IDMC, 2019). The country is experiencing rapid urbanisation as well as poverty, which are considered to be major drivers of disaster and displacement risks. IDMC also outlines how climate change is making the country more vulnerable to internal displacement. Between 2008 and 2018, an annual average of 3.6 million people were displaced due to disasters.

During the Special Rapporteur visit in July 2015, the government of the Philippines was commended for its reconstruction efforts after Typhoon Haiyan (known as 'Yolanda'), which killed thousands and displaced more than 4 million people. It was, however, noted that attention to those displaced was waning prior to durable solutions being achieved, with a lack of basic services or adequate housing found in many cases.

IDPs in the Philippines face similar challenges to other populations. These include access to safe housing and basic services such as education and health, as well as difficulties in generating income in new locations due to a lack of livelihood opportunities (IDMC, 2019).

In terms of statistics, the Philippines is one of the most reliable countries for data on internal displacement. The government publishes regular and reliable updates and reports through field offices across the country. This Disaster Response Operations Monitoring and Information Centre (DROMIC)[3] gathers, consolidates and disseminates information related to all phases of disasters to promote a safe and resilient Filipino society.

The needs of IDPs

Regardless of whether IDPs have been displaced through conflict or as a result of disasters, they have a number of needs in common. People should be protected against being displaced in the first instance (Kalin, 2014). This means that people should be able to enjoy all the relevant guarantees of human rights applicable to the rest of the population of a given country. As outlined earlier, the protection of IDPs ultimately comes down to 'primarily national protection' (UNHCR, 2012:120) through domestic legislation due to State sovereignty and the lack of a legal or institutional basis for the international community to provide protection or assistance, unless invited to do so.

Should national protection not be feasible, the next need is to be able to leave danger zones to reach a safe location and not be forced to return to the danger zone. Evacuation from these areas is often fraught with difficulties and different understandings between different agencies of when and how this should be done. This leads to the next need – the need to find a place to stay temporarily, pending a durable solution. As with refugees, if finding a durable solution is delayed, displacement may become protracted and this affects people's ability to move forward in their lives.

There is also a need to protect IDPs against discrimination due to displacement (Kalin, 2014). People who are displaced should have the same ability to access services, employment or education as the rest of the population. In practice, this is often not the case with numerous examples of discrimination against those who have been displaced. For example, in Myanmar, ethnic minority groups have been discriminated against for over half a century by the ruling military regime that is often the cause of their displacement due to military campaigns and land appropriation. Internal displacement within Myanmar has mostly resulted from systematic patterns of human rights abuses associated with the conflicts in ethnic minority areas. Many have crossed international borders, but those remaining within the country may migrate to forest areas to avoid further persecution. In this way discrimination serves a purpose, with proposed development projects and use of land made available. Return in these instances is invariably not possible.

Practically, any documentation that has been lost during displacement needs to be replaced. This applies to adults and children, with the need to replace birth and educational certificates to children. Being able to register to vote and participate in any future elections is also needed.

There are examples of internal displacement wherein property left behind during periods of conflict is taken by others – be this property housing or other assets. Some form of restitution for lost property is required. Since 2005 there have been principles designed for this purpose – the Principles on Housing and Property Restitution for Refugees and Displaced Persons (the Pinheiro Principles). These have the restitution of property as their aim to overcome previous assumptions that the land, homes and other possessions of conflict were somehow just the spoils of war. These Principles do not stop this issue from being complex, as houses may have been destroyed, built over and/or rebuilt by those now occupying them. Official records of ownership may have been destroyed or, in some cases, forged. Following the conflicts in the former Yugoslavia, for example, those driven out of their homes often found it difficult to prove ownership and also found other people living in their houses upon return.

Finally, there is a need to find a durable solution to displacement, be this by invoking a process of 'sustainable return' or 'sustainable local integration' in another part of the country (Kalin, 2014). As seen earlier, return to areas of origin may not be feasible if the reasons for displacement in the first instance mean that homes, property or means of livelihood have been made into development projects or, in some known but peculiar cases, golf courses for military generals.

Impacts from this type of displacement need to take the degree, reasons and scale of initial coercion around displacement into account. It is impossible to underestimate the fragmentation of communities, the splitting of families, the individual losses associated with relocation and in conflict-related displacement and the mistrust generated by people who have been relocated (Harris, 1998). However, forced relocation may also be used by state agents to change the ethnic balance in politically sensitive areas, and the impact of this might be felt for generations.

Points for discussion – the needs and risks of IDPs

- Should IDPs be treated as a category of concern distinguished from other people who have experienced internal human rights violations?
- What other specific needs do you think IDPs have?
- What other future impacts do you think subsequent generations will have following the fragmentation of communities and/or internal displacement of families?

Further risks and needs

Kalin (2014) suggests that many IDPs also face problems that are not only limited to being displaced in the first place but related to the contexts in which they are displaced to. For example, they may have a higher risk of hunger or malnutrition in their new locations, requiring food assistance. There are a range of other risks and needs, both of adults and children.

Children might be recruited into state or non-state armies, invoking a need for child protection (Kalin, 2014). Child sexual exploitation can become part of displacement and humanitarian contexts (Radford et al., 2015). For adults and children, sexual and gender-based violence (SGBV) may be prevalent prior to, during and after displacement (Hynes, 2017). Ideas around specific gendered vulnerabilities can sometimes lead to women and children being identified as weak dependents without any agency of their own. This has been one critique of the human trafficking discourse and international law, which will be explored further in the next chapter. However, adults and children are also trafficked from humanitarian and displacement contexts (UNODC, 2016).

People may become separated from family members (Kalin, 2014), requiring family reunification programmes. People may also be excluded from education or health services, and access to these may become more difficult over time (Kalin, 2014). In such cases, literacy and other educational projects will be required and, as often happens in camp settings for refugees, parallel systems of provision of health services may be necessary. If poverty or extreme socio-economic deprivations are part of the experience of internal displacement, access to employment or livelihood opportunities becomes essential (Kalin, 2014).

Key Thinker Box 3.2   Chaloka Beyani – Protecting the Internally Displaced

Chaloka Beyani is the former United Nations Special Rapporteur on the Human Rights of Internally Displaced Persons, having been appointed in 2010 and remaining in this role until 2016 (Beyani, 2011).

During his time as Special Rapporteur, he was one of the key drafters of the **Great Lakes Protocol** on Internally Displaced Persons (discussed earlier) and was also involved in drafting and negotiating a planned African Union Convention on internal displacement in Africa. Research published in 2000 also underpinned the African Union Convention for the Protection and Assistance of Internally Displaced Persons – the **Kampala Convention** (discussed earlier) – adopted in 2009, coming into force in 2012 after being ratified by 15 African states. This Convention was the first to create binding obligations on signatories for protecting and assisting persons displaced within states.

In the role of Special Rapporteur he undertook field research and produced official reports which were presented each year to the UN Human Rights Council and the General Assembly. During this time he made country visits to Kenya (2011), Sudan (2012), Georgia (2013), Serbia, Kosovo (2013), Sri Lanka (2013), Haiti (2014), Ukraine (2014), Syria (2015), the Philippines (2015) and Nigeria (2016) amongst other countries. Reports of these and other visits can be found at: www.ohchr.org/EN/Issues/IDPersons/Pages/Visits.aspx

His academic works include collected essays on the use of international law and a book-length exposition of the standards of human rights which are applicable to the right of freedom of movement within States (Beyani, 2000). This latter book recognises that most displacement is within States, and people's ability to exercise their rights depends upon their ability to move and choose a place of residence within States.

Subsequently, freedom of movement is therefore crucial to the protection and enjoyment of all other rights.

Beyani's expertise in international human rights law has also led to his practical involvement in helping African nations draft new constitutions. For example, the African Union Panel of African Eminent Personalities, led by former UN Secretary-General Kofi Annan, invited Beyani to participate in drafting Kenya's new constitution, after the turbulent presidential elections in 2007 had failed to produce a clear winner. He served in Kenya from 2009 to 2010, helping to draft the constitution and undertaking civic education across Kenya. He is performing a similar role in Zambia and South Sudan.

Beyani was also part of a team of experts that formulated the **Responsibility to Protect** principle, adopted in 2005 and designed to avoid a repetition of atrocities committed in the 1990s in Srebrenica and Rwanda, which the international community failed to prevent. The UN Secretary-General has taken steps to guide the practical implementation of this principle. This Responsibility to Protect was inspired by Francis Deng's ideas around state sovereignty as a responsibility, with States having positive responsibilities for their population's welfare.

Chaloka Beyani is now an Associate Professor of International Law in the London School of Economics.

Key references – Chaloka Beyani

Beyani, C. (2000) *Human Rights Standards and the Movement of People within States*, Oxford University Press, Oxford.

The possibility of 'durable solutions'?

There are **three possible options available for internally displaced persons**. These are:

1   Local integration in the place of refuge within a country of origin
2   Settlement in another part of a country of origin
3   Sustainable return to the place of origin or habitual residence

These three settlement options constitute only part of a durable solution to the issue of internal displacement. Option 1 involves settling permanently in the place of refuge. Option 2 involves moving to another part of the same country. Both options 1 and 2 are sometimes the only reasonable option available to IDPs. Option 3 can only happen if there has been a change in the conditions that caused the displacement in the first instance. It is sometimes considered to be the ideal option, but it is not always a possibility. For a durable solution to be reached, other factors need to be addressed, and the challenges of reaching such a durable solution for IDPs cannot be underestimated.

A durable solution can only be achieved when IDPs no longer have specific assistance needs as a result of their displacement and when their need for protection has also been addressed in a sustainable way. People need to be able to live without discrimination and have their fundamental human rights respected. Akin to location integration for refugees, circumstances should include the receipt or re-receipt of citizenship documents of the country of origin. Employment, livelihoods, access to basic, education and health services are a part of this.

As IDMC outlined in a 2015 training module that can be found on its webpage, the achievement of durable solutions includes both visible and invisible challenges:

- 'Vulnerable' IDPs tend to remain in displacement longer
- Extended families have different intentions
- Multiple waves of displacement occur
- Solutions become more elusive over time
- Political cooperation is lacking
- Development work begins late
- Funding is inadequate
- Data (on displacement) is scarce

Points for discussion – the visible and invisible challenges of finding solutions for IDPs

- Discuss each of the points above from the IDMC 2015 training module,[4] and think about what types of challenges each of these would bring when finding durable solutions for IDPs.
- Why do you think they are considered challenges?
- Can you think of any particular examples of where these points are most relevant?
- Who would you consider to be a 'vulnerable' IDP?

On the point about solutions becoming more elusive over time, there is no equivalent definition to PRS (see Chapter 2) of what constitutes a **protracted IDP situation**. However, there are a number of contexts in which this description is used. For example, within Columbia, there have been five decades of internal armed conflict over control of land and resources (Brookings-Bern Project on Internal Displacement, 2011[5]). It has been estimated that as many as one in ten Columbians have been displaced at least once in their lives (IDMC, 2014). The **indigenous population** make up a high percentage of IDPs in Columbia. Some displaced by conflict are later displaced by disasters (Crawford *et al.*, 2015). In the Darfur region of Sudan, conflict that emerged in 2003 has affected all levels of society and led to several million IDPs as a result of conflict and violence (Crawford *et al.*, 2015). As Crawford *et al.* (2015) outline, as a result the **civilian population** has:

> borne the brunt of the conflict, which has had an enormous impact in terms of displacement, physical insecurity, loss of livelihoods and social networks, morbidity, malnutrition and loss of life.

Crawford *et al.* (2015) go on to describe how civilians have fled their homes to escape violations of human rights including torture, destruction of property, sexual violence and forced conscription. They outline how Janjaweed militias have been notorious in their mass killings, rape, looting of villages and extortion and how both government forces and armed groups have restricted the movement of local populations, cutting off their livelihood options.

As can be seen, seeking solutions to IDP issues is complex, and in thinking about these a range of political, economic, social and cultural rights considerations are involved. Addressing the causes of displacement in the first instance are a part of this, and durable solutions for IDPs will remain elusive if political as well as economic issues are not addressed in a lasting and sustainable way.

Internal 'human trafficking'

Beyond the displacement of people due to conflict or disasters, there are also those who are displaced within their countries of origin due to forced migration as a result of human trafficking (see Chapter 4 for further details of the definition and scope of human trafficking). The topic of human trafficking is often focused on those who cross international borders, but it can equally apply to those who are trafficked within a country. Human trafficking can include exploitation in the form of sexual exploitation, forced labour and domestic servitude. Those subjected to forced labour can include a number of sectors such as the fishing industry, mining and agricultural work. As Martin (2006) outlines:

> Internal trafficking shares many common elements with internal displacement and one could argue that internal trafficking victims are internally displaced persons (IDPs). The Guiding Principles on Internal Displacement describe IDPs as 'persons or groups of persons who have been forced or obliged to flee or leave their homes or places of habitual residence . . . and who have not crossed an internationally recognized international boundary'. The Handbook for Applying the Guiding Principles on Internal Displacement makes clear that 'the distinctive feature of internal displacement is coerced or involuntary movement that takes place within national borders. The reasons for flight may vary and include armed conflict, situations of generalized violence, violations of human rights, and natural or human-made disasters'. Human trafficking involves forced or coerced movements.

Martin (2006) goes on to consider how internal displacement and internal trafficking intersect in other ways. For those who have been displaced by conflict, other human rights violations or disasters, vulnerability to trafficking might be a consequence if protective factors are not present. The Guiding Principles outlined earlier do call for protection from slavery, including sale into marriage, sexual exploitation and forced labour.

Points for discussion – IDPS and internal trafficking

- How do you think that internal displacement and internal trafficking may differ in practice?
- Do you think that becoming an IDP might make someone more 'vulnerable' to being trafficked?
- If yes, why?

Researching internal displacement – methodological, data collection and statistical challenges

There are a considerable number of methodological challenges involved in collecting data or estimated statistics about IDPs. For example, the internally displaced remain within their own countries but are, by the nature of their displacement, often made invisible within the local populations and within statistics. People may move to places that make them difficult to find and/or difficult to reach. If people are escaping violence and conflict, they may be moving around at night and in small groups to avoid detection (see Figure 3.1). This makes people difficult to identify as IDPs, and identifying people on the move is also challenging.

Areas to carry out fieldwork may well be inaccessible due to security considerations. The use of local researchers to carry out fieldwork may also involve a number of ethical and security related considerations (see Chapter 7 for details of ethical considerations when carrying out research in these areas). If people have been involved in disasters, they may have lost their homes and possessions as well as members of their family.

Statistics may be provided by either the government or those involved in providing aid to people who have been displaced. In some instances, estimates of those displaced will vary in range dependent upon political exigencies of those collecting data. Data may have been collected from a range of sources wherein different methodologies may have been used. As such, the quality, reliability and comparability of data should always be a key consideration. Reported data may also be incomplete and not adequately represent the changing picture of displacement.

In recent years there has been a focus on profiling IDP situations – a process of collaborating across agencies to generate more reliable data. This allows for data collection and analysis to take place and for generating agreement about definitions of who is an IDP, what the causes of displacement are and understanding the key needs and risks involved. This exercise is context specific and,

Figure 3.5 Internally Displaced Persons
Source: Hynes, 2020

as such, takes into account perceptions of displacement, including those of the people who have themselves been affected.

Reliable sources of data should always be sought. The Internal Displacement Monitoring Centre (IDMC) is a good place to start when thinking about estimates of the displaced. View at: www.internal-displacement.org

Point for discussion – data collection

- How would you collect data about IDPs given the range of challenges involved in this activity (refer to Figure 3.1)?
- How would you be able to keep yourself safe in areas affected by conflict?
- What problems do you see with statistics collected by the government involved or those involved in providing aid to people displaced by disasters?

Notes

1 View the country report of the Special Rapporteur at: www.ohchr.org/EN/Issues/ IDPersons/Pages/Visits.aspx
2 View at: www.internal-displacement.org/countries/philippines

3 View at: https://dromic.dswd.gov.ph
4 View at: https://www.internal-displacement.org/sites/default/files/inline-files/3.-IDMC-DS-Module-DS-Criteria-Facilitator-Notes.pdf
5 View at: https://www.brookings.edu/project/brookings-lse-project-on-internal-dis placement/

Further reading

Beyani, C. (2011) *Report of the Special Rapporteur on the Human Rights of Internally Displaced Persons, Chaloka Beyani*, UN Doc. A/HRC/19/54, 26 December 2011. [check]

Crawford, N., Cosgrave, J., Haysom, S. and Walicki, N. (2015) *Protracted Displacement: Uncertain Paths to Self-reliance in Exile*, Humanitarian Policy Group, Overseas Development Institute, London.

Kalin, W. (2014) Internal Displacement, in Fiddian-Qasmiyeh, E., Loescher, G., Long, K. and Sigona, N. (Eds.), *The Oxford Handbook of Refugee and Forced Migration Studies*, Oxford University Press, Oxford.

Martin, S. (2006) Internal Trafficking, *People Trafficking: Upholding Rights and Understanding Vulnerabilities*, University of Oxford, Oxford.

United Nations Office for the Coordination of Humanitarian Affairs (2008, reprinted 2004) *Guiding Principles on Internal Displacement*, United Nations, New York.

UNODC (2016) *Global Report on Trafficking in Persons*, United Nations Office on Drugs and Crime, New York.

References

Harris, P. (1998) Myanmar, in *Internally Displaced People: A Global Survey*, Earthscan, London.

Hynes, P. (2017) Trust and Mistrust in the Lives of Forcibly Displaced Women and Children, *Families, Relationships and Societies*, 6(2), 219–238.

Internal Displacement Monitoring Centre (IDMC) (2014) *Global Report on Internal Displacement*, IDMC and Norwegian Refugee Council, Geneva, Switzerland.

Internal Displacement Monitoring Centre (IDMC) (2019) *Global Report on Internal Displacement*, IDMC and Norwegian Refugee Council, Geneva, Switzerland.

Internal Displacement Monitoring Centre (IDMC) (2020) *Global Report on Internal Displacement*, IDMC and Norwegian Refugee Council, Geneva, Switzerland.

Radford, L., Allnock, D. and Hynes, P. (2015) *Preventing and Responding to Child Sexual Abuse and Exploitation: Evidence Review*, UNICEF, New York.

UNHCR (2012) *The State of the World's Refugees: In Search of Solidarity*, Oxford University Press, Oxford.

Key web pages

Internal Displacement Monitoring Centre (IDMC):
www.internal-displacement.org/global-figures
For global IDP estimates see: www.internal-displacement.org
Various other reports from the UN Special Rapporteur on Internally Displaced Persons:
www.ohchr.org/EN/Issues/IDPersons/Pages/IDPersonsIndex.aspx

4   Who is a 'victim' or 'survivor' of trafficking?

Introduction

People who are forced to migrate as a result of threat, the use of force or other forms of coercion, abduction, fraud, deception, the abuse of power or the abuse of a position of vulnerability for the purposes of exploitation represent another form of forced migration defined within international law as the crime of 'human trafficking'. Although rarely studied through a forced migration lens, people who are trafficked are subject to degrees of force, coercion or coercive control, with debates about agency and consent ongoing in this field. There is also a degree of confusion between 'human trafficking' and 'human smuggling', with the terms often used interchangeably by governments and the media. This confusion has consequences in policy, practice and in responses to people involved.

This chapter begins by exploring the internationally recognised definition of human trafficking as contained within the 2000 Protocol to Prevent, Suppress and Punish Trafficking in Persons, Especially Women and Children (otherwise known as the Palermo Protocol). This Protocol formed part of the UN Convention Against Transnational Organised Crime, adopted by the UN General Assembly in 2000, to promote cooperation between states to combat organised crime. Two other Protocols were adopted under this Convention, one on human smuggling and another on trafficking of firearms. Some of the key issues with the human trafficking definition are then explored, such as its focus on borders and how it pertains to women and children only. Thereafter the contested and often binary terminology of who is a 'victim', 'potential victim' or 'survivor' of human trafficking and the distinctions between human trafficking and human smuggling are also highlighted.

Difficulties around the provision of accurate and reliable statistics and/or estimates are often highlighted in debates around human trafficking and associated areas such as slavery or forced labour, and these issues are explored. Key forms of exploitation, such as sexual exploitation, forced labour and domestic servitude are outlined. Thereafter, the geography of human trafficking – both across and within borders – is described, highlighting how the estimated numbers of people trafficked within their country of origin outnumbers international estimates. Key concepts such as 'collateral damage', case studies and the work of key thinkers are included throughout this chapter.

Who is a 'victim' of human trafficking?

The first internationally recognised definition of human trafficking as contained within Article 3 of the 2000 Protocol to Prevent, Suppress and Punish Trafficking in Persons, Especially Women and Children (otherwise known as the Palermo Protocol) defines *trafficking in persons* as:

> the recruitment, transportation, transfer, harbouring or receipt of persons, by means of the threat or use of force or other forms of coercion, of abduction, of fraud, of deception, of the abuse of power or of a position of vulnerability or of the giving or receiving of payments or benefits to achieve the consent of a person having control over another person, for the purpose of exploitation.

This definition is regularly broken down into three distinct elements – the **act**, **means** and **purpose** of human trafficking:

1   The **act** of trafficking relates to the recruitment, transportation, transfer, harbouring or receipt of persons. In other words, the way in which trafficking takes place.
2   The **means** relates to the threat or use of force or other forms of coercion, of abduction, of fraud, of deception, of the abuse of power or of a position of vulnerability or of the giving or receiving of payments or benefits. This is about how trafficking takes place. Under this definition, children under the age of 18 years cannot give valid consent to any of the means of trafficking due to their age. Therefore, for children, only the 'act' and 'purpose' aspects of the definition apply in law and practice.
3   The **purpose** in this definition relates to exploitation. This is about why trafficking takes place which, as outlined in the Palermo Protocol, 'shall include, at a minimum, the exploitation of the prostitution of others or others forms of sexual exploitation, forced labour or services, slavery or practices similar to slavery, servitude or the removal of organs'.

Represented diagrammatically in Figure 4.1, these three elements make up the current view of human trafficking:

Exploitation is a contested term and can cover a very broad range of sectors across construction, agriculture, beauty, cleaning, manufacturing, waste disposal, textile, food processing and other factory-based industries as well as domestic work. As the Palermo Protocol definition outlines, people might also be trafficked for forced labour, the removal or organs and/or sexual exploitation. People trafficked for forced marriage, forced begging and to be child soldiers are also regularly included in human trafficking discourse.

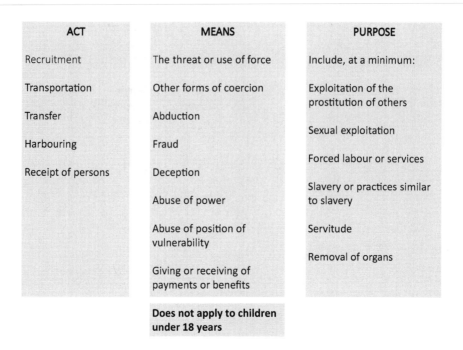

ACT	MEANS	PURPOSE
Recruitment	The threat or use of force	Include, at a minimum:
Transportation	Other forms of coercion	Exploitation of the prostitution of others
Transfer	Abduction	Sexual exploitation
Harbouring	Fraud	Forced labour or services
Receipt of persons	Deception	Slavery or practices similar to slavery
	Abuse of power	Servitude
	Abuse of position of vulnerability	Removal of organs
	Giving or receiving of payments or benefits	
	Does not apply to children under 18 years	

Figure 4.1 Elements of the Human Trafficking Definition

This list of forms of exploitation continues to grow. In a recent report of the Special Rapporteur on contemporary forms of slavery – which explored **current and emerging forms of slavery** – expected changes in the future of work, the environment, migration and emerging demographics were considered in respect of future forms of exploitation (United Nations General Assembly, 2019). For example, it was found that with the advent of new technologies, new forms of exploitation are emerging, such as online sexual exploitation.

As with any definition that has an element of ambiguity, the Palermo Protocol definition has been criticised for including vague terms (Gallagher, 2015). This includes the term *exploitation* which has meant the inclusion of multiple practices – from sexual exploitation to forced begging, illegal adoptions to surrogacy and other forms that expand the concept of trafficking and lead to what Chuang (2014) has described as a form of **'exploitation creep'**. Chuang (2014) warns against growing forms of exploitation included under human trafficking that enables a recasting of human trafficking as modern-day slavery, something that makes defining the concept's legal parameters problematic. Chuang also suggests that the increasing number of actors in this area have led to forced labour being included in human trafficking work and all forms of trafficking being labelled as slavery (2014:611). Others, such as Anderson (see

Key Thinker Box 4.1) have argued that such **loose definitions conceal both practical and philosophical problems** and that, in the UK, trafficking has been framed as an immigration issue by the State with very different understanding of the term by those advocating for people who have experienced human trafficking (Anderson, 2007).

As Allain (2018) recounts, the **conflation between human trafficking and slavery** does not take into account distinct 'genealogies' of the two concepts, with each having its own history and there being little in common other than both address the issue of exploitation. The two concepts are also distinct in the way in which slavery was once legal and facilitated by States, whereas human trafficking has emerged out of language around 'white slave traffic' during the 19th century to describe prostitution. However, as Allain has argued:

> Yet these two very different genealogies would converge, in the year 2000, with the end product being no longer focused on prostitution and exploitative practices therein, but rather on exploitation writ large, within the context of human trafficking. The Victorian impulse to address prostitution, both forced and otherwise, remains at the heart of contemporary human trafficking, though its impulse has diminished as States recognise that exploitation can exists not only in sex work, but in any labour situation.
>
> (Allain, 2017)

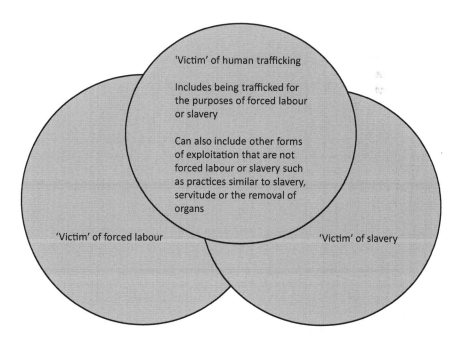

Figure 4.2 Overlaps between 'Victims' of Trafficking, Forced Labour and Slavery

The Palermo Protocol brought together these two concepts as well as forced labour – which itself had another history, largely considered through the International Labour Organisation (ILO). ILO's definition of forced labour relates to **all work or service** which is **exacted under menace of penalty** and which is **carried out involuntarily**.

Whilst the concepts are distinct, there are important overlaps between trafficking, forced labour and slavery as shown diagrammatically in Figure 4.2 which require ongoing consideration.

Key Thinker Box 4.1   Bridget Anderson –
Motherhood, Apple Pie and Slavery

Bridget Anderson is a Professor of Migration, Mobilities and Citizenship at the University of Bristol and Director of a research grouping – Migration Mobilities Bristol – that seeks to bring together an interdisciplinary network of academics to engage with migration theory, policy and practice. Anderson's initial research considered the lives of migrant domestic workers in the European Union, in particular the racialisation of paid domestic labour and the challenges this posed to feminism, political theory and community organisations. Over the past two decades she has been engaged with debates around human trafficking, 'modern-day slavery', state enforcement, deportation and immigration controls. Her work now explores the tension between labour market conditions and citizenship rights.

In a book published in the year 2000, Anderson looked at domestic work in Europe and the American South – *Doing the Dirty Work? The Global Politics of Domestic Labour*. This book considered issues around race, class and domestic oppression. The book **challenges the notion that domestic work is the great leveller among feminists**, arguing instead that the feminisation of the labour market results in middle-class white women in the North pushing responsibility for domestic work onto women from the South.

In a notable contribution in 2007 – *Motherhood, Apple Pie and Slavery: Reflections on Trafficking Debates* – Anderson argued that loose definition of terms such as *human trafficking* conceals both practical and philosophical problems. It was also argued that human trafficking has been framed by the state as an immigration issue, whereas there are different understandings of the term from those advocating for people who have experienced human trafficking. In this working paper, Anderson points out that challenging the actions of those seeking to 'stamp out' human trafficking 'is akin to saying that one endorses slavery or is against motherhood and apple pie' (2007:3) but that **a critical consideration of trafficking requires viewing the positions, priorities, conflicting agendas and different lenses of the different actors involved**. Three actors in particular – States, feminist 'abolitionist' NGOs and migrant worker organisations – are examined, and **themes around consent, choice and agency** are explored. The distinctions between voluntary and forced migration, as well as forced or free engagement in sex work, are also outlined in a nuanced way that illustrates how thinking beyond such binary distinctions is essential.

Anderson is also the author of a 2013 contribution – *Us and Them? The Dangerous Politics of Immigration Control* – which examines the construction of differences between the foreigner and the citizen and theorises immigration debates. With a focus on the borders between citizens (us) and migrants (them), Anderson delves into the history of the creation of the homogenised migrant figure within liberal democracies. Chapter 7 is devoted to the language and policy around human trafficking. There is a useful tracing of the development of anti-trafficking policy (mainly within the UK) and account of the usage of the language of slavery and the recent terminology of *modern-day slavery*. Questions around consent, choice and agency are reiterated, as is the role of the State in not only the protection of victims of trafficking, but also in creating and producing vulnerability through legislation, policy and practice resting on border controls.

Amongst many other papers and contributions, in 2019 Anderson engages with the ethical and epistemological challenges of the way migration is constructed as a problem and how this relates to political and methodological nationalism. She considers the growth of migration research and provides a sophisticated contribution around work on transnationalism, the 'mobilities turn' in the social sciences and methodological nationalism. The distinctions and overlaps between migrants and citizens are drawn out and, as has been seen across Europe in the past few years, 'crimes of solidarity' by citizens who assist people who cross borders and are subsequently accused of 'smuggling, trafficking and even being 'slave-traders' are helpfully explored (2019:9).

Key references – Bridget Anderson

Anderson, B. (2000) *Doing the Dirty Work? The Global Politics of Domestic Labour*, Zed Books, London.

Anderson, B. (2007) *Motherhood, Apple Pie and Slavery: Reflections on Trafficking Debates*, Working Paper No.48, Centre on Migration, Policy and Society (COM-PAS), University of Oxford, Oxford.

Anderson, B. (2013) *Us & Them? The Dangerous Politics of Immigration Control*, Oxford University Press, Oxford.

Anderson, B. (2019) New Directions in Migration Studies: Towards Methodological De-nationalism, *Comparative Migration Studies*, 7(36), 1–13.

What are the key issues with the Palermo Protocol definition?

The Palermo Protocol has been successful in gaining signatories and providing the first internationally agreed-upon definition of human trafficking. However, the Palermo Protocol is **not a human rights instrument**; rather it was designed to facilitate cooperation between states to combat organised crime (Anderson, 2007, 2013; Gallagher, 2015). As such, border controls rather than human rights protection lie at the heart of this Protocol. The logic behind this piece of anti-trafficking legislation being devised by the Organisation for Security Cooperation in Europe (OSCE) has attracted considerable concern given the **focus on security above the rights** or protection of victims (Gould, 2010; Palmary, 2010). Consequently, an appreciation of the more structural 'harms' and 'collateral damage' (see Key Concept Box 4.1) of State policies wherein vulnerability to exploitation is created and/or exacerbated by State policies and legislation is also essential to an understanding of human trafficking (Anderson, 2012; GAATW, 2007; O'Connell Davidson, 2013).

Gallagher (2015) has argued that two key critiques of the Palermo Protocol – that, as stated earlier, it is **not a human rights treaty** and also that it **does not have a credible enforcement mechanism** – have been overcome because the Protocol provides an 'impetus and template' for legal and political developments that have subsequently ameliorated these weaknesses. Gallagher (2015) discussed the criminal justice focus of the Protocol, arguing that the alternative – a human rights treaty on trafficking – was never viable due to lack of political support but that States were willing to create an international instrument around human trafficking as an issue of transnational crime which, over time, has seen human rights protections added.

Shortly after the adoption of this Protocol, the UN High Commissioner for Human Rights issued principles to integrate a human rights perspective and provide practical guidance on the prevention of trafficking and the protection of victims of trafficking – the Recommended Principles and Guidelines on Human Rights and Human Trafficking. As Gallagher (2015) outlined, this extension of the Palermo Protocol has allowed for international law around human trafficking to evolve. For example, within Europe, the 2005 Council of

Europe Convention reiterated provisions of the Protocol but also incorporated concepts and language contained with the UN Recommended Principles. It is **now accepted that victims of human trafficking have rights** relating to identification, protection and support, the right not to be detained and not to be prosecuted for offences relating to their trafficking experiences.

Gallagher (2015) also commented that although there were challenges of weak implementation of the Protocol, without regular reports from States, this has been improved by external developments. Examples again include the 2005 Council of Europe Convention with regular and rigorous oversight mechanisms including country visits and the advent of the Special Rapporteur on Trafficking in Persons, especially Women and Children.

Another key consideration that emerged shortly after the advent of the Palermo Protocol was that the focus of discussion – including within the title of the Protocol – was on 'Women and Children'. As Gould recounted in 2010:

> Historically, and currently, the focus of discussion, research and indeed national and international legislation is on countering, and preventing, the trafficking of 'women and children' for the purposes of sexual exploitation. While lip service is paid to other forms of trafficking, it is trafficking for prostitution that has grabbed the attention of policy makers, researchers, advocacy organisations and the media.
>
> (Gould, 2010:32)

Some commentators suggest that this focus on sexual exploitation in human trafficking debates has now been broadened out to include other forms of exploitation (Allain, 2017; Gallagher, 2015).

Debates around sexual exploitation are themselves often highly polarised. On one side feminists argue that sex work should be legalised and a rights approach adopted (Andrijasevic, 2010; Doezma, 2010). On the other side, feminists argue that prostitution is a symptom of patriarchy, and voluntary consent is not possible. Agustin (2007) (see Key Thinker Box 4.2) and others argue that the label of 'human trafficking' itself invokes a victimising discourse and does not accurately describe those who do sex work. She also argued that 'helpers' and moral agendas surrounding 'rescuing' those involved deny agency, making those involved into passive victims (Gould, 2010).

Critiques around **consent, choice and agency** are critical within human trafficking debates and relate to what some commentators have termed *infantilised femininity* and concerns about women or children who 'move' (Anderson, 2007, 2013; Gould, 2010; Palmary, 2010). As Palmary (2010) suggests:

> It is a concern over women who move – with all the associated implications of leaving home and children – where home is considered the most appropriate place for women and for expressions of female sexuality.
>
> (Palmary, 2010:53)

The conflation of these issues around agency, and representations of **women and children as passive victims**, is something which has been explored in relation to gender in broader contexts of forced migration including refugee and IDP camps (Fiddian-Qasmiyeh, 2014). In a literature review on vulnerabilities to human trafficking Brodie *et al.* (2018) outlined a significant gap in the number of studies exploring the perspectives of those who have themselves experienced trafficking, often referred to as the 'survivors' of human trafficking, which could provide gendered and nuanced understandings.

In a study on the trafficking of children into, within and out of the UK, Pearce *et al.* (2013:53–56; Hynes, 2010) also considered the **difficulties of identifying where exploitation begins and ends** within a trafficking process. Trafficking was found to have no clear, easily identifiable beginning, middle or end. It could also be hidden in the day-to-day activities of a child, occurring over a long period of time. A key finding of their research was that trafficking is a *process* occurring over the longer term, rather than being a one-off and sometimes nationally bounded *event* in the life of a young person. They argued that the identification of trafficking therefore also needed to be understood as a process, rather than relying on one-off disclosure, and that recovery could be a lengthy process requiring adequate resources over a period of time.

Perhaps due to the history of the term, or the ways in which States interpret it, there are many other issues around who constitutes a victim, potential victim or survivor of human trafficking beyond those recounted here (see Further reading below).

Key Concept 4.1   'Collateral Damage' following Anti-Trafficking Campaigns

The term *collateral damage* was first used by the Global Alliance Against Traffic in Women (GAATW) in a 2007 publication looking at the impact of anti-trafficking measures on human rights around the world (Dotteridge, 2007, see also Dottridge, 2018). *Collateral damage* describes the risk of anti-trafficking measures taken that affect the rights and freedoms of people who are experiencing human trafficking. The term describes how harm may be inflicted upon victims of trafficking as a result of anti-trafficking campaigns and actions – for example, detention in immigration centres, prosecution of individuals for offences around illegal work, raids and rescues that do not adequately consider the protection of those involved as well as forced repatriation. In other words, collateral damage occurs when the victim of human trafficking is not placed at the centre of actions designed to combat human trafficking and which do not respect the dignity of these same individuals. The preface of the 2007 anthology also outlines how those involved in anti-trafficking may misrepresent the interests of individuals:

A plethora of actors on the anti-trafficking terrain do their work from the perspective of human rights including those who bundle off the trafficked and migrant women back to where they came from in the name of protection.

(2007:vii)

Pollock (2007) described the human rights impact of the trafficking responses within Thailand following raids, often conducted at night, where personal possessions were confiscated and not returned and those 'rescued' were locked into cramped police detention cells under frightening conditions and/or deported under unsafe conditions (2007:174–175). Pollock also outlined how the causes of human trafficking were often shifted from State responsibilities onto those facilitating movement:

Although most trafficking reports have pointed to economic, political, and social reasons for the prevalence of trafficking from certain countries, countries of origin blamed the brokers, transnational crime gangs, and anything other than their own policies.

(Pollock, 2007:175–176)

Pollock outlines how national initiatives around trafficking began in Thailand as a response to child labour, HIV/AIDS and an international focus on the sex industry in the country. Whilst arrests and prosecution of offenders remained consistently low (for example, 352 arrests and 74 convictions in 2005) the numbers of people deported, repatriated, held in shelters or assistance programmes that denied them any freedom of movement were considerably higher (Pollock, 2007:191–196).

Denial of freedom of movement, deportation and repatriation continue today in many parts of the world in the name of preventing trafficking, including in Libyan detention centres. Dottridge (2018) questions why such levels of collateral damage remain after more than a decade of awareness of the unintended side effects of anti-trafficking policies and legislation. He concludes that this may be due to ignorance of policy makers, lack of training for law enforcement personnel but also potentially due to deliberate decisions by policy makers to not pay attention to some forms of migrants if not politically expedient to do so (2018:351–352). He also suggests that anti-trafficking practitioners tend not to listen to people who have gone through this experience, although they can be:

happy to hear testimony about the misery caused to trafficking victims by criminals, they do not listen to feedback provided by the same people about their experiences while supposedly being

protected and assisted by law enforcement officials or others assisting
trafficked persons.

(2018:352)

Key references – 'Collateral Damage'

Dottridge, M. (2018) Collateral Damage Provoked by Anti-Trafficking Measures, in
Piotrowicz, R., Rijken, C. and Uhl, B.H. (Eds.), *Routledge Handbook of Human
Trafficking*, Routledge, Abingdon and New York.
Global Alliance Against Traffic in Women (GAATW) (2007) *Collateral Damage: The
Impact of Anti-Trafficking Measures on Human Rights around the World*, GAATW,
Bangkok, Thailand.

Points for discussion – key issues in human trafficking debates

- What key issues do you consider most important in thinking about the
  exploitation and/or trafficking of people?
- Why do you think the Palermo Protocol emphasises women and children,
  and what does this mean for men and boys who are trafficked?
- Why is movement important in these debates?
- How do you think the term *collateral damage* helps us understand legislation, policy and practices around human trafficking?

Key Thinker Box 4.2   Laura Agustin – *Sex at the Margins* and the 'Rescue Industry'

Laura Agustin is an anthropologist who studies cultural and postcolonial
issues linking commercial sex, trafficking, migration, informal economies
and feminist theory. She blogs as The Naked Anthropologist at: www.
lauraagustin.com

Agustin wrote the highly acclaimed text – *Sex at the Margins* – in 2007.
It sought to explode the myth that sex work is different from other kinds of
work and that migrants who sell sex are passive victims. It also explored the
idea that those involved in the 'rescuing' of people from human trafficking,
in what has been termed the 'rescue industry', are necessarily benevolent and
without self-interest. The book explored how such stereotypes work and
how the 'victimising discourse known as "trafficking"' (2007:8) is disem-
powering and does not accurately describe the lives of those given this label.

Agustin is critical of the conflation of the terms *human trafficking* and
prostitution, arguing that those ascribed 'victim' status by helpers in the
rescue industry are often people who have made conscious and rational
decisions to migrate and would never consider themselves to be 'victims'.

Key reference – Laura Agustin

Agustin, L. (2007) *Sex at the Margins: Migration, Labour Markets and the Rescue Industry*, Zed Books, London.

What are the differences between 'human trafficking' and 'human smuggling'?

The differences between trafficking and smuggling are often misrepresented or absent in debates, media accounts and reports, with the two terms often used interchangeably. Under the UN Convention Against Transnational Organised Crime, adopted by the UN General Assembly in 2000, the two Protocols – one around human trafficking and another around human smuggling – are often the source of confusion. Anderson (2007) has argued that the two Protocols suggest two distinct 'groups of wrongdoers' (Anderson, 2007:6) – traffickers and smugglers – but that the networks of these two are not distinct in practice.

However, there are distinctions in law. Figure 4.3 gives an overview of the distinctions between human trafficking and human smuggling and also the

Human Trafficking	Human Smuggling
Involves the violation of human rights	May involve violation of human rights
Can involve coercion and deceit	No coercion or deceit involved
Can happen within a country and across international borders	Always involves crossing an international border
Can be brought into a country legally	Moving a person across a border illegally
Violation of a person's freedom	Violation of state sovereignty
Exploitation of a human being for financial gain or other benefits	No ongoing exploitative relationship involved
People who are trafficked are considered a victim of crime and therefore should not be punished or deported and should be protected from further harm	People who are smuggled are not considered a victim of crime but in some way complicit and may be punished and deported without further protection

Human Trafficking and Human Smuggling - Similarities
Involve movement from one place to another
Defined as a punishable offence
May involve transnational organised criminal groups

Figure 4.3 Trafficking and Smuggling: Distinctions and Similarities

similarities, which go some way to explain the confusion between the two Protocols on human trafficking and human smuggling.

As can be seen, a key distinction is that trafficking involves coercion and some form of deceit, whereas smuggling does not. Trafficking is considered to involve a relationship that involves exploitation for financial gain or other benefit, whereas in smuggling cases, there is no ongoing exploitative relationship involved post-movement.

Both trafficking and smuggling can involve the violation of human rights, with human trafficking considered a violation of a person's freedom. People who experience trafficking are considered to be victims of crime and, therefore, should not be punished or deported as a result. People who are smuggled are not considered in the same way but are rather often considered to be in some way complicit and can be punished or deported. Further protections for people who have experienced human trafficking is an expectation in law, although this does not always occur in practice.

The crossing of an international border is also relevant. Human trafficking can, and does, occur within countries as well as across borders. A victim of trafficking can be brought into a country legally and then go on to experience exploitation. For example, seeking asylum may involve the use of smugglers and, as van Liempt (2007) has suggested, smuggling can and often does become trafficking *en route* to safety and sanctuary. People who experience trafficking may have predominantly been labelled as migrants, refugees or others but can be vulnerable to situations of exploitation due to lack of opportunities in destination countries and the need to repay costs associated with their movement (UNODC, 2016:17). The crime of human smuggling has to involve the crossing of an international border, and that movement across a border is carried out illegally.

Both involve movement from one place to another and are defined in law as punishable offences. Both may involve transnational organised crime groups, but, as outlined later in this chapter may also involve individuals who facilitate movement, family members, *ad hoc* and opportunistic actors within broader networks. As UNODC outlined in their 2016 global trends: 'Most of the time, the trafficking is not committed by highly organized criminal networks, but rather by family members, acquaintances and neighbours' (UNODC, 2016:61). Bringing this factor into the debate about who is trafficked versus who is smuggled highlights how any focus on organised criminal networks does not always reflect the realities of these forms of movement.

Evidence, statistics, estimates and monitoring mechanisms

Chuang has suggested that the anti-trafficking field is a 'rigor-free zone' (2014:609) in terms of the concept of trafficking's legal parameters. Evidence, statistics and estimates have lacked rigour in the past, and there is ongoing debate around how statistics and estimates can be provided around human trafficking. There is also an overall lack of empirical studies and considerable unevenness in terms of methodological quality and diversity in the evidence around human trafficking (Brodie *et al.*, 2018).

Over the past few decades, the estimated global prevalence of trafficking has been fervently debated, particularly around the lack of empirical data for statistics cited (Laczo and Gramengna, 2003; Salt, 2000; Tyldum, 2010). Measuring human trafficking poses a considerable challenge as collecting data in this area is fraught with methodological difficulties. There are significant differences between estimates from different actors in the human trafficking field, some of which are reproduced uncritically. The Palermo Protocol does, however, oblige States to collect and share information on trends around human trafficking (Dijk and Campistol, 2018). The monitoring body of the Council of Europe Convention on Action against Trafficking in Human Beings – the Group of Experts on Action against Trafficking in Human Beings (GRETA) – also recommends the maintenance of comprehensive statistics around all aspects of human trafficking for countries which have ratified the Convention (Dijk and Campistol, 2018).

Several agencies now claim to be the authoritative source of trafficking statistics. Currently the United Nations Office on Drugs and Crime (UNODC) Global Report is one international source of information on trafficking in persons. Since 2010 UNODC has been mandated to collect data and produce biennial reports on trafficking in persons and of patterns and flows at national, regional and international levels (UNODC, 2014:6). Global trend reports in 2014, 2016 and 2018 provide details of detected numbers of people trafficked. UNODC's 2018 edition is based on information from 142 countries, around 94% of the world's population (2018:15), plus a separate overview of human trafficking in contexts of conflict. The reports provide an overview of patterns and flows of human trafficking at global, regional and international levels. In the 2018 report details of ascertaining national estimates through Multiple Systems Estimation (MSE) techniques were detailed, a methodology that is being used by governments to generate estimates of the hidden population of people who have experienced human trafficking (UNODC, 2018:34).

During the period 2002–2011, the International Labour Organization (ILO) estimated that there are 20.9 million people who are victims of forced labour globally at any one time (ILO, 2012).

In 2017, the Walk Free Foundation and the ILO, together with the International Organization for Migration (IOM), developed the Global Estimates of Modern Slavery. The 2017 estimates focus on two main issues – forced labour and forced marriage. Forced labour includes both state-imposed and forced labour in the private economy as well as sexual exploitation of adults and children. The methodology combined survey research involving face-to-face interviews with administrative data on victims of trafficking who had been assisted by the IOM. In these estimates, some 40.3 million people are considered to be living in some form of modern slavery as of 2016. This estimate has been widely debated and disputed amongst commentators. Statistics and estimates continue to evolve in this area.

IOM, Polaris and Liberty Asia have recently launched a global data repository on human trafficking – the Counter Trafficking Data Collaborative (CTDC) – which holds data on over 90,000 individual cases of trafficking from 172 countries, contributed by counter-trafficking organisations around the world.

In terms of monitoring, the US State Department produces Trafficking in Persons reports (known as TiP reports) which rank governments based on their anti-trafficking efforts around prosecution, protection and prevention. This system of ranking divides countries into different tiers according to compliance with a US piece of legislation – the 2000 Trafficking Victims Protection Act (TVPA). Tier 1 countries are those that comply with this legislation; Tier 2 are those not fully compliant; Tier 2 (Watchlist) are those making efforts to comply; Tier 3 are those that do not comply with the minimum standards advocated. According to the US State Department, the TiP Report is considered to be:

> the world's most comprehensive resource of governmental anti-human trafficking efforts and reflects the U.S. Government's commitment to global leadership on this key human rights and law enforcement issue. It represents an updated, global look at the nature and scope of trafficking in persons and the broad range of government actions to confront and eliminate it.
>
> (US State Department webpage, n.d.)[1]

GRETA's monitoring of the Council of Europe Convention is led by 15 independent experts. Country evaluation reports cover the treaty obligations of each State and, if found to be non-compliant, GRETA urges change. In cases where States are compliant, GRETA considers that changes should be made.

Why are people trafficked?

Human trafficking is a 'multifaceted phenomenon' (UNODC, 2016), and several references in the SDGs emphasize this. *Trafficking* appears in Targets 5.2, 8.7 and 16.2 plus, arguably, 5.3 if early and forced marriages are regarded as a form of exploitation.

The former Special Rapporteur on Trafficking in Persons, Joy Ngozi Ezeilo has outlined how little is being done to prevent and/or address the root causes of human trafficking across the African continent (Ezeilo, 2018:57) (see Key Thinker Box 4.3). These root causes – or drivers – of human trafficking relate to intertwining factors, and it is therefore not easy to specify the specific risk factors without thorough examination of particular contexts. Conflict can also make people vulnerable to human trafficking (UNODC, 2018).

Risk factors can cut across individual, household, family, community and structural levels and vary from country to country (Hynes *et al.*, 2019). In a study on human trafficking from Albania, Viet Nam and Nigeria, it was found that factors at family and household levels appeared to be particularly significant in the lives of people who had experienced trafficking. These included households affected by social issues such as domestic violence, substance abuse and physical violence as well as broader societal issues such as gender inequalities (Hynes *et al.*, 2019). It was also found that social norms that enabled early marriage and moral codes around divorce, pregnancy out of marriage and the shame and stigma associated with domestic violence in some instances could also be drivers – as well as the more known outcome – of human trafficking (Hynes *et al.*, 2019).

The reasons why trafficking occurs are invariably context-specific and may include some or a constellation of the following reasons:

- People may be living in contexts where human rights violations occur with impunity and there are few safety nets available to protect against trafficking
- People may be living in extreme and protracted socio-economic deprivation and need to find ways out, which can involve risk
- People may be living in debt
- Families may be separated from each other due to conflict, war or natural disasters or be placed in situations of vulnerability to trafficking
- Family backgrounds that are abusive or harmful might create vulnerability to trafficking
- People are sometimes 'kidnapped' for trafficking purposes, but this is sometimes over-represented in accounts of trafficking
- Children who are orphaned can sometimes be targeted for trafficking purposes
- Children without anyone with 'parental responsibility' for them may become vulnerable
- Control mechanisms of traffickers may be based on an intimate and sometime subtle knowledge of specific familial, socio-economic or civil and political vulnerabilities
- Control mechanisms may also be based on neglect, physical, sexual or emotional abuse

The Palermo Protocol identifies the **purposes** of human trafficking as including sexual exploitation, forced labour, slavery, practices similar to slavery, servitude or the removal of organs. As outlined earlier, exploitation can occur across a broad range of sectors, and different forms of exploitation continue to become known.

Human trafficking is now associated across a range of forms, including:

- Sexual exploitation
- Forced labour

- Domestic servitude
- Forced begging and/or petty crimes
- Enforced criminality (e.g. drug production or street crime)
- Forced or early marriage
- Child soldiers
- Seasonal employment
- Organ harvesting
- Trafficking for ritual purposes
- Illegal inter-country adoption or intra-country adoption
- Surrogacy (also known as 'baby factories' in some contexts)
- Orphanage trafficking

Multiple forms of exploitation may also arise wherein people are exploited in multiple ways, such as daytime enforced criminality and night-time sexual exploitation.

Exploitation has been explained by Skrivankova (2018) as constituting: 'a sphere that stretches from the optimum (decent work) to the worst (forced labour). This sphere has been described as the *continuum of exploitation*'. This **'continuum of exploitation'** captures the complexity of work conditions and allows for consideration that the journey of an individual can begin with deceptive recruitment and then develop into a situation where there is an extreme misbalance of power between the victim and the exploiter. As Skrivankov (2018) suggests, it is **the combination of the abuse of power and the position of vulnerability of the individual involved that leads to a situation of exploitation**.

Key Thinker Box 4.3   Joy Ngozi Ezeilo – Former Special Rapporteur on Trafficking in Persons

Professor Joy Ngozi Ezeilo is a Law Professor and Dean within the University of Nigeria and was appointed to be the Special Rapporteur on Trafficking in Persons, especially Women and Children, between 2008 and 2014. During this time as Special Rapporteur, country visits were made to Japan, Gabon, Thailand, the Philippines and a range of others.

In 2015, Ezeilo considered the achievements of the Palermo Protocol, based on her experiences whilst Special Rapporteur. In an article, Ezeilo outlines how the Protocol was a watershed moment in 'galvanising the global movement against human trafficking' (2015:144) in that it provided a legal framework around which an anti-trafficking movement could operate. Ezeilo notes how States continue to grapple with promoting or integrating a human-rights and/or child-centred approach that pays attention to the causes and vulnerabilities of trafficking. She also notes gaps in the practice of States around accurate identification, protection and provision of assistance to people who have been trafficked.

When addressing the root causes of human trafficking across the African continent, several key causes are suggested (Ezeilo, 2018:57). The first of these being 'poverty linked to high unemployment, livelihood challenges and human insecurity – i.e. freedom from fear and want' (2018:56). Other key causes outlined are (Ezeilo, 2018):

- Gender inequalities and sex discrimination in education and employment
- The cultural and religious practice of fostering children, particularly the practice of sending children to other relatives for the purpose of education or apprenticeship and beliefs around traditional oaths and rites
- Weak legislation, gaps between jurisdictions and discrimination in law and practice
- War, conflict and terrorist activities
- Poor governance
- A lack of, or incomplete, data

Ezeilo is also a lawyer, feminist and teacher of law at the University of Nigeria. Her work in the Civil Society Movement in Nigeria, particularly around human rights, democracy and good governance has resulted in the conferment of the national honour of Officer of the Order of Niger (OON) in 2006.

Key references – Joy Ngozi Ezeilo

Ezeilo, J.N. (2015) Achievements of the Trafficking Protocol: Perspectives from the Former UN Special Rapporteur on Trafficking in Persons, *Anti-Trafficking Review*, (4), 144–149.

Ezeilo, J.N. (2018) Trafficking in Human Beings in the African Context, in Piotrowicz, R., Rijken, C. and Uhl, B.H. (Eds.), *Routledge Handbook of Human Trafficking*, Routledge, Abingdon and New York.

Who is trafficked worldwide?

Trafficking is a gendered phenomenon, from the ways in which recruitment occurs through to the consequences of gendered exploitation and within gendered laws and policy responses. Predominant narratives around trafficking only involving women trafficked into richer countries for the purposes of exploitation are being dismantled as the phenomena is better understood, including issues around demand (Anderson and O'Connell-Davidson, 2002).

As awareness is raised, both male and female cases are being recorded, and the trafficking of children and young people is also becoming better known (Craig, 2010). It is estimated that around one-quarter of people trafficked are children (UNODC, 2016).

According to UNODC (2018), women make up 49% and girls make up 23% of detected victims of human trafficking as of 2016. As outlined earlier, the Palermo Protocol has historically had a focus on women and children, so it is unsurprising that structures around identification of females are more developed in practice.

There is an emerging picture of men making up 21% and boys making up 7% of detected victims of human trafficking as of 2016. Given the limited attention to men and boys throughout anti-trafficking work, this statistic is likely to under-represent actual percentages involved beyond the cases reviewed to establish this figure. For example, in the UK, Leon and Raws (2016) have argued that recognition of child sexual exploitation across the country has been focused on girls but that boys and young men seeking asylum are also targeted when placed in local authority care. Leon and Rawls (2016) outline how sexual exploitation has occurred during journeys to the UK but also, once in the country:

> how sexual exploitation may be embedded with multiple forms of exploitation which can obscure its existence from authorities. The criminalization of trafficked boys – for activities they have been forced to undertake

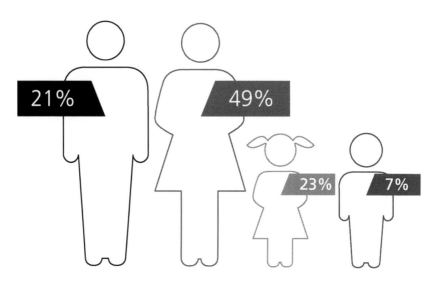

Figure 4.4 Share of Detected Victims of Trafficking in Persons, by Age Group and Sex: 2016
Source: UNODC (2016)

as part of their exploitation – can also shift the focus of interventions away from inquiry into potential trafficking or sexual exploitation.

(Leon and Raws, 2016:14)

They found that multiple forms of exploitation were a common experience for boys and young men, linking this with being seen as versatile to different forms of exploitation such as forced labour, forced criminality and domestic servitude (2016:16).

When these global figures are compared against regional breakdowns, it becomes clear that there are geographical differences (UNODC, 2018). As can be seen in Figure 4.5, when sub-regions are charted, numbers of women and girls detected in North and Central America as well as West and Central Europe are high. In Southeast Asia, men account for more than 30% of detected victims. In Sub-Saharan Africa, children account for 55% of victims detected, with an almost equal split between girls and boys.

These regional differences relate not only to local conditions but also to differences in identification, recording and reporting around human trafficking. As outlined by UNODC:

Europe, some parts of Asia, as well as the Americas, detect the largest numbers of victims. Additionally, most of the women victims considered in

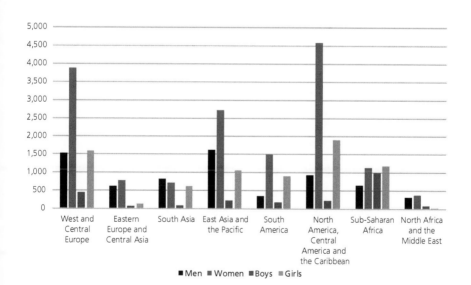

Figure 4.5 Detected Victims of Trafficking in Persons, by Age Group and Sex, by Sub-Region of Detection: 2016

Source: UNODC (2016)

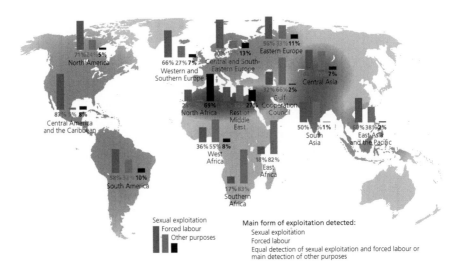

Map 4.1 Share of Detected Trafficking Victims by Form of Exploitation and by Sub-Region of Detection: 2016

Source: UNODC (2016)

this report were detected in these regions. With regard to males, in absolute numbers, most of the detected boy victims were detected in Africa, whereas adult male victims were often detected in South Asia and the Middle East.

(2018:26)

The ability of Europe and North America to carry out more detention therefore affects the overall data analysis and overall picture of human trafficking worldwide. In other words, if detection capabilities in Sub-Saharan African countries were similar to Europe or North America, this picture may look very different. It is also worthwhile linking this regional picture with the differing forms of exploitation outlined earlier in this chapter, as shown in Map 4.1.

From this same UNODC data (2018), sexual exploitation is the main form of exploitation detected in North, Central and South America as well as Europe and parts of Southeast Asia. Forced labour is the main form in most of Africa, the Middle East as well as parts of South Asia and, for men, in Eastern Europe and Central Asia. In North Africa, begging and other forms of exploitation are key forms.

Point for discussion – regional differences

- Why do you think there are differences in the detection of human trafficking across the globe?

- How does the history of concentrating on women and children affect this picture?
- What forms of exploitation do you think are most prevalent in your country?
- Why might the identification, reporting and recording of human trafficking affect this picture?

Who are the 'traffickers'?

According to UNODC (2016), traffickers and their victims often **come from the same place, speak the same language or have the same ethnic background**. It is also outlined how traffickers tend to recruit victims from within their country of origin, where they are usually citizens or within destination countries where they are either citizens of that country or have the same citizenship as the victims. For example, in Thailand's fishing industry, Boll (2018) outlines details of an ILO study into how for migrant workers from Burma/Myanmar, **brokers** were essential in recruiting workers, including those deceived or coerced into working on fishing boats:

> In the absence of attractive (or any) regular migration opportunities for work in the Thai fishing industry, brokers and social networks were key for both voluntary and involuntary recruitment amongst Cambodian and Myanmar nationals. For those deceived or coerced into work on fishing boats . . . most were recruited by brokers, either from their country of origin or Thailand, with a smaller share suggesting that their relatives forced them to take up such work. Deceptive broker practices typically involved misinformation about the sector, nature or conditions of work.
>
> (Boll, 2018:71)

Disaggregating networks of brokers and/or agents that involve practices around smuggling rather than trafficking is important in such cases. It is also important to note that family ties can also be utilised. Rather than trafficking being about organised criminal networks, relatives may be entrusted with the care of a family member, which can lead to broken promises and exploitative outcomes.

It has also been found that women are commonly involved in the trafficking of women and girls. Whilst most detected 'victims' of trafficking are female and most detected 'perpetrators' of trafficking male, women comprise a large shared of convicted offenders in comparison to other crimes (UNODC, 2016). Women are often used to recruit other women. In their 2018 report, 35% of people prosecuted for human trafficking offences were female. Again, there are interesting regional differences with, for example, Eastern Europe and Central Asia having higher proportions of female convictions than males (UNODC, 2018).

Current geography of human trafficking

People can be **trafficked both across borders and within their countries of origin**. People who are trafficked include those who are moved within their own countries, and there is increasing recognition that domestic trafficking accounts for higher numbers than those who are trafficked across international borders.

Internal or Domestic trafficking

As with refugees and the higher number of IDPs worldwide, estimates around human trafficking reveal that there are **more people trafficked within their countries of origin** than those who experience trafficking across borders. UNODC's 2018 global trends report outlines how 58% of the total figure of 'victims' detected are domestic cases, and 28% of cases remain within the sub-region of origin. There has been a steady increase in detection within countries of origin which may be the result of improved awareness, identification and recording or, in the words of UNODC:

> In countries characterized to be more typically destinations of cross border trafficking, this may be the result of improved controls at borders, hence more difficulties to traffic victims from abroad. In typical origin countries, improved border controls could also result in more victims being intercepted during the process to be transferred abroad. In this scenario, victims could be recruited for the purpose of being exploited abroad, but detected before leaving the country.
>
> (UNODC, 2018:41)

As outlined in Chapter 3, Martin (2006) has argued that those who have been trafficked within their own countries could be considered to be IDPs. It is unclear whether this rise in recognition of domestic trafficking has resulted in additional efforts around identification of trafficking or provision of protective structures by governments. There are also questions around the building of additional skills for practitioners, provision of specialist shelters for those trafficked domestically and/or considerations of what it means to return 'home' after being trafficked within a country of origin. As can be seen on Map 4.2, there are parts of the world with a high percentage of cases of trafficking detected domestically (UNODC, 2016).

Cross-border or international trafficking

UNODC's 2018 global trends report also provides an overview of flows of trafficking across international borders (Map 4.3).

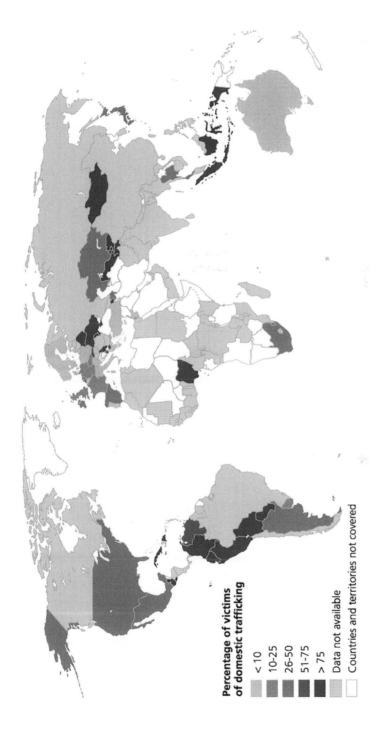

Map 4.2 Share of Detected Victims Trafficked Domestically: 2012–2014

Source: UNODC (2016)

**Percentage of victims
of domestic trafficking**

< 10
10-25
26-50
51-75
> 75
Data not available
Countries and territories not covered

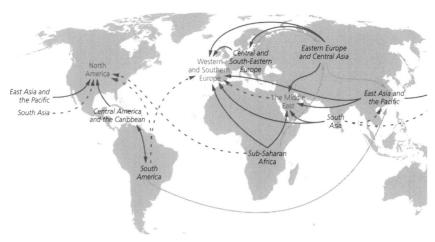

→ Transregional flows: detected victims in destination countries
- → Transregional flows: less than 5% of detected victims in destination countries
— Transregional flows: victims repatriated from destination countries

Map 4.3 Main Detected Transregional Trafficking Flows: 2014–2017

Source: UNODC (2016)

As can be seen, trans-regional flows relate to detected victims in destination countries as well as, perhaps more controversially, 'victims' who have repatriated from destination countries. There is very little research available exploring the repatriation of victims of human trafficking, unlike within refugee studies. However, it is clear that some victims of trafficking may well fall within the definition of a refugee and may therefore be entitled to international refugee protection under the 1951 Refugee Convention (see Chapter 2).

Case Study 4.1 of the UK's National Referral Mechanism and cases of cross-border and cases of domestic or internal trafficking illustrate how people can be trafficked across borders or within their own countries of origin.

Case Study 4.1   The UK's National Referral Mechanism, International and Internal Trafficking

The United Kingdom signed the Palermo Protocol in December 2000 and the 2005 Council of Europe Convention on Actions Against Trafficking in Human Beings in 2008, establishing a National Referral Mechanism (NRM) on 1 April 2009 to meet its commitments towards people who had experienced trafficking into, within and out of the UK. The Modern Slavery Act received Royal Assent and became law in March 2015 – 'Modern Slavery' under this Act included human trafficking along with slavery, servitude and forced or compulsory labour.

In the UK statistics are available on the number of adults and children, both non-UK and UK-born, who have been identified as 'trafficked' and have been referred to a National Referral Mechanism. These statistics are presented quarterly and annually as a 'snapshot' in time and include the numbers of people trafficked into the UK as well as within the UK. Both people born in the UK and those who cross borders to reach the UK can be trafficked internally, with the movement and exploitation occurring within the borders of the UK. However, there are no statistics available of the number of people who are trafficked out of the UK, although known cases of this do exist (Pearce *et al.*, 2009, 2013).

To operationalise the NRM, a series of first responders including the police, border forces, immigration enforcement, local authorities, certain non-governmental organisations and other agencies were able to refer cases of individuals who they had identified as having experienced 'modern slavery'.

As can be seen in Figure 4.6, the numbers of referrals have steadily risen year-on-year from just over a thousand referrals in 2012 to 10,627 referrals as of end 2019. Whether this is because more people are being trafficked, experiencing servitude or forced labour is unclear. Certainly, there is increasing knowledge of the issue within the UK in the past

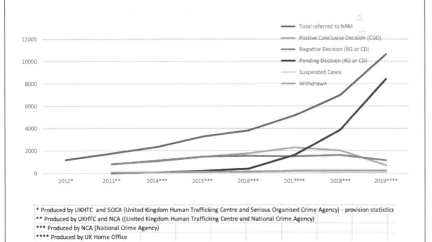

* Produced by UKHTC and SOCA (United Kingdom Human Trafficking Centre and Serious Organised Crime Agency) - provision statistics
** Produced by UKHTC and NCA ((United Kingdom Human Trafficking Centre and National Crime Agency)
*** Produced by NCA (National Crime Agency)
**** Produced by UK Home Office

Figure 4.6 Referrals, Decisions and Pending Cases in the UK's National Referral Mechanism (NRM): 2012–2019

decade, but these figures may also relate to increased reporting as a result of this increased knowledge.

Numbers of positive or negative decisions have not kept pace, but what is apparent is the rise in pending cases – in other words, people awaiting a decision. As Burland suggests, with 2019 referrals and historical cases between 2014 and 2018, there are:

> more than 11,000 people in limbo waiting for a . . . decision with no idea when it could arrive. A decision which could help them move forwards in their life and help provide closure.
>
> (Burland, 2020)

Craig and Burland also describe how positive decisions are mainly for UK nationals (83%), with EU (45%) and non-EU (17%) nationals not being recognised to the same extent. Also, as can be seen in Figure 4.7, the top nationalities of people referred for such 'modern slavery' are not necessarily similar to populations of refugees, asylum seekers or IDPs outlined in earlier chapters. Between 2012 and 2019, the UK had the highest number of referrals, followed by Albania and Vietnam (27%, 16% and 8% respectively, as of end of year 2019).

Referrals of adults and children – with children referred to as 'minors' in this instance – highlight how there has been a steady increase over time of both adults and children (see Figure 4.8). To some extent, the increasing number of children being referred into

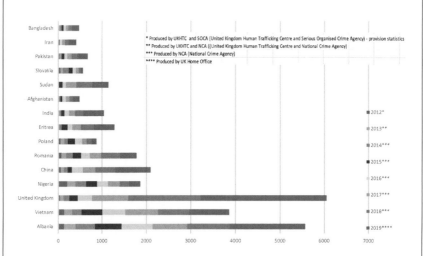

Figure 4.7 Referrals into the UK's National Referral Mechanism (NRM) by Highest Nationalities: 2012–2019

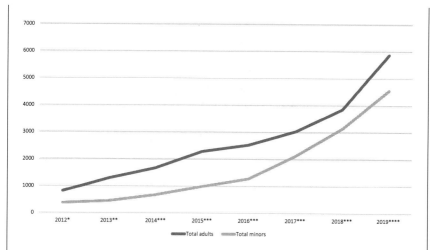

Figure 4.8 Referrals into the UK's National Referral Mechanism (NRM) by Adult/
Minor Categories: 2012–2019

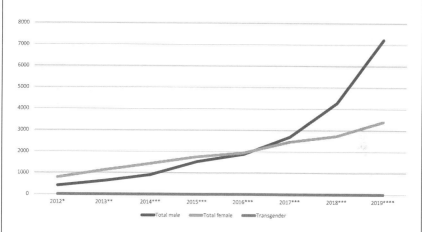

Figure 4.9 Referrals into the UK's National Referral Mechanism by Gender Categories: 2012–2019

the NRM from the UK for forms of criminal exploitation explains
this parallel rise.

Breaking these figures down by gender illustrates how the numbers
of male referrals began to exceed female referrals from 2017 onwards
(Figure 4.9). This is revealing, as human trafficking and other forms of
exploitation have historically been focussed on female victims.

The work of two Key Thinkers – Rebecca Surtees and Cathy Zimmerman – provide further insights into who is trafficked, the consequences of this and resulting needs.

Key Thinker Box 4.4   Rebecca Surtees – Exploring the Experiences and Needs of Trafficking Victims, including Under Considered Profiles of Victims and Forms of Trafficking

Rebecca Surtees is an anthropologist and researcher at the NEXUS Institute in Washington DC and focusses on human trafficking.

Surtees, together with Anette Brunovskis, carried out research in 2007 in three south-eastern European countries to understand why some victims of trafficking decline or avoid support and assistance (Brunovskis and Surtees, 2007). Reasons included their personal circumstances such as seeing assistance standing in the way of further migration; difficulties in protection systems such as the 'one size fits all' nature of assistance provided and differing social contexts and personal experiences such as the stigma of receiving assistance; and problems around identification and lack of trust in those providing assistance.

Her research also includes some of the first studies on trafficked men, who are often overlooked in discussions of human trafficking and under-considered in research (Surtees 2008a, 2008b) in spite of indications in many countries and regions that male migrants are also exploited and violated in ways that constitute human trafficking. Surtees has also researched trafficking in the fishing industry.

Together with Anne Gallagher, Surtees (2012) has also looked at measuring the success of counter-trafficking interventions in the criminal justice sector, finding that determinants of success (or failure) vary according to who is consulted and their role in the intervention, the criteria against which success is measured and the assumptions built into that criteria. Overall they note:

> the lack of an overarching vision of what 'success' might look like allows mediocre or even harmful interventions to flourish and good work to go unrecognised and unrewarded.
>
> (Gallagher and Surtees, 2012:10)

They outline how quality evaluations, including impact evaluations, are vital to the anti-trafficking sector, which has historically lacked rigorous and transparent evaluations of successes and failures. This, they suggest, is especially required in criminal justice responses that may have been developed 'on the run' and 'through trial and error' (Gallagher and Surtees, 2012:28).

In one of the few longitudinal studies of trafficking victims, conducted in Indonesia, Surtees *et al.* (2016) explored the nature of reintegration assistance, identifying critical challenges including that most reintegration assistance is of a 'one-off' nature, the provision of assistance is uneven and victims are generally unaware of assistance available to them. The same longitudinal project in Indonesia has outlined the range of short- and long-term assistance needs, directly related to and often caused by trafficking as well as those caused by underlying and pre-existing vulnerabilities that contributed to being trafficked and which also have the potential to undermine reintegration. Surtees (2017a, 2017b) discusses what Indonesian trafficked persons identified as their issues, vulnerabilities and resiliencies at different stages of their lives (before, during and after trafficking) and how vulnerability and resilience are influenced by external factors like the family and community setting and may fluctuate and change over time. Surtees (2018a, 2018b) has also written about how Indonesian men returning after trafficking often feel like failures, and assistance and reintegration support do not adequately take into account problems within their families due to long separations, fractured relationships, blame over 'failed' migration and unfulfilled expectations and blame within communities.

More recent research has been on identifying and assisting trafficked persons amongst refugees in Serbia in what has been termed the 'refugee crisis' (see Chapters 2 and 10). Brunovskis and Surtees (2019) outline the challenges of operationalising an anti-trafficking framework in this context, focussing on the established and well-known 'Balkan route' from the Middle East to the EU through Turkey and Southeast Europe, via potentially deadly journeys by sea from Turkey to Greece, overland to Macedonia or Bulgaria and onward to the EU via Serbia and Hungary or Serbia, Croatia and Slovenia. They found that the anti-trafficking framework in this context is difficult to apply and does not always fit with peoples' experiences, with protections on offer against an individual's self-interest in reaching a place of sanctuary through onward migration (2019:82). They also outlined how the 'role' of being a 'victim' of trafficking does not always align with people's self-identity (2019:83).

Surtees has also written on research methods and ethics including how the heavy reliance on assisted victims in trafficking research may limit our understanding of the issue and possible avenues for safely and ethically sampling unidentified and/or unassisted trafficking victims which will, in turn, serve to respond to the needs of both visible and less visible trafficking victims (Surtees, 2014, see also Surtees and Craggs, 2010). In 2010 Surtees (with Anette Brunovskis; see also McAdam *et al.*, 2019) discussed methodological and ethical issues arising when conducting research with trafficked persons, including unrepresentative samples, access to respondents, selection biases by 'gatekeepers' and self-selection by potential respondents. Such considerations should inform not only how research is undertaken but also how this information is read and understood. A chapter on ethics discusses the importance of providing information about assistance when conducting research with trafficking victims, as a means of preventing and mitigating research harm while also noting the practical obstacles in identifying assistance options and offering referral information to respondents, both in terms of the actual existence of services and their appropriateness and desirability for respondents. More recent work has explored good practice in TIP research and data collection (Surtees *et al.*, 2019a, 2019b).

This is a small selection of Surtees's work to date, with further publications and articles on the exploitation of fishermen, victims' experiences of protection and assistance, reintegration of trafficked persons in the Balkans, Indonesia and the greater Mekong region, amongst others (Brunovskis and Surtees, 2019; Surtees, 2008b, 2018a, 2018b).

Key references – Rebecca Surtees

Brunovskis, A. and Surtees, R. (2007) *Leaving the Past Behind? When Victims of Trafficking Decline Assistance*, Fafo AIS and NEXUS Institute, Oslo and Vienna.

Brunovskis, A. and Surtees, R. (2010) Untold Stories: Biases and Selection Effects in Research with Victims of Trafficking for Sexual Exploitation, *International Migration*, 48(4).

Brunovskis, A. and Surtees, R. (2019) Identifying Trafficked Migrants and Refugees along the Balkan Route: Exploring the Boundaries of Exploitation, Vulnerability and Risk, *Crime, Law and Social Change*, 73–86.

Gallagher, A.T. and Surtees, R. (2012) Measuring the Success of Counter-Trafficking Interventions in the Criminal Justice Sector: Who Decides – and How? *Anti-Trafficking Review*, 1(1), 10–30.

McAdam, M., Surtees, R. and Johnson, L.S. (2019) *Legal and Ethical Issues in Data Collection on Trafficking in Persons*, NEXUS Institute, Washington, DC.

Surtees, R. (2008a) *Trafficking in Men, a Trend Less Considered: The Case of Belarus and Ukraine,* IOM Migration Research Series, No.36, IOM, view at: https://nexushumantrafficking.files.wordpress.com/2015/03/trafficking-in-men-the-case-of-belarus-ukraine-surtees-2008.pdf

Surtees, R. (2008b) Trafficked Men as Unwilling Victims, *St Antony's International Review*, 4(1).

Surtees, R. (2014) Another Side of the Story. Challenges in Research with Unidentified and Unassisted Trafficking Victims. *Human Trafficking in Asia*, Routledge, London and New York.

Surtees, R. (2017a) *Moving on. Family and Community Reintegration against Indonesian Trafficking Victims*, NEXUS Institute, Washington, DC, view at: https://nexushumantrafficking.files.wordpress.com/2020/02/moving-on-nexus-institute-2017.pdf

Surtees, R. (2017b) *Our Lives. Vulnerability and Resilience among Indonesian Trafficking Victims*, NEXUS Institute, Washington, DC, view at: https://nexushumantrafficking.files.wordpress.com/2020/02/our-lives-nexus-institute-2017.pdf

Surtees, R. (2018a) At Home: Family Reintegration of Trafficked Indonesian Men, *Anti Trafficking Review*, (10), 70–87.

Surtees, R. (2018b) Exploring Family Reintegration amongst Trafficked Indonesia Domestic Workers, in R. Piotrowicz, C. Rijken and B.H. Uhl (Eds.), *Routledge Handbook of Human Trafficking*, Routledge, Abingdon and New York.

Surtees, R. and Brunovskis, A. (2016) Doing No Harm. Ethical Challenges in Research with Trafficked Persons, in D. Siegal and R. de Wildt (Eds.), *Ethical Concerns in Research on Human Trafficking*, Springer International Publishing, Switzerland.

Surtees, R., Brunovskis, A. and Johnson, L. (2019a) *The Science (and Art) of Understanding Trafficking in Persons: Good Practice in TIP Data Collection*, NEXUS Institute, Washington, DC, view at: https://nexushumantrafficking.files.wordpress.com/2020/02/good-practice-tip-data-collection-nexus-institute.pdf

Surtees, R., Brunovskis, A. and Johnson, L.S. (2019b) *On the Frontlines: Operationalizing Good Practice in TIP Data Collection*, NEXUS Institute, Washington, DC.

Surtees, R. and Craggs, S. (2010) *Beneath the Surface. Methodological Issues in Trafficking Research*, NEXUS Institute, Washington, DC, and IOM, Geneva, view at: https://nexushumantrafficking.files.wordpress.com/2015/03/beneath-the-surface_methodological-issues_nexus.pdf

Surtees, R. and Johnson, L.S. (2019) *Good Practice in TIP Data Collection: Recommendations for Donors and Funders*, NEXUS Institute, Washington, DC.

Surtees, R. Johnson, L.S., Zulbahary, T. and Caya, S.D. (2016) Going Home: Challenges in the Reintegration of Trafficking Victims in Indonesia, NEXUS Institute, Washington DC.

Key Thinker Box 4.5   Cathy Zimmerman – Conceptualising Human Trafficking through a Public Health Approach

Professor Cathy Zimmerman is a founding staff member of the Gender Violence and Health Centre at London School of Hygiene and Tropical Medicine in London, where she leads research on migration and health, including research on human trafficking, mobile populations and gender-based violence. Her research has put the physical and mental health of women who had experienced trafficking for sexual exploitation firmly on the international agenda.

Between 2000 and 2003, Zimmerman's study into women's health and trafficking in the EU began highlighting the health risks and consequences of trafficking. A second study conducted between 2003 and 2005 – *Stolen Smiles* (Zimmerman *et al.*, 2006) – was the first to use epidemiological methods to investigate the physical, sexual and mental health of women and adolescents who had experienced trafficking. This study found that women's physical and sexual health problems included high levels of injury and pain for which they were often unable to seek treatment. This work was influential in extending a 'recovery and reflection' period – the period people are given to decide on whether to cooperate with any criminal investigation in the UK – from 30 to 45 days. She is also the co-author of the World Health Organization's *WHO Ethical and Safety Recommendations for Interviewing Trafficked Women* (Zimmerman and Watts, 2003).

Published in 2011, Zimmerman *et al.* devised a conceptual model to inform policy, interventions and research into human trafficking and health. This highlighted a multi-staged trafficking process, from recruitment, travel/transit, exploitation, integration and/or reintegration stages plus, for some people, detention and re-trafficking stages. As such, trafficking and health can be conceptualised as a multi-staged process of cumulative harm.

In 2015, Kiss *et al.* (including Zimmerman) produced findings from the largest cross-sectional study to date on the health of over 1,100 women, men and children in post-trafficking services in the Mekong. These survey results were particularly important because they included survivors who had been exploited in over 15 different labour sectors, including fishing, forced sex work, forced marriage, manufacturing, agriculture and forced street-begging. Findings highlighted the high levels of violence, exploitation, unsafe working conditions and resultant serious harm that occurs across labour sectors and to men, women and children.

In a report for the Freedom Fund, Zimmerman *et al.* (2015) discuss the state of the evidence for programming for safer labour migration and community-based prevention of exploitation. In this they identify the potential for theory-based approach for research and programming to be applied, such as theories of change, behaviour change theory and ecological frameworks.

In 2016, McAlpine, Hossain and Zimmerman provide a systematic review of sex trafficking and sexual exploitation in settings affected by armed conflicts in Africa, Asia and the Middle East. Their findings were that various forms of human trafficking and sexual exploitation in conflict-affected settings primarily occur as early or forced marriage, forced combatant sexual exploitation and sexual slavery. They also suggest that terminology around 'sex trafficking' and 'sexual exploitation' requires clarification, with inconsistent definitions limiting the evidence base in this area of study. A further systematic review by Ottisova *et al.* with Cathy Zimmerman (2016) on the prevalence, risk of violence and mental, physical and sexual health problems associated with human trafficking also found differences in definitions across a range of mostly low- and middle-income countries. This review also found limited but emerging evidence on the health of trafficked men and the health consequences of forms of exploitation beyond sexual exploitation.

By 2017, Zimmerman and Kiss argued that human trafficking – and labour exploitation more generally – comprises a public health problem of global magnitude and that public health intervention approaches that target the underlying drivers of exploitation are necessary. A public health approach to preventing exploitation in the first instance would involve addressing structural determinants, as with other public health problems. It would also take the stages of pre-departure, destination and return across a migration process into consideration, alongside structural drivers such as inequalities and globalisation.

Cathy Zimmerman and colleagues recently completed five-year intervention evaluation research: the DFID-funded Study on Work in Freedom Transnational (SWIFT) Evaluation of the International Labour Organization's 'Work in Freedom' programme in South Asia (SWIFT: http://same.lshtm.ac.uk/projects-2/swift/).

Cathy Zimmerman's current work focuses on child domestic workers and violence against women and girls in Southeast Asia.

Key references – Cathy Zimmerman

Kiss, L., Pocock, N.S., Naisanguansri, V., Suos, S., Dickson, B., Thuy, D., Koehler, J., Sirisup, K., Pongrungsee, N., Nguyen, V.A., Borland, R., Dhavan, P. and Zimmerman, C. (2015) Health of Men, Women, and Children in Post-trafficking Services in Cambodia, Thailand and Vietnam: An Observational Cross-sectional Study, *The Lancet Global Health*, 3, 154–161, view at: www.thelancet.com/journals/langlo/article/PIIS2214109X(15)70016-1/fulltext

McAlpine, A., Hossain, M. and Zimmerman, C. (2016) Sex Trafficking and Sexual Exploitation in Settings Affected by Armed Conflicts in Africa, Asia and the Middle East: Systematic Review, *BMC International Health and Human Rights*, 16(34), 1–16.

Ottisova, L., Hemmings, S., Howard, L.M., Zimmerman, C. and Oram, S. (2016) Prevalence and Risk of Violence and the Mental, Physical and Sexual Health Problems Associated with Human Trafficking: An Updated Systematic Review. *Epidemiology and Psychiatric Sciences*, 25(4), 317–341, https://doi.org/10.1017/S2045796016000135

Zimmerman, C., Hossain, M. and Watts, C. (2011) Human Trafficking and Health: A Conceptual Model to Inform Policy, Intervention and Research, *Social Science & Medicine*, 73(2), 327–335.

Zimmerman, C., Hossain, M., Yun, K., Roche, B., Morison, L. and Watts, C. (2006) *Stolen Smiles: The Physical and Psychological Health Consequences of Women and Adolescents Trafficked in Europe*, London School of Hygiene and Tropical Medicine and Daphne Programme of the European Commission, London.

Zimmerman, C. and Kiss, L. (2017) Human Trafficking and Exploitation: A Global Health Concern, *PLOS Medicine*, 14(11), 1–11.

Zimmerman, C. and Watts, C. (2003) *WHO Ethical and Safety Recommendations for Interviewing Trafficked Women*, London School of Hygiene and Tropical Medicine and Daphne Programme of the European Commission, London.

Note

1 View at: https://www.state.gov/trafficking-in-persons-report/

Further reading

Allain, J. (2017) Genealogies of Human Trafficking and Slavery, in Piotrowicz, R., Rijken, C. and Uhl, B.H. (Eds.), *Routledge Handbook of Human Trafficking*, Routledge, Abingdon and New York.

Anderson, B. (2007) *Motherhood, Apple Pie and Slavery: Reflections on Trafficking Debates*, Working Paper No.48, Centre on Migration, Policy and Society (COMPAS), University of Oxford, Oxford.

Anderson, B. (2012) Where's the Harm in That? Immigration Enforcement, Trafficking and the Protection of Migrants' Rights, *American Behavioral Scientist*, 56(9), 1241–1257.

Andrijasevic, R. (2010) *Migration, Agency and Citizenship in Sex Trafficking*, Palgrave Macmillan, London.

Brunovskis, A. and Surtees, R. (2007) *Leaving the Past Behind? When Victims of Trafficking Decline Assistance*, Fafo AIS and NEXUS Institute, Oslo and Vienna.

Chuang, J.A. (2014) Exploitation Creep and the Unmaking of Human Trafficking Law, *The American Journal of International Law*, 108(4), 609–649.

Craig, G. (Ed.) (2010) *Child Slavery Now: A Contemporary Reader*, Policy Press, Bristol.

Doezma, J. (2010) *Sex Slaves and Discourse Masters: The Construction of Trafficking*, Zed Books, London.

Gallagher, A.T. (2015) Two Cheers for the Trafficking Protocol, *Anti-Trafficking Review*, (4), 14–32.

Hynes, P. (2010) Global Points of 'Vulnerability': Understanding Processes of the Trafficking of Children and Young People into, within and Out of the UK, *The International Journal of Human Rights*, 14(6), 952–970.

O'Connell Davidson, J. (2013) Troubling Freedom: Migration, Debt and Modern Slavery, *Migration Studies*, 1(2), 176–195.

Pearce, J.J., Hynes, P. and Bovarnick, S. (2013) *Trafficked Young People: Breaking the Wall of Silence*, Routledge, New York.

Ross, C., Dimitrova, S., Howard, L.M., Dewey, M., Zimmerman, C. and Oram, S. (2015) Human Trafficking and Health: A Cross-sectional Survey of NHS Professionals' Contact with Victims of Human Trafficking, *BMJ Open*, 5, 1–7.

Skrivankova, K. (2018) Defining Exploitation in the Context of Trafficking – What is a Crime and What is not? in Piotrowicz, R., Rijken, C. and Uhl, B.H. (Eds.), *Routledge Handbook of Human Trafficking*, Routledge, Abingdon and New York.

Tyldum, G. (2010) Limitations in Research on Human Trafficking, *International Migration*, 48(5), 1–13.

References

Agustin, L.M. (2007) *Sex at the Margins: Migration, Labour Markets and the Rescue Industry*, Zed Books, London and New York.

Allain, J. (2018) Genealogies of Human Trafficking and Slavery, in R. Piotrowicz, C. Rijken, and B.H. Uhl (Eds.), *Routledge Handbook of Human Trafficking*, Routledge, New York and Abingdon, Oxfordshire.

Anderson, B. (2013) *Us & Them? The Dangerous Politics of Immigration Control*, Oxford University Press, Oxford.

Anderson, B. (2019) New Directions in Migration Studies: Towards Methodological Denationalism, *Comparative Migration Studies*, 7(36), 1–13.

Anderson, B. (2000) *Doing the Dirty Work? The Global Politics of Domestic Labour*, Zed Books, London.

Anderson, B. and O'Connell-Davidson, J. (2002) *Trafficking – A Demand-Led Problem?* Save the Children, Stockholm.

Boll, S. (2018) Human Trafficking in the Context of Labour Migration in Southeast Asia: The Case of Thailand's Fishing Industry, in R. Piotrowicz, C. Rijken and B.H. Uhl (Eds.), *Routledge Handbook of Human Trafficking*, Routledge, New York and Abingdon, Oxfordshire.

Brodie, I., Spring, D., Hynes, P., Burland, P., Dew, J., Gani-Yusuf, L., Tran, H.T., Lenja, V. and Thurnham, A. (2018) *'Vulnerability' to Human Trafficking: A Study of Viet Nam, Albania, Nigeria and the UK*, University of Bedfordshire and International Organization for Migration (IOM), London.

Brunovskis, A. and Surtees, R. (2007) *Leaving the Past Behind? When Victims of Trafficking Decline Assistance*, Fafo AIS and NEXUS Institute, Oslo and Vienna.

Brunovskis, A. and Surtees, R. (2019) Identifying Trafficked Migrants and Refugees along the Balkan Route: Exploring the Boundaries of Exploitation, Vulnerability and Risk, *Crime, Law and Social Change*, 73–86.

Burland, P. (2020) *OPINION: What Can New Survivor Statistics Tell Us About Modern Slavery in the UK?*, view at: https://news.trust.org/item/20200408093233-8ao4k

Dijk, J.V. and Campistol, C. (2018) Work in Progress: International Statistics on Human Trafficking, in Piotrowicz, R., Rijken, C. and Uhl, B.H. (Eds.), *Routledge Handbook of Human Trafficking*, Routledge, Abingdon and New York.

Dotteridge, M. (2007) *Introduction in Global Alliance Against Traffic in Women (GAATW) Collateral Damage: The Impact of Anti-Trafficking Measures on Human Rights around the World*, GAATW, Bangkok, Thailand.

Fiddian-Qasmiyeh, E. (2014) Gender and Forced Migration, in E. Fiddian-Qasmiyeh, G. Loescher, K. Long and N. Sigona (Eds.), *The Oxford Handbook of Refugee and Forced Migration Studies*, Oxford University Press, Oxford.

Gallagher, A.T. and Surtees, R. (2012) Measuring the Success of Counter-Trafficking Interventions in the Criminal Justice Sector: Who Decides – and How? *Anti-Trafficking Review*, (1), 10–30.

Gould, C. (2010) The Problem of Trafficking, in Palmary, I., Burman, F., Chantler, K. and Kiguwa, P. (Eds.), *Gender and Migration: Feminist Interventions*, Zed Books, London.

Hynes, P., Burland, P., Thurnham, A., Dew, J., Gani-Yusuf, L., Lenja, V. and Hong Thi Tran with Olatunde, A. and Gaxha, A., (2019) *'Between Two Fires': Understanding Vulnerabilities and the Support Needs of People from Albania, Viet Nam and Nigeria Who Have Experienced Human Trafficking into the UK*, University of Bedfordshire and International Organization for Migration (IOM), London.

International Labour Office (ILO) (2012) *ILO Global Estimate of Forced Labour: Results and Methodology*, ILO, Geneva.

Laczo, F. and Gramengna, M. (2003) Developing Better Indicators of Human Trafficking, *Brown Journal of World Affairs*, (1), 179–194.

Leon, L. and Raws, P. (2016) *Boys Don't Cry: Improving Identification and Disclosure of Sexual Exploitation among Boys and Young Men Trafficked to the UK*, The Children's Society, London.

Martin, S. (2006) *Internal Trafficking*, Forced Migration Review, No. 25, University of Oxford, Oxford.

McAdam, M., Surtees, R. and Johnson, L.S. (2019) *Legal and Ethical Issues in Data Collection on Trafficking in Persons*, NEXUS Institute, Washington, DC.

Ottisova, L., Hemmings, S., Howard, L.M., Zimmerman, C. and Oram S. (2016) Prevalence and Risk of Violence and the Mental, Physical and Sexual Health Problems Associated with Human Trafficking: An Updated Systematic Review, *Epidemiology and Psychiatric Sciences*, 25(4), 317–341, https://doi.org/10.1017/S2045796016000135

Palmary, I. (2010) Sex, Choice and Exploitation: Reflections on Anti-Trafficking Discourse, in Palmary, I., Burman, F., Chantler, K. and Kiguwa, P. (Eds.), *Gender and Migration: Feminist Interventions*, Zed Books, London.

Pearce, J.J., Hynes, P. and Bovarnick, S. (2009) *Breaking the Wall of Silence: Practitioners' Responses to Trafficked Children and Young People*, NSPCC and University of Bedfordshire, London.

Pollock, J. (2007) *Thailand in Global Alliance Against Traffic in Women (GAATW) Collateral Damage: The Impact of Anti-Trafficking Measures on Human Rights around the World*, GAATW, Bangkok, Thailand.

Salt, J. (2000) Trafficking and Human Smuggling: A European Perspective, *International Migration*, 38(3), 31–56.

Surtees, R. (2008a) Trafficked Men as Unwilling Victims, *St Antony's International Review*, 4(1).

Surtees, R. (2008b) *Trafficking in Men, a Trend Less Considered: The Case of Belarus and Ukraine*, IOM Migration Research Series, No. 36, IOM, view at: https://nexushumantraffick ing.files.wordpress.com/2015/03/trafficking-in-men-the-case-of-belarus-ukraine-sur tees-2008.pdf

Surtees, R. (2014) Another Side of the Story. Challenges in Research with Unidentified and Unassisted Trafficking Victims. *Human Trafficking in Asia*, Routledge, London and New York.

Surtees, R. (2017a) *Moving on. Family and Community Reintegration against Indonesian Trafficking Victims*, NEXUS Institute, Washington, DC, view at: https://nexushumantrafficking. files.wordpress.com/2020/02/moving-on-nexus-institute-2017.pdf

Surtees, R. (2017b) *Our Lives, Vulnerability and Resilience among Indonesian Trafficking Victims*, NEXUS Institute, Washington, DC, view at: https://nexushumantrafficking.files.word press.com/2020/02/our-lives-nexus-institute-2017.pdf

Surtees, R. (2018a) At Home: Family Reintegration of Trafficked Indonesian Men, *Anti Trafficking Review*, (10), 70–87.

Surtees, R. (2018b) Exploring Family Reintegration amongst Trafficked Indonesia Domestic Workers, in Piotrowicz, R., Rijken, C. and Uhl, B.H. (Eds.), *Routledge Handbook of Human Trafficking*, Routledge, Abingdon and New York.

Surtees, R. (2018c) Exploring Family Reintegration amongst Trafficked Indonesia Domestic Workers, in Piotrowicz, R., Rijken, C. and Uhl, B.H. (Eds.), *Routledge Handbook of Human Trafficking*, Routledge, Abingdon and New York.

Surtees, R. and Brunovskis, A. (2016) Doing no Harm. Ethical Challenges in Research with Trafficked Persons, in *Ethical Concerns in Research on Human Trafficking*, Springer, Switzerland.

Surtees, R., Brunovskis, A. and Johnson, L.S. (2019a) *On the Frontlines: Operationalizing Good Practice in TIP Data Collection,* NEXUS Institute, Washington, DC.

Surtees, R., Brunovskis, A. and Johnson, L. (2019b) *The Science (and Art) of Understanding Trafficking in Persons: Good Practice in TIP Data Collection,* NEXUS Institute, Washington, DC, view at: https://nexushumantrafficking.files.wordpress.com/2020/02/good-practice-tip-data-collection-nexus-institute.pdf

Surtees, R. and Craggs, S. (2010) *Beneath the Surface. Methodological Issues in Trafficking Research,* NEXUS Institute, Washington, DC and IOM, Geneva, view at: https://nexushumantrafficking.files.wordpress.com/2015/03/beneath-the-surface_methodological-issues_nexus.pdf

Surtees, R., Johnson, L.S., Zulbahary, T. and Caya, S.D. (2016) *Going Home: Challenges in the Reintegration of Trafficking Victims in Indonesia*, NEXUS Institute, Washington, DC.

United Nations General Assembly (2019, July) *Current and Emerging Forms of Slavery*, Report of the Special Rapporteur on Contemporary Forms of Slavery, Including Its Causes and Consequences, 42nd Session, Human Rights Council, A/HRC/42/44.

United Nations Office on Drugs and Crime (UNODC) (2014) *Global Report on Trafficking in Persons 2014*, UNODC, Vienna.

United Nations Office on Drugs and Crime (UNODC) (2016) *Global Report on Trafficking in Persons 2016*, UNODC, Vienna.

United Nations Office on Drugs and Crime (UNODC) (2018) *Global Report on Trafficking in Persons 2018*, UNODC, Vienna.

van Liempt, L. (2007) *Navigating Borders: Inside Perspectives on the Process of Human Smuggling into the Netherlands*, Amsterdam University Press, Amsterdam.

Zimmerman, C., McAlpine, A. and Kiss, L. (2015) *Safer Labour Migration and Community-Based Prevention of Exploitation: The State of the Evidence for Programming*, Freedom Fund and London School of Hygiene & Tropical Medicine, London.

5 Mixed movements of people and human rights

Introduction

As outlined in Chapter 1, it has been asserted that we now live in **an 'age of migration'** (Castles *et al.*, 2014). Simultaneously, it has been asserted that we live in both **an 'age of genocide'** (Kushner and Knox, 1999) and **an 'age of rights'** (Bobbio, 1996). This chapter considers the intersections of these, in relation to forced migration as outlined in the preceding chapters when looking at who is defined as a refugee, stateless, an internally displaced person or 'victim' of human trafficking. This chapter considers how human displacement is related to human rights in relation to these different legal statuses.

In some ways, this chapter could have sat more easily at the beginning of this book, as rights violations often precede mobility, movement or displacement from a country of origin towards a country of asylum, resettlement or, in the case of IDPs, internal displacement. This chapter will consider how debates about 'root causes', or drivers, of forced migration are discussed. Human displacement is related to struggles to dominate the social order within nation-states. Zolberg *et al.* (1989) links human displacement to the 'root causes' that may have taken place over several decades prior to movement to the restructuring of the social order within nation-states in what is termed a 'refugee-generating process' (1983). A range of political, demographic, environmental, economic, conflict and violence-related drivers have been used to understand internal displacement (IDMC, 2015). As already outlined in Chapter 4, Ezeilo (2018) has also called for a 'root causes' debate in respect of human trafficking.

This chapter then provides a short history and forms of human rights, outlining negative and positive rights and the key distinctions between civil and political rights on the one hand and, on the other, social, economic and cultural rights. Key critiques are discussed, and details of key thinkers in these areas are provided. How human rights relate to forced migration will then be considered as well as emerging understandings of how motivations for migration are often mixed, with resulting mixed movements, and how mixed migration occurs and incorporates a range of legal statuses.

'Root causes' or drivers of forced migration

The creation of **nation-states as a refugee-generating process**, with **refugees as by-products of social change**, were explored in depth by Zolberg (see Key Thinker Box 5.1). As outlined by Zolberg *et al.* (1989), a 'root causes' debate in the early 1980s related to the underlying social and international forces that generated refugees. An assumption within this debate was that addressing these underlying causes would avert refugee flows. Poverty and inequality were widely considered as being at the root of international refugee flows, much of which related to economic under-development as a result of colonialism. Zolberg *et al.* (1989) disputed this idea that economic under-development was itself a major cause of refugees, pointing out that it was often the most poor who were last to leave a country. They also suggest that a focus on root causes: 'ignores the historical connection between social change and refugees. To avert flows would be the equivalent of trying to oppose social change' (1989:262).

'Root causes' of forcible displacement are often linked to legislation and social norms that are tolerant of discrimination and persecution and, simultaneously, often allow impunity for perpetrators of such violence. This can include contexts where there is conflict and a breakdown of the social order. It can also include repressive, unfair, discriminatory practices that legitimise the persecution of those perceived as 'other' or in some way 'outside' national constructions of identity. It is not, however, straightforward – or some say possible (Richmond, 1988) – to clearly distinguish between political, economic or social determinants of migration.

This 'root causes' debate also appears in other forms of forced migration. For example, when addressing the root causes of human trafficking across the African continent, Ezeilo (2018:57) suggests several key causes (see also Key Thinker Box 4.3). Calling for a debate about root causes of human trafficking, Professor Ezeilo advised:

> root causes are escalating in the face of socio-economic crisis, extreme poverty, insurgency, inequalities, discrimination and gender-based violence. Ignoring these root causes and failure to squarely confront them through international cooperation and development paradigms would amount to paying lip service to efforts to fight human trafficking.
>
> (Ezeilo, 2018, quoted in Hynes, 2018)

For example, within Nigeria, the actions of Boko Haram in the Northeast and the realities of IDPs in that region directly relate to insecurity, conflict, sexual and gender-based violence with resulting livelihood challenges and internal displacement. As can be seen in Figure 5.1, the IDMC provides a range of political, demographic, environmental, economic, conflict and violence related drivers to explain this displacement.

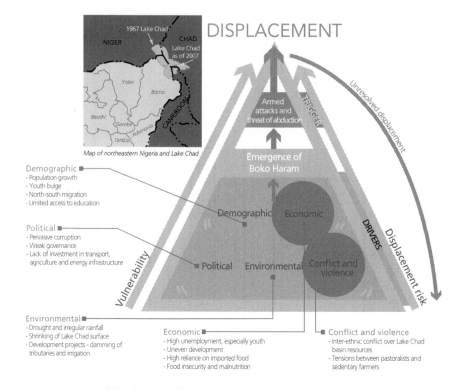

Figure 5.1 Internal Displacement Drivers in Northeast Nigeria: 2015
Source: IDMC, 2015

Key Thinker Box 5.1   Aristide Zolberg – The Formation of New States as a 'Refugee-Generating Process'

Professor Aristide R. Zolberg has been a leading voice on the politics, history and ethics of immigration at The New School for Social Research in New York. As a scholar of comparative politics, the history of international migration, national and ethnicity, he served for many years as the founding Director of the International Center for Migration, Ethnicity and Citizenship at The New School.

In a now much-quoted 1983 paper, the late Aristide Zolberg outlined how the transformation of empires into secular nation-states contributed to the creation of refugees. This compelling idea was that the formation of the modern system of sovereign nation-states are themselves a driver of forced migration. Zolberg outlined how persecution – as well as relating to political persecution – is often directed against groups based upon 'race', religion, nationality or their social group was based on 'accidents of birth' (1983:24) to which individuals belong without choice.

Zolberg suggested that an obvious point about refugee flows is that they are the result of events such as civil strife, abrupt changes of regime and arbitrary governmental decisions – each of which are events likely to occur in 'some parts of the contemporary world than in others' (1983:25). He suggested that it is therefore possible to view refugees as a phenomenon of world politics. Drawing on the work of Hannah Arendt, Zolberg pointed out the inherent dangers of linking rights with nationality. For both minorities and the stateless, these rights could not be assumed.

It is suggested that processes of imperialism and subsequent processes of decolonisation and dismantling of colonial empires resulted in sudden adoption of the nation-state as a form of political organisation by new indigenous rulers. Within these new countries, victim groups emerged as a by-product of this sometimes rapid social change, based around 'race', religion, nationality or membership of a particular social group as well as those in opposition to the emerging rulers who were persecuted based upon their political opinions. It was suggested that **refugees are a by-product of nationalism** that demands individuals to be transformed into sharing a common nationality and myths.

In a 1989 seminal text with Astri Suhrke and Sergio Aguayo, Zolberg continued these themes. Three distinct categories of refugees during the 20th century were distinguished. The first was the **refugee as an activist**, engaging in political activities that stood in opposition, and therefore problematic, to the State. The second was the **refugee as a target** as a result of the misfortune of belonging, often by 'accident of birth' (1989:30), to a 'race', religion, nationality or membership of a particular social group based on the 1951 Refugee Convention. The third was the **refugee as a mere victim**. This related to people displaced by societal or international violence, not necessary directed at them as individuals but sufficient to make continued presence in their own country impossible. This third category was not included in the 1951 Refugee Convention or the 1967 Protocol. As such, uninvolved bystanders caught in the crossfire of conflict were not included within the legal categorisation of what it means to be a 'refugee' within the legal definitions. They were, however, included in the subsequent 1969 OAU Convention and 1984 Cartagena Declaration.

With chapters on new State formation and refugee contexts across Sub-Saharan Africa, South Africa, Ethiopia, South Asia, East Asia, Latin

America and Central America during the 1970s and 1980s, Zolberg argued that each of these contexts began in the years immediately after World War II. Partition in India, separatism in the Horn of Africa, revolution in East Asia and social conflict and revolutions in Latin and Central America are each considered to be **refugee-generating processes as a result of the formation of new states**.

Further reading – Aristide Zolberg

Zolberg, A.R. (1983) The Formation of New States as a Refugee-Generating Process, *Annals of the American Academy of Political and Social Science*, 467, 24–38.

Zolberg, A.R., Suhrke, A. and Aguayo, S. (1989) *Escape from Violence: Conflict and the Refugee Crisis in the Developing World*, Oxford University Press, Oxford and New York.

What are human rights?

Where, after all, do universal human rights begin? In small places, close to home – so close and so small that they cannot be seen on any maps of the world. Yet they are the world of the individual person; the neighbourhood he lives in; the school or college he attends; the factory, farm, or office where he works. Such are the places where every man, woman, and child seeks equal justice, equal opportunity, equal dignity without discrimination. Unless these rights have meaning there, they have little meaning anywhere. Without concerted citizen action to uphold them close to home, we shall look in vain for progress in the larger world.

(Eleanor Roosevelt on the UDHR)

There are traces of **the idea of human rights within all major philosophies and religions across all parts of the globe**, as far back as 539 BC when the troops of Cyrus the Great freed Babylonian slaves and declared all people had the right to choose their own religion and establish equality. These and other precepts were recorded onto a backed-clay cylinder known as the **Cyrus Cylinder**, which then served as inspiration for the first four Articles of the Universal Declaration of Human Rights in 1948. The **Magna Carta in England of 1215** is another moment in time when principles of equality before the law, a right to property and elements of religious freedom were documented in a selective manner (Smith, 2005). For some, this document marked the start of modern democracy as we know it today.

In the early 18th century in Europe, a concept of human rights emerged that distinguished between 'classic' and 'social' rights. *Classic rights* looked broadly at what governments should refrain from doing. For example, governments should not restrict the freedom of individuals. *Social rights* referred broadly to how governments should provide certain guarantees such as the right to education, the right to welfare and the right to work. Early statements about rights, such as the United States Declaration of Independence (1776) and the French Declaration of the Rights of Man (1789), articulated rights to be enjoyed by all citizens.

Towards the end of the 19th century, when industrialising countries began to introduce exploitative practices for their workers, legislation was introduced to protect people. The creation of the International Labour Organization (ILO) in 1919 was motivated by humanitarian concerns and working conditions of the early 20th century (Smith, 2005). States came together to ensure workers were not exploited, costs of labour were not undercut and competitive positions in relation to countries that did not have similar labour laws were not lost. This economic necessity forced states to consult with each other and through this, adopted measures addressed working hours and working conditions for women and children.

At the end of the Second World War, states gathered together to ensure that future generations would be saved from future wars and to ensure the promotion of human rights worldwide. The Universal Declaration of Human Rights (UDHR) was adopted in 1948, introduced by the United Nations to recognise the rights of all humans. The UDHR was originally formulated and agreed upon by Western states, China, the Soviet Union, Chile and Lebanon. This was made up of 30 Articles with its first Article stating that: 'all human beings are born free and equal in dignity and rights'.

Rights are outlined as applying to everybody on the basis of their being 'human'. The idea of human rights is that each one of us, no matter who we are or where we are born, is entitled to the same basic rights and freedoms. Some authors assert that human rights are enjoyed by individuals on the basis of their being human but also as a 'consequence of their shared vulnerability' (Turner, 1993, 2006:3). In other words, the frailty of human beings is key to sympathy for all required, a key foundation of the provision of rights to all. Others have suggested that human rights are social constructs based on particular sets of circumstances and contexts and less to do with such embodied notions (Waters, 1996; Woodiwiss, 1990, 2005; see also Nash, 2012).

Regardless of how they are viewed, it is clear that the UDHR has now: 'far surpassed the expectations of the drafters and it is widely accepted as the consensus of global opinion on fundamental rights' (Smith, 2005:38). The UDHR was not a legally binding document; rather it was a set of ethical demands and a starting point for a movement that has steadily grown since 1948 (Sen, 2004). It was also a set of conclusions derived from the international community and built up through international consensus about:

- What governments should not do to people (negative rights)
- What governments should do for people (positive rights)
- *De jure* (rights in principle)
- *De facto* (rights in practice)

These final two points are very important. There is a considerable gulf between human rights ideals in principle and in practice across the globe. In other words, human rights ideals and the lived experiences of people are often very different and dependent upon state-based approaches to recognising and addressing rights, with or without impunity.

In theory, human rights are considered to be **universal**, in that they belong to each and every one of us regardless of age, gender, race, ethnicity, religion, political conviction or the type of government within which we live (O'Byrne, 2003). However, this principle is contested, with many authors suggesting that the **universality of rights** ignores differences between cultures. It has also been suggested that, because the UDHR was developed by Western countries in the first instances, that it imposes 'Western values' on other cultures and traditions. Others point to the way that different versions of human rights might clash with, for example, the rights of individuals assuming more importance over the collective rights.

It is also suggested that human rights are **indivisible**, in that they cannot be separated from each other and belong together as a package. The principle is that the implementation of all rights at the same time is necessary for a fully functioning system of human rights to work and that any other approach would be incomplete, arbitrary or allow for states to pick and choose which rights they wished to emphasise at any given point in time. However, in practice, some categories of rights are treated as more important than others in practice. For example, there is a bias towards civil and political rights (see later text) over social, economic or cultural rights in many international human rights instruments. Some rights are more fully realised than others, and it is argued that some rights are less available to some countries that have less resources.

Rights are also considered to be **inalienable**, or unable to be taken away from an individual or group. However, rights are regularly taken away from individuals and groups in some cases. For example, the rights of the Rohinyga to be citizens of Burma have been stripped over the past few decades, with their basic rights regularly violated in practice. Their 'right to have rights' (Arendt, 1951) has been taken away throughout this process, leaving them stateless without any tangible access to rights or recourse. As outlined earlier in the discussion around Zolberg *et al.'s* discussion of nationalism creating refugees, the 'right to have rights' is linked to being part of a nation-state in a concrete way that allows for access to rights.

As such, characterisation of human rights as universal, indivisible and inalienable is not consistent with the way human rights are enacted in practice. To many they remain an ideal and not a reality.

Such slow, grinding realities and denials of basic human rights are very much a part of the refugee regime. As such we need to avoid the assumption that spaces for the protection for refugees are always supportive or offer sanctuary from persecution. For example, refugee camps, urban centres, places where people are living in protracted refugee situations or, in recent decades, host countries that have ratified refugee law but have increasingly narrow interpretations of this law. These spaces may themselves be sites of slow and grinding denials of basic human rights.

Points for discussion – human rights

- Can rights be universal beyond the right to life?
- Do you think there is such a thing as 'Asian values' that emphasise community over the individual?
- What do you think about arguments saying that human rights are a Eurocentric idea?
- Some say human rights is just an ideology, and it legitimises the role of a 'Western' idea of what constitutes 'civilisation'. Do you agree?

The International Bill of Rights and subsequent international instruments

Following the UDHR, two 1966 International Covenants – the International Covenant on Civil and Political Rights and the International Covenant on Economic, Social and Cultural Rights – formed the foundation of international human rights protection. Together these are often referred to as the International Bill of Rights. These two Covenants elaborated on the rights contained within the UDHR in a legally enforceable way.

Another Convention includes the **1948 Convention on the Prevention and Punishment of the Crime of Genocide** following the Nuremberg Tribunal and Tokyo War Crimes Trials, where individuals were found guilty of war crimes and crimes against humanity. Genocide is the most extreme form of 'population cleansing' (O'Byrne, 2003:299). The term *genocide* was coined by Raphael Lemkin – literally meaning the killing (*cide*, from Latin) of a race or tribe (*genos*, from Greek) – to describe an act or attempted act of destruction aimed at a particular social grouping (Short, 2010). This Convention was meant to be only in effect for 10 years but, with further acts of genocide in places like Cambodia, Rwanda and the former Yugoslavia, it remains in force today. The establishment of a permanent International Criminal Court following the Rome Statute of 2002 has been a logical next step for holding individuals to account. Kushner and Knox (1999) (see Key Thinker Box 5.3) outline refugee movements over the past century linked to genocide.

Other key Conventions to consider include the:

- 1966 International Convention on the Elimination of all Forms of Racial Discrimination
- 1979 Convention on the Elimination of All Forms of Discrimination against Women
- 1984 Convention against Torture and other Cruel, Inhuman, or Degrading Treatment or Punishment
- 1989 Convention on the Rights of the Child

Points for discussion – human rights instruments

- Why do you feel these Conventions in particular are relevant to people who are forced to migrate?
- How do they relate to the 1951 Refugee Convention and its 1967 Protocol?

What form do human rights take?

There are a large range of rights – civil, political, economic, social and cultural – set out in international law and other regional mechanisms. These include those shown in Figure 5.2:

These rights are categorised by type:

- **Civil**: e.g. the right to life, the right to not be tortured or suffer inhuman treatment, not to be arbitrarily arrested.
- **Political**: e.g. freedom of expression, the right to vote.
- **Social**: e.g. the right to an adequate standard of living, the right to education.
- **Economic**: e.g. the right to work, trade union rights, right to a fair wage.
- **Cultural**: e.g. the right to participate in the cultural life of your community

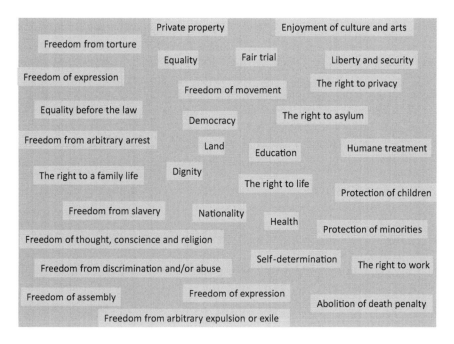

Figure 5.2 Human Rights

Table 5.1 Civil, Political, Social, Economic and Cultural Rights

	Positive (what states should do through policies)	Negative (what states should refrain from doing)
Civil and political	Invest in judiciary, prisons, police and elections	Torture, extra-judicial killings, disappearances, arbitrary detention, unfair trial, electoral intimidation, etc.
Economic, social and cultural	Invest in health, education and welfare	Ethnic, racial, gender or linguistic discrimination in health, education and welfare

As per the two Covenants that make up the International Bill of Rights, there is an important distinction between civil and political rights, on the one hand and, on the other, social, economic and cultural rights. These rights are often broadly divided into two categories with, arguably, the priority having been civil and political rights over other forms of rights.

Certainly, the adoption of two distinct categories perpetuated the belief that human rights existed in a hierarchy or different 'generations' of rights, with civil and political rights considered regarded as 'first generation' (Smith, 2005:46). What this meant in practice was that civil and political rights such as the rights to life, liberty, fair trials and freedoms were considered fundamental to participation in a democratic society.

'Second generation' rights – economic, social and cultural rights – include the right to health, education, safe working environments and social security. A recent 'third generation' of rights – group rights, such as the right to self-determination or the right to development – is aimed at the creation of conditions to realise all other human rights (Smith, 2005:46).

This framework was established within the UDHR with Articles 1–18 outlining civil rights, Articles 19–21 political rights, Articles 22–26 social and economic rights and Articles 27–28 cultural rights. As can be seen in Table 5.1 these rights encompass a range of positive and negative rights.

Key critiques of human rights

It is important to remember that human rights have a long history of being fought for; they are difficult to get, involving slow and incremental gains and, when in place, are constantly under attack. Promotion of human rights is a continuous struggle and about unrelenting effort, even if only limited results are achieved. As outlined by Hynes *et al.* (see also Hynes *et al.*, 2010):

> Impunity, denial and neglect remain central characteristics within the struggle to realise human rights in practice, with a gulf between human rights ideals and lived experiences continuing across the world.
>
> (Hynes *et al.*, 2012:788)

At the heart of this reality is a key issue – **in practice it is difficult to ensure human rights standards are maintained**. Although the atrocities of World War II put an end to the view that States alone should have a say in the treatment of their own citizens, valid questions about enforcement of human rights and how acceptable it is for one country to interfere in another country's internal affairs to ensure human rights standards remain. Regardless of how extreme human rights violations can be within a country, **it is rarely possible to enforce compliance with human rights in another sovereign State** or to interfere with the actions of another sovereign State. Historically, when there has been intervention from one State into another, these have not necessarily been effective. There are therefore no perfect guarantees for respect of human rights, and impunity – a lack or exemption from punishment for an injurious action against another person – can be enjoyed by the ruling parties of a State.

Key Concept Box 5.1   Fighting Impunity across National Boundaries

A key example of how the fight against impunity and the challenges of operating across different national jurisdictions is outlined by O'Byrne (2016) in relation to the trial of Slobodan Milosevic in 1999:

> On May 27, 1999, Slobodan Milosevic, the president of the Federal Republic of Yugoslavia, was indicted of war crimes at the International Criminal Tribunal for the Former Yugoslavia in The Hague. The tribunal had been established under the auspices of the Security Council of the United Nations in 1993 and was one of a number of developments that built on, and extended, the understanding of 'war crimes', 'crimes against humanity' and the crime of genocide. Since the deliberations of the International Military Tribunal at Nuremberg in 1945, these legal concepts had been subject to considerable debate and wide interpretation. Where does the jurisdiction of one legal system end, and another begin? Must absolute legal authority rest with the nation-state, or might that be subject to a higher authority? If so, what defines that higher authority, or what gives it legitimacy? Under what circumstances can one legal system take primacy over another?
>
> Milosevic was more than aware of this controversy. His opening statement to the International Criminal Tribunal was a direct assault on its legitimacy. 'I consider this Tribunal a false Tribunal and [this] indictment a false indictment' . . . 'You are not [a] juridical institution', he went on, 'you are [a] political tool'.
>
> (Lombardi, 2003:887, cited in O'Byrne, 2016:113)

The post-World War II Nuremberg Trials and Tokyo War Crimes Trials enshrined the importance of bringing war criminals to justice (Neier, 1998, 2012). Despite this, until recent tribunals in The Hague and Tanzania began hearing testimonies about war crimes in the former Yugoslavia and Rwanda, there had been no international effort for this fight against impunity for nearly 50 years. Aryeh Neier (2012), in an influential text, asked how these atrocities occur while the world is watching and, if they do occur, what can be done to ensure offenders are captured and punished. Neier called for a permanent war crimes tribunal to hear evidence against perpetrators when war crimes are committed anywhere in the world. Neier also explored instruments available to hold people accountable such as truth commissions, local trails, dismissals from government positions or demotion in military rank. He also explored the role of the UN and the way in which countries that fear an erosion of national sovereignty within such a permanent tribunal would object.

Civil society organisations such as Human Rights Watch, Amnesty International and a whole range of domestically based human rights organisations have key roles in reporting the abuse of rights and tackling both impunity and denial. Less interested in the conceptual issues of rights, human rights organisations and individual human rights defenders regularly tackle violations of rights and deprivations worldwide.

Much has been written about the **poor and infrequent monitoring mechanisms** available to translate the principles of human rights into practice after states have signed and/or ratified international Conventions. These mechanisms are often legally non-binding or weak in practice, relying on 'naming and shaming' governments into changing their own practices. As Cohen (2001) has suggested, **states of denial** are well documented, outlined on the back cover of his seminal test – *States of Denial: Knowing About Atrocities and Suffering*:

> Blocking out, turning a blind eye, shutting off, not wanting to know, wearing blinkers, seeing what we want to see . . . these are all expressions of 'denial'. Alcoholics who refuse to recognize their condition, people who brush aside suspicions of their partner's infidelity, the wife who doesn't notice that her husband is abusing their daughter, are supposedly 'in denial'. **Governments deny their responsibility for atrocities**, and plan them to achieve 'maximum deniability'. **Truth Commissions try to overcome the suppression and denial of past horrors**. Bystander nations deny their responsibility to **intervene**, whether in Bosnia or Rwanda'.

> (Cohen, 2001: my emphasis)

There is considerable critique of the notion of human rights, with questions about where the values that make up these rights come from and how they can be justified in ethical terms. For some commentators, a key critique is not about where human rights come from that matters, nor the fact that they clash with other ideas about right and wrong, but rather that **human rights just do not work in practice**. For example, McIntyre argues that believing in human rights is akin to having a belief 'in witches and in unicorns' (2007:69), fictional ideas that exist but are not based in fact. Questions then arise about the use of such fictions.

Ignatieff (2001) drew attention to **three key challenges to the claims of universality** of human rights – from resurgent Islam, from within the West itself and from East Asia. Ignatieff outlines how, firstly, the challenge from Islam, based around both choice of marriage and freedom of religion, were present from the time the UDHR was being drafted. Secondly, the argument that rights are a Western construct, with limited applicability beyond the USA, UK and France has been influential within debates on rights. Thirdly, Western human rights standards have been criticised by leaders in East Asia, on the basis that 'Asian values' involve putting community and family ahead of individual rights, democracy and individual freedoms. Alongside this view, some leaders suggest that authoritarian government and authoritarian family structures provide a route to development and prosperity. Sen also questions how 'Asian values' have been invoked to provide justification for authoritarian political arrangements (1999:231–248). These critiques focus on disaggregating generalisations about societies, questioning the 'cross-cultural validity – and hence legitimacy – of human rights norms' (Ignatieff, 2001:102).

The Nobel Peace Prize laureate and development economist, Amartya Sen, has drawn attention to the **'rhetoric of human rights'** (1999:227, 2004). Sen has questioned duties and obligations that a universal set of human rights generate. Sen also questions whether economic and social rights – 'second generation rights' (see earlier text) – can be included as human rights given a lack of resources to achieve these in many parts of the globe. Sen links these and other questions to development, specifically to the process of expanding the real freedoms people enjoy throughout the world. Development, he suggests, requires **the removal of 'unfreedoms'** such as poverty and social deprivation, pointing out how 'a great many people in different countries of the world are systematically denied political liberty and basic civil rights' (1999:15) and how economic insecurity relates to the lack of rights. Sen's seminal focus on 'capabilities' relates to expansion of freedoms (see Key Thinker Box 5.2):

> The analysis of development presented in this book treats the freedoms of individuals as the basic building blocks. Attention is thus paid particularly to the expansion of the 'capabilities' of persons to lead the kind of lives they value – and have reason to value.

> (1999:18)

This emphasis on positive capabilities aligns with other commentators who suggest the idea of human rights benefitting many. For Bobbio (1996), a positive sign of the 'age of rights' is the **increasing importance given to recognising human rights in international debates**. Bobbio has argued for a historically sensitive approach to human rights, suggesting that rights are constructed based on prevailing conditions of modernity and that they reflect universal struggles and universal human needs (O'Byrne, 2003:40–41). For O'Byrne (2012), the **socially constructed language structure of rights** itself frames social actions and gives meaning to these actions. These language structures are themselves historically dependent, reflecting wider political concerns, within which social actors concerned about rights operate.

Fascinating debates about the role of human rights across the world today continue to emerge, and suggestions for further reading can be found at the end of this chapter.

Key Thinker Box 5.2   Amartya Sen – a 'Capabilities Approach'

The Nobel Peace Prize laureate and development economist, Amartya Sen, is a Professor at Harvard University and was until 2004 the Master of Trinity College, Cambridge. He is also Senior Fellow at the Harvard Society of Fellows. Earlier on he was Professor of Economics at Jadavpur University Calcutta, the Delhi School of Economics and the London School of Economics and Drummond Professor of Political Economy at Oxford University. He was also formerly Honorary President of OXFAM and is now its Honorary Advisor. His research has ranged over social choice theory, economic theory, ethics and political philosophy, welfare economics, theory of measurement, decision theory, development economics, public health and gender studies. Sen's books include *On Economic Inequality* (1973, 1999), *Commodities and Capabilities* (1985), *The Standard of Living* (1987), *On Ethics and Economics* (1987), *Hunger and Public Action* (with Jean Drèze, 1989), *Inequality Re-examined* (1992), *The Quality of Life* (with Martha Nussbaum, 1993), *Development as Freedom* (1999) and *Rationality and Freedom* (2002).

From the mid-1970s, Sen worked on the causes and prevention of famines, publishing *Poverty and Famines: An Essay on Entitlement and Deprivation* in 1981. This work addressed not only how people bought food, but also inequalities built into the distribution of food – who was and who was not entitled to that food. Sen's interest in famine stemmed from his personal experiences of witnessing the Bengal famine of 1943, which did not arise out of a lack of food supply but due to particular groups of people not having the means to buy food. Famine and starvation were not about people not *having* or their not *being* enough food to eat. Rather, these were about the *relationship* of persons to that food, ownership of that food and, importantly, *entitlement* to the food.

Sen's work has been influential in informing the UNDP Human Development Index (HDI), which is a composite index of life expectancy, education and per capital income indicators informed by Sen's pioneering work on poverty as 'the deprivation of basic capabilities' (1999:87) or 'capability' approach to examining human development. In his book on *Development as Freedom* (1999), Sen's central argument is that the expansion of freedom is the primary end to a principal means of development, rather than a focus on economic growth or GDP. This approach compares levels of education, health and standard of living across countries, emphasising that people and their capabilities should be the ultimate criteria for assessing the development of any given country. Sen suggests that expanding the real freedoms people enjoy throughout the world is linked to such development, requiring the removal of 'unfreedoms' such as poverty and social deprivation.

This engagement with the devastating penalties of economic unfreedoms were partially based around a childhood experience whilst playing in the garden of his family home in Dhaka. A man came through the gate screaming after being knifed in his back at a time when Hindus and Muslims were in the throes of communal riots. The knifed man, a Muslim day labourer, was called Kader Mia. Kader Mia had been in the area to carry out work in a neighbouring house – for a tiny reward. As he was being taken to the hospital, he outlined how his wife had told him not to go into a hostile area during the riots but, as the family had nothing to eat, he had set out in search of work. Sen sets out how:

> The penalty of his economic unfreedom turned out to be death, which occurred later on in the hospital. The experience was devasting for me. It made me reflect . . . on the terrible burden of narrowly defined identities, including those firmly based on communities and groups. . . . But more immediately, it also pointed to the remarkable fact that economic unfreedom, in the form of extreme poverty, can make a person a helpless prey in the violation of other kinds of freedom. Kader Mia need not have come to a hostile area in search of little income in those terrible times had his family been able to survive without it.
>
> (1999:8)

Sen's subsequent emphasis on the positive capabilities of people to achieve development sits closely alongside ideas about human rights, although Sen provides three distinct critiques of human rights. Firstly, the *legitimacy critique* of the demands of human rights are queried. Sen asks how human rights have any real status except through individual states. Secondly, Sen asks about the *form* rights take and the way in which rights as entitlements that require a duty to provide them and, in the absence of this duty, are hollow – a *coherence critique*. Thirdly, Sen considers rights to be in the domain of social ethics, questioning whether every culture regards rights valuable compared to other virtues or qualities. This *cultural critique* is at the heart of the universality debate within human rights as outlined earlier in this chapter. For these critiques in full see *Development as Freedom* (1999), pages 227–248.

Sen (2004) has also worked on the elements of a theory of human rights, questioning where rights come from, what makes them important, what duties they generate and through what forms of actions human rights can be promoted. He also questions whether economic and social rights or 'second generation rights' (see earlier text) can be included given the lack of resources available to achieve these goals in many parts of the world. Sen also asks how proposals of human rights can be defended, the challenges faced and how any claim to universal status can be assessed in a world with both cultural variation and diverse practice.

Key references – Amartya Sen

Sen, A. (1981) *Poverty and Famines: An Essay on Entitlement and Deprivation*, Clarendon Press, Oxford.

Sen, A. (1999) *Development as Freedom*, Oxford University Press, Oxford.

Sen, A. (2004) Elements of a Theory of Human Rights, *Philosophy and Public Affairs*, 32(4), 315–356.

Human rights and forced migration

> Refugees are human rights violations made visible.
>
> (Reid, 2005:4)

So, how do human rights relate to refugees, IDPs, stateless persons, asylum seekers and people who have experienced human trafficking? If refugees are, as Reid suggests, human rights violations made visible, what of those who experience enforced displacement in small groups, moving surreptitiously to avoid detection, potentially within their own nation-states, and are thus invisible to possibilities of protection? If crossing a border, what rights do people have if they are outside citizenship structures and do not have access to the rights others enjoy? What type of rights are prioritised in these situations? What of those crossing borders under duress, having been deceived or misled and now invisible to all but a few people who do not have their human rights at heart?

Understanding human rights, and the ways in which violations of human rights do and do not become visible, is vitally important within the study of forced migration (Neier, 2012). As Reid suggests, the human rights violations of refugees become visible upon crossing a border. Others forced to migrate remain invisible in terms of international protection. Tracing the rise of human rights, the eminent Conor Gearty suggests that human rights are a 'visibility project' (2005, 2009), about seeing every person as someone who counts and that:

> we are each equally worthy of esteem . . . not on account of what we do, or how we look, or how bright we are, or what colour we are, or where we come from, or our ethnic group: it is simply on account of the fact that we are.
>
> (2005:4)

Gearty goes on to suggest that it follows that: 'at its core, human rights is a subject that is concerned with the outsider, with the marginalised, and with the powerless' (2005:5). He continues, describing how individuals and groups of individuals who become invisible or are pushed out of vision, are often viewed as 'non- or sub-human if they are seen. It is these people who need human rights protection the most' (2005:5). This resonates with what Zolberg and Arendt suggest about the inherent dangers of linking rights with nationality – as outlined earlier in this chapter – wherein the rights of minorities and the stateless cannot be assumed. People living outside the structures of citizenship rarely have access to the rights citizens enjoy. Gaps in protection of people outside citizenship structures remain to this day. In the words of Arendt, the right to belong to some kind of an organised community and gain 'the right to have rights' (1951) is an anchor of what might otherwise be abstract notions of human rights.

In theory, under international law, every person has human rights, and violations of these rights are addressed by a range of international treaties, Conventions and Covenants as well as national Bills, Charters and human rights Acts. Under these laws, people who are forced to migrate are entitled to the full range of rights – civil, political, economic, social and cultural – set out in international law and regional mechanisms surrounding protection.

However, rights are frequently violated during human displacement and upon arrival into a host country. Historical processes and practices described here have and do – in the eyes of the State – legitimise the persecution of those perceived as 'other' or in some way 'outside' national constructs of identity.

For refugees persecuted on the basis of their race, religion, nationality or membership of a particular social group, as well as those in opposition to the emerging rulers who experience persecution based upon their political opinions, the right to have rights is contained with the 1951 Refugee Convention and its 1967 Protocol. International refugee law is complimented and buttressed by a range of human rights instruments in practice, often drawing on similar principles and wording (Reid, 2005). For IDPs, human rights instruments within nation-states are essential components of protection, often around the legal duties of states to refrain from committing human rights abuse against their own populations, but also in protecting people from rights violations in the first instance. For people who experience human trafficking, rights to protection and comprehensive processes to identify 'victims' are key any subsequent recovery strategy put in place. The stateless, denied the protection of any citizenship anywhere in the world, live with the implications of lack of access to education, health, housing and the basic necessities meant to be available to all on the basis of membership of the human family.

It is also the case that the types of rights prioritised is important. The 1951 Refugee Convention and the 1967 Protocol:

> 'represent a politically partisan view of human rights to the extent that they prioritise civil and political rights over socio-economic and cultural rights. Such prejudice is evident in the textual definition of a refugee as one who flees a violation of civil and political rights *only*.
>
> (Reid, 2005:15)

As can be seen, connecting forced migration to human rights is not a straightforward exercise, with 'first generation' rights often emphasised in law, policy and practice. There has also been a historical tension around individual rights over collective rights as outlined previously, which can be seen within the definition of who is a refugee and the need to prove individualised persecution. Some have argued that although preventing human rights abuses is key to preventing refugee movements, the discourse around human rights rather than a more explicit discourse around persecution is less powerful (Zetter, 2007).

One obvious linkage between forced migration and human rights relates to the Universal Declaration of Human Rights (UDHR). The General Assembly of the United Nations adopted and proclaimed the UDHR on 10 December 1948. This Declaration had its origins in the Holocaust, wherein there was a mass displacement of millions and Genocide of some 6 million Jews and other populations within Europe.

Eleanor Roosevelt's speech – *'On the Adoption of the Universal Declaration of Human Rights'* – outlined the right to be human, the protection of individuals from state tyranny regardless of differences, how peace between nations be fostered and the promotion of understanding of the inherent dignity and equal worth of 'all members of the human family'. View at: www.americanrhetoric.com/speeches/eleanorrooseveltdeclarationhumanrights.htm

The right to asylum

Article 14 of the UDHR outlines how **everyone has the right to seek and to enjoy** in other countries **asylum from persecution**. This is one of the most important obligations in international law. This principle protects people around the world who are at risk of persecution by their own State. It recognises how there is a need for countries to provide a safe place for people to live.

However, there is no mention of the right to be granted asylum in the UDHR or in other international Conventions. In contemporary terms, the process of reconciling these two positions is through Refugee Status Determination (RSD) processes that people seeking asylum ('asylum seekers') move through to obtain 'refugee' or another form of legal status that recognises their need to be protected from persecution. This process is subject to interpretation of international obligations by States. For example, in the UK, the Home Office handles this RSD process within what is widely considered to be a 'hostile environment' towards people seeking asylum. For people in refugee camps, UNHCR, or the government of the country of asylum, might handle this RSD process in what is now a global environment where resettlement options are limited.

As outlined in Chapter 2, a key principle in the 1951 Refugee Convention is found in Article 33 on the principle of ***non-refoulement***. This is also a cornerstone of international law more broadly. This obliges states to not return anyone to the country of origin if they are likely to be tortured or subject to cruel, inhuman or degrading treatment. Similar wording is found in the UDHR and other international and domestic human rights law.

Key Thinker Box 5.3   Tony Kushner and Katharine Knox – *Refugees in an Age of Genocide*

Tony Kushner is a Professor of the History of Jewish and non-Jewish Relations at Southampton University and former historian for the Manchester Jewish Museum. His interests and research are around British Jewish history in the late 19th and 20th centuries, UK immigration history and refugee movements. His books include, with Katharine Knox, *Refugees in an Age of Genocide* (1999) and *Journeys from the Abyss: The Holocaust and Forced Migration from the 1880s to the Present* (2017). Katharine Knox is a consultant, based in the UK, and currently also works for the Joseph Rowntree Charitable Trust, supporting funding on issues of power and accountability. She has a background in academia and has worked in policy and research roles to address a range of human rights and social justice issues, including formerly working for the Refugee Council and Equally Ours, a human rights and equality NGO.

Kushner and Knox's 1999 text – *Refugees in an Age of Genocide* – traces the history of global refugee movements throughout the 20th century, relating these to the history of refugees in the UK. During the course of writing this text, the authors recounted how surprising it was that, with few exceptions, refugee histories had been neglected and often forgotten. Resurrecting these histories, this 1999 text outlined the ways in which refugees have been a part of the British landscape for centuries. This work emphasised the importance of 'the local' for both refugees and for those receiving them, connecting the local with national and global events and processes. The book begins with the origins of the Jewish refugee movement from 1881, when Tsar Alexander II was assassinated, seeing some 2.5 million Jews leaving the Russian Empire through to the turn of the 21st century when asylum seekers from the former Yugoslavia arrived in the UK.

Kushner and Knox also detail responses to the arrival of refugees in the form of dispersal polices, including Belgian refugees between 1914 and 1918, Polish refugees from the 1940s to early 1950s and post-1956 Hungarian refugees. Thereafter Ugandan Asian, Chilean and Vietnamese 'quota refugees' arriving via agreed resettlement schemes experienced enforced dispersal during the 1970s and 1980s. They detail how, in the case of Ugandan Asians in places like Leicester, the lack of welcome upon arrival had by the end of the century turned into descriptions of their being 'central' to revitalisation efforts and creating employment for others (1999:287). They also detail the arrival of the Kurds, refugees from former Yugoslavia and from former Zaire in the 1990s, describing the 'closing doors of western Europe, and especially Britain, in granting a safe haven to refugees' (1999:336) and 'charges of racism' (1999:375) towards many African countries during the 1980s and 1990s (see also Knox, 1997).

Kushner's 2017 subsequent text – *Journeys from the Abyss: The Holocaust and Forced Migration from the 1880s to the Present* – explores how history has been largely neglected within the field of refugee studies and forced migration. Using a wide variety of governmental papers, film, novels, memorials and archival material, this book details the 'then' (Jewish refugee journeys) and 'now' (contemporary forced migration), providing a view of forced migration in historical context and allowing for memories to be captured. In a 2018 paper, Kushner goes on to discuss how Britain's response to the recent refugee 'crisis' in the Mediterranean is marked by its absence. Child refugees are discussed, and comparisons drawn (and then rejected) to the Kindertransport, when close to 10,000 mainly Jewish children came to Britain before the Second World War.

Kushner is now working on the construction of ethnicity and further books relating to the Holocaust and co-edits the journal *Patterns of Prejudice*, which provides a forum to explore the historical roots and contemporary varieties of social exclusion and the stigmatisation of racial, ethnic, national or religious 'others' across the world.

Further reading – Tony Kushner and Katherine Knox

Knox, K. (1997) *Credit to the Nation: A Study of Refugees in the UK*, Refugee Council, London.

Kushner, T. (2017) *Journeys from the Abyss: The Holocaust and Forced Migration from the 1880s to the Present* (Migrations and Identities), Liverpool University Press, Liverpool.

Kushner, T. (2018) Truly, Madly, Deeply . . . Nostalgically? Britain's On-off Love Affair with Refugees, Past and Present. *Patterns of Prejudice*, 52(2–3), 172–194.

Kushner, T. and Knox, K. (1999) *Refugees in an Age of Genocide*, Frank Cass, London and Portland, ON.

Mixed movements and mixed migration

The connection between human rights and forced migration is not straightforward and understanding that **motivations for migration and resulting movements are often mixed** is important. It is becoming increasingly more recognised that people migrate with a range of legal statuses and labels – some of which may well not capture the complex mix of civil, political, social, economic or cultural reasons for migration.

Theoretically, Kunz (1973, 1981) proposed a kinetic model of refugee movements which distinguished refugees into two kinetic types – 'anticipatory' and 'acute' – which began to recognise mixed motivations. Anticipatory refugees were those who anticipated future persecution and planned their flight accordingly. Acute refugees were those coerced, often at gunpoint, and forced to flee. This model has since been critiqued for its simplicity, but it did allow for further theorisation (Bloch, 2020; see also Chapter 1). It also allowed for the recognition that often-used terms such as *push* and *pull* models of migration are inadequate and do not address the complex causes, motivations or drivers of migration.

As outlined in Key Thinker Box 1.2, Anthony Richmond challenged the simplistic dichotomies of forced/voluntary and push/pull by suggesting a continuum between 'proactive' and 'reactive' migration, as well as between sociopolitical and economic in a matrix illustrating the complex mix of determinants of migration (see also Kunz, 1973, 1981). For Richmond, proactive migrants have choices that include whether to move at all, when to move, where to go, long or short distances and whether to cross an international border. For those with less choice and coercive contexts, reactive migration was associated with forced migration.

Van Hear (1998) discusses 'mixed motives' for migration, highlighting how migration is rarely either voluntary or forced, there being choice or compulsion involved in both. Zetter (2018) also outlines how **multiple drivers**

produce 'mixed movements' of people who do not fit the definition of a refugee. Zetter provides points out that:

> voluntary migrants, putative refugees, former IDPs, other forcibly displaced people, and trafficked and smuggled persons, may often be travelling together, along the same routes and with the same aspirations.
>
> (2018:35)

He also notes that the pejorative term *irregular migration* is increasingly being used to describe mixed movements. This term is often found in debates around human trafficking, wherein people who left their countries of origin as 'regular migrants' who then are rendered 'vulnerable' due to being exposed to situations of exploitation *en route*. This has been picked up by the Mixed Migration Centre of the Danish Refugee Council (view at: www.mixedmigration.org). It outlines how not everyone forced to move is without agency during their journey but that people who start their migration journey voluntarily do not necessarily maintain agency during their journeys.

They define such mixed migration as:

> **cross-border movements of people** including refugees fleeing persecution and conflict, victims of trafficking and people seeking better lives and opportunities. **Motivated to move by a multiplicity of factors**, people in mixed flows have **different legal statuses** as well as a **variety of vulnerabilities**. Although entitled to protection under international human rights law, they are **exposed to multiple rights violations along their journey**. Those in mixed migration flows travel along **similar routes**, using similar means of travel − often travelling irregularly and wholly or partially assisted by migrant smugglers.

Such a focus from pre-departure to destination as well as return migration is useful in that it captures a full range of people on the move or in transit and how they may face similar risks and vulnerabilities en route. It recognises a range of drivers for movement, often intertwined and influencing each other. These include persecution, conflict, discrimination, lack of access to rights, lack of access to decent work, violence, gender inequality, separation from family, poverty, individual or family aspirations as well as the consequences of climate change.

Further reading

Arendt, H. (1951) *The Origins of Totalitarianism*, Penguin Books, London.

Bloch, A. (2020) Reflections and Directions for Research in Refugee Studies, *Ethnic and Racial Studies*, 43(3), 436–459.

Bobbio, N. (1996) *The Age of Rights*, Polity Press, Cambridge.

Cohen, S. (2001) *States of Denial: Knowing about Atrocities and Suffering*, Polity Press, Cambridge.

Hynes, P., Lamb, M., Short, D. and Waites, M. (2012) Special Issue: The Sociology of Human Rights, *Sociology*, 46(5).

IDMC (2015) *Briefing: Understanding the Root Causes of Displacement: Towards a Comprehensive Approach to Prevention and Solutions*, IDMC, Norway.

Neier, A. (1998) *War Crimes: Brutality, Genocide, Terror and the Struggle for Justice*, Times Books, New York and Toronto.

Neier, A. (2012) *International Human Rights Movement: A History*, Princeton University Press, Princeton, NJ and Oxford.

O'Byrne, D.J. (2003) *Human Rights: An Introduction*, Pearson, Harlow.

O'Byrne, D.J. (2012) On the Sociology of Human Rights: Theorising the Language-structure of Rights, in Hynes, P., Lamb, M., Short, D. and Waites, M. (Eds.), Special Issue, The Sociology of Human Rights, *Sociology*, 46(5).

Reid, C. (2005) *International Law and Legal Instruments*, Forced Migration Online, University of Oxford, Oxford.

Sen, A. (1981) *Poverty and Famines: An Essay on Entitlement and Deprivation*, Clarendon Press, Oxford.

Sen, A. (1999) *Development as Freedom*, Oxford University Press, Oxford.

Smith, R.K.M. (2005) *International Human Rights*, Oxford University Press, Oxford.

Turner, B. (1993) Outline of a Theory of Human Rights, *Sociology*, 27(3), 489–512.

Zetter, R. (2018) Conceptualising Forced Displacement: Praxis, Scholarship and Empirics, in Bloch, A. and Dona, G. (Eds.), *Forced Migration: Current Issues and Debates*, London: Routledge.

Zolberg, A.R., Suhrke, A. and Aguayo, S. (1989) *Escape from Violence: Conflict and the Refugee Crisis in the Developing World*, Oxford University Press, Oxford.

References

Castles, S., de Haas, H. and Miller, M. (2014) *The Age of Migration: International Population Movements in the Modern World* (5th ed.), Guildford Press, New York.

Ezeilo, J.N. (2018) Trafficking in Human Beings in the African Context, in Piotrowicz, R., Rijken, C. and Uhl, B.H. (Eds.), *Routledge Handbook of Human Trafficking*, Routledge, Abingdon and New York.

Gearty, C. (2009) *Can Human Rights Survive?* Cambridge University Press, Cambridge.

Hynes, P., Gani-Yusuf, L., Burland, P., Dew, J., Olatunde, A., Thurnham, A., Brodie, I., Spring, D. and Murray, F. (2018, October) *'Vulnerability' to Human Trafficking: A Study of Viet Nam, Albania, Nigeria and the UK: Report of a Shared Learning Event Held in Lagos, Nigeria*, University of Bedfordshire and International Organization for Migration (IOM), London.

Hynes, P., Lamb, M., Short, D. and Waites, M. (2010) Special Issue, Sociology and Human Rights: New Engagements, *The International Journal of Human Rights*, 14(6).

Hynes, P., Lamb, M., Short, D. and Waites, M. (2012) Special Issue, New Directions in the Sociology of Human Rights, *The International Journal of Human Rights*, 16(8).

Ignatieff, M. (2001) The Attack on Human Rights, *Foreign Affairs*, 80(6), 102–116.

Kunz, E.F. (1973) The Refugee in Flight: Kinetic Models and Forms of Displacement, *International Migration Review*, 7, 125–146.

Kunz, E.F. (1981) Exile and Resettlement: Refugee Theory, *International Migration Review*, 15, 42–51.

Lombardi, G.P. (2003) Legitimacy and the Expanding Power of the ICTY, *New England Law Review*, 37(4), 887–901.

McIntyre, A. (2007) *After Virtue: A Study in Moral Theory*, University of Notre Dame Press, Notre Dame, IN.

Nash, K. (2012) Towards a Political Sociology of Human Rights, in Nash, K., Amenta, E. and Scott, A. (Eds.), *The New Blackwell Companion to Political Sociology*, Wiley-Blackwell, Malden, MA, Oxford and West Sussex.

O'Byrne, D.J. (2016) *Human Rights in a Globalizing World*, Palgrave Macmillan, London and New York.

Richmond, A.H. (1988) Sociological Theories of International Migration, *Current Sociology*, 36(2), 7–25.

Sen, A. (2004) Elements of a Theory of Human Rights, *Philosophy and Public Affairs*, 32(4), 315–356.

Short, D. (2010) Cultural Genocide and Indigenous Peoples: A Sociological Approach, in Hynes, P., Lamb, M., Short, D. and Waites, M., Sociology and Human Rights: New Engagements, *The International Journal of Human Rights*, 14(6), 833–848.

Turner, B. (2006) *Vulnerability and Human Rights*, Pennsylvania University Press, Pennsylvania.

Van Hear (1998) *New Diasporas: The Mass Exodus, Dispersal and Regrouping of Migrant Communities*, University of Washington Press, Washington, DC.

Waters, M. (1996) Human Rights and the Universalisation of Interests, *Sociology*, 30(3), 593–600.

Woodiwiss, A. (1990) *Rights v. Conspiracy: A Sociological Essay on the Development of Labour Law in the United States*, Berg, Oxford.

Woodiwiss, A. (2005) *Human Rights*, Routledge, London and New York.

Zetter, R. (2007) More Labels, Fewer Refugees: Remaking the Refugee Label in an Era of Globalization, *Journal of Refugee Studies*, 20(2), 172–192.

6 'Children on the move' and the 'displaced child'

Introduction

There is no single piece of legislation that systematically addresses the issue of children on the move in the world today (Bhabha *et al.*, 2016). The 1989 United Nations Convention on the Rights of the Child (UNCRC) is a comprehensive compilation of legal standards for the protection of children, defining children as being below the age of 18 years, and the most widely ratified international human rights treaty today. The pre-history of the UNCRC involves a vision of the kind of 'childhood' that children everywhere should be able to enjoy (Hart, 2006).

Within 54 Articles that spell out the basic human rights of children, children seeking refugee status and children temporarily or permanently separated from their family environments are discussed (Articles 20 and 22). Special protections for separated children end upon their 18th birthday, or in some cases earlier. This chapter will consider these rights and the parallel evolution of terminology around the migration of children. This chapter will look at ideas of who is a 'child', what is 'childhood', who are 'children on the move' and what are their 'migration pathways'. The approach of viewing children as inherently 'vulnerable' is questioned, particularly around past approaches that viewed women and children as homogenous, 'vulnerable' groups of 'victims'. This chapter also briefly engages in broader discourses about gender related to the causes, consequences and protection of women, men, girls and boys who experience displacement. 'Safe spaces' and the roles of Advocates or Guardians for children are then explored.

At the end of 2019, an estimated **40% of 79.5 million people forcibly displaced were children**. This means that between 30–34 million children and young people below the age of 18 years are displaced (UNHCR, 2020). This chapter provides a sketch of this population, refugee children, children in IDP situations, stateless children and the historical evolution of international legal responses to the trafficking of children (Faulkner, 2019) and emerging work on child sexual exploitation in humanitarian contexts. The work of key thinkers in these areas is provided for further reference, and further readings are suggested for further elaboration.

The United Nations Convention on the Rights of the Child

The 1989 United Nations Convention on the Rights of the Child (UNCRC) defines children as being below the age of 18 years. The UNCRC has been widely ratified – by all Member States except for the USA and Somalia – with governments recognising the survival, development, protection and participation rights of children and the subsequent need for special assistance and protection. As Hart (2006) outlines, the work of Eglantyne Jebb, a champion of children's rights and founder of the Save the Children Fund, was fundamental within its pre-history. In 1924, the General Assembly of the League of Nations had adopted a Declaration of Children's Rights, as championed by Jebb. This Declaration was a milestone and was subsequently expanded into the 1959 UN Declaration on the Rights of the Child, which was then replaced in 1989 by the UNCRC. This pre-history of the UNCRC involved a vision of the kind of 'childhood' that children everywhere should be able to enjoy (Hart, 2006).

The basic human rights of children are spelled out in 54 Articles around four key principles found in the UNCRC – Articles, 2, 3, 6 and 12. Article 2 ensures all children have the same rights as others, without discrimination of any kind. Article 3 outlines that the 'best interests' of children should be a primary consideration in all actions concerning children. Article 6 recognises that every child has the inherent right of life and State Parties should ensure the survival and development of children. Article 12 is about the right to participation, that children capable of forming their own views have the right to express those views freely.

The 54 Articles also include children temporarily or permanently separated from their family environment (Article 20) and children seeking refugee status (Article 22):

> Article 20: 'A child temporarily or permanently deprived of his or her family environment, or in whose own best interests cannot be allowed to remain in that environment, shall be entitled to special protection and assistance provided by the State.'
>
> Article 22: 'State Parties shall take appropriate measure to ensure that a child who is seeking refugee status . . . shall, whether unaccompanied or accompanied by his or her parents or by any other person, receive appropriate protection and humanitarian assistance. . . .'
>
> 'State Parties shall provide, as they consider appropriate, co-operation . . . to protect and assist such a child and to trace the parents . . . to obtain information necessary for reunification with his or her family. In cases where no parents or other members of the family can be found, the child shall be accorded the same protection as any other child permanently or temporarily deprived of his or her family environment.'

These special protections for separated children end upon their 18th birthday, or in some cases earlier. Member States are bound by this Convention, which sets out the range of civil, political, economic, social and cultural rights of children. Children have not always been seen or accepted as holders of rights, but as 'possessions' of parents or, in some cases, an economic resource. The Committee on the Rights of the Child (CRC) was set up to monitor the UNCRC and in 2005 issued General Comment No.6, which stated that the best interests of children should be respected throughout the different stages of displacement. How this is operationalised in practice remains, however, less clear.

As Bhabha (2014; see also Key Thinker Box 6.2) suggests, it was only in the late 1990s that policy makers began to ask about the reasons why children migrated, or who made key decisions regarding their journeys, wellbeing, rights and futures. Bhabha suggests this is a result of child welfare specialists being 'absorbed by their domestic preoccupations with issues such as abuse and neglect' (2014:2) but also how the UNCRC's increasing importance meant that children began to feature as rights-bearers. This included children who were not citizens of a given signatory.

In reality, there is a connection between the age of a child, child protection policies and procedures and immigration policies. In practice, in different countries and across different regions, children are not always treated in accordance with the principles and Articles of the UNCRC. For example:

- Article 20 outlines how children should not be temporarily or permanently deprived of a family environment, but children with families in the UK are regularly denied access to the country when arriving alone in Calais and other port areas of France where they are forced to sleep rough, depend on volunteers for food and clothing, and be exposed to violence from the authorities and other inhabitants of informal camps (Beddoe, 2017; UNICEF, 2016). Article 10 outlines how children have the right to travel to a different country to be in contact with their family; this is also not the case in this context.
- Article 22 outlines how children without parents who are seeking asylum should be accorded the same protections as other children, but this is most often not the case (Bhabha, 2014).
- Articles 19, 25, 34 and 39 address the sale and sexual exploitation of children but, to date, change has been slow (UN Special Rapporteur on the sale of children, n.d.).
- Detention of children is against the best interests of children, as contained in Article 3 of the UNCRC, but many governments continue to detain children who are unaccompanied, separated or in families for immigration-related purposes, including children who are refugees and/or seeking asylum, despite strong evidence that detention has a profoundly negative impact on children's health and development (UNHCR, 2017).
- Article 35 discusses preventing the abduction of, sale or trafficking of children but this continues (Hynes, 2010, 2015; Setter, 2017).

Like other laws that purport universality, the UNCRC has been critiqued on the basis of enshrining Western notions of 'childhood' and who is a 'child', upon which its rights were constructed. It has also been critiqued on the basis of excluding the legacy of colonialism and imperialism within its construction and subsequently not adequately representing the world's children (for an overview, see Faulkner and Nyamutata, 2020). Hart (2006) has also compared its stance with that of the famous anthropologist, Margaret Mead, who aimed to enhance appreciation for the diversity and understand the differences of children's lives, potentially ascribable to specific settings in which they grow up.

Laws are sometimes inadequate to address the immediate needs of children who migrate. For example, although international law prohibits returning children to their countries of origin unless there are adequate reception facilities to return them to, several countries have been found to (or try to) do this. For example, Gladwell *et al.* (2016) found, when looking at the lives of 25 care leavers forcibly removed to Afghanistan from the UK, they had experienced a range of difficulties on return, including problems with families, insecurity, stigma, fragmented social networks and, for some, being targeted simply due to their status as a 'returnee'.

Points for discussion − what is 'childhood'?

- Do you think there can be a universal version of 'childhood' as encapsulated within the UNCRC?
- What does the diversity of children's lives mean in terms of the rights they may or may not be entitled to?
- What rights are (or should) children be entitled to during the different stages of their movement or displacement?

Terminology shifts

Prior to the development and ratification of the UNCRC, children were often considered to be the possessions of others − parents or families − rather than accepted holders of rights. Parallel to the evolution of children being seen as rights-holders, terminology and labels have evolved around children on the move from simple 'dependents' (Bhabha, 2014). Different terms are linked to different conceptualisations of policy and practice with **terms constructed in a way that does not always match the lived experiences of children and young people**.

Children arriving into a country without parents were and are still often referred to as **'unaccompanied minors' or 'unaccompanied children'** and assumed to be in need of asylum. Bhabha (2014) outlines how this terminology was gradually seen as being inadequate as it was not only children arriving without a parent, but also those not cared for by a responsible adult. As such, it was the 'lack of care rather than unaccompanied status' that required attention. In the US, terminology changed to reflect this, with 'unaccompanied and separated child asylum-seekers' replacing this initial description. Children accompanied were not assumed as being protected if separated from their customary caregivers and, as a result, children being trafficked or in some way exploitation by others were seen as in need of protection by the State.

By the mid-2000s it became increasingly recognised that children and young people were not all asylum seekers, but were **crossing borders due to mixed drivers, mixed motivations and factors unrelated to a fear of persecution** (Bhabha, 2014). In other words, like adults, the complexity of migration was being increasingly recognised. As with adults, the binary approach or duality of being a 'child refugee' or a 'child migrant' does not capture such lived experiences. Over time, **the term 'children on the move' replaced previous labels** assigned, reflecting the realities of mixed migrations to find safety, refuge as well as aspirational reasons such as educational and economic prospects. Sometimes referred to as **independent child migrants** who do not necessarily want the 'rescue' or care of the State, young people may encounter their aspirations to earn or undertake education hindered by immigration concerns. D'Costa outlines how:

> we simply do not know enough about the dynamics and complexities of children and young people on the migration pathway. There are a lot of assumptions about children's migration and displacement but not enough research-informed understanding of this phenomenon.
>
> (D'Costa, 2018)

For D'Costa, the term *children on the move* is considered to exclude some groups, such as children unable to move, left behind by parents, children with disabilities and/or stateless children. The term *migration pathway* is used to explore both individual aspirations and larger-scale experiences related to the constraints and possibilities of migration or movement. D'Costa questions **who is visible and invisible on such migration pathways**, but also who is **hyper visible**, given preference in policy and practice. An example of this hypervisibility could be young women and girls, often defined by their perceived 'vulnerability'.

Migration journeys undertaken by children remain largely untold, with few accounts centring on the experiences of children or the backstories of their motivation to migrate (Bhabha, 2014). The UNCRC also contains the notion of children's evolving capabilities, taking the **different stages – rather than ages – of children** into account, alongside the progressive empowerment of children and their specific needs. Children's evolving capacities can, however, be a cause of mistreatment if overestimated or underestimated. An example of overestimating a child's capacities could be around criminal responsibility where a child knows they have done something wrong but have the right to have their 'unevolved capacities' taken into account. Underestimating a child's capacities can be related to their understanding and competency to make their own decisions, including before and during migration journeys.

This may include children who have chosen to leave home to escape situations of abuse or exploitation, **challenging cosy notions of what 'home'**

means. Equally, it may include **children who undertake journeys, motivated by parents, out of love.** As Gulwali Passarlay outlines in the prologue of an autobiographic novel of his journey from Afghanistan when 12 years old:

> Before I died, I contemplated how drowning would feel. It was clear to me now; this was how I would go: away from my mother's warmth, my father's strength, and my family's love.
>
> (2016:1)

> It helped to try to focus on my mother's steely determination and imagine her voice urging me not to give up: 'Be safe, and do not come back.' They had been her last words to me and my brother before she had sent us away to find sanctuary in strange lands. She wanted to save our lives, to help us escape from men who had wanted us dead.
>
> (2016:4)

Who is a child? Who are children on the move? What are their migration pathways?

Socially constructed notions of 'childhood' differ across time and context and evolve as societies change (Aries, 1973; Hart and Tyrer, 2006; James and Prout, 1997; Seeberg and Goździak, 2016; Wells, 2009).

As Aries (1973) outlined, the notion of 'childhood' did not exist in medieval society; people passed from infancy – when little notice was taken of them – to full participation in adult life. From the age of 7, most young people were expected to work, learn or play alongside adults. Across time, attitudes began to change and from the 15th century onwards, 'childhood' began to emerge as **a time of innocence and vulnerability**, justifying separating children from adults in daily life (Aries, 1973):

> Henceforth it was recognised that the child was not ready for life, and that he had to be subjected to a special treatment, a sort of quarantine, before he was allowed to join the adults.
>
> (Aries, 1973:396)

However, this happened slowly and selectively dependent upon a person's position in society. It did not, for example, prevent children being employed in heavy and dangerous work in factories or mines. Differing constructions over time included **Locke's portrayal of children as *tabula rasa* (blank slates)** with knowledge coming from their experiences throughout life. In the second half of the 18th century, the Romantic poets (such as Blake, Coleridge and Wordsworth) considered the concept of *original innocent* to best describe a child. For Blake, **'childhood' was the source of innocence,** to be kept alive as long as possible.

In the 18th century and during the onset of the industrial revolution, few voices were raised against child labour, with labouring considered a condition which would teach children principles. This view began to be challenged by the end of the 18th century at a time when 'climbing-boys', apprentices in cotton mills and children were employed in factories. Perceptions began to shift, with **children regarded as 'victims', 'slaves' and 'innocents'** who had been forced into 'unnatural' employment and therefore denied a 'childhood' (Hendrick and Horn, 1997). By around **the 1840s, the wage-earning child was no longer considered the norm in industrialised nations** (Henrick and Horn, 1997). The 1850s and 1860s saw the growth of charitable organisations that raised awareness and campaigned against the use of children in employment. Reformers drew on the anti-slavery movement to make this case.

During this same period, in 1874, a 9-year-old child in the US – Mary Ellen McCormack – had experienced extreme physical abuse, starvation and neglect (Radford et al., 2011). Due to a lack of laws to protect children, a case was brought by the American Society for the Prevention of Cruelty to Animals. Thereafter, the world's first organisation against child cruelty, the New York Society for the Prevention of Cruelty to Children (SPCC) and subsequently, in England, the National Society for the Prevention of Cruelty to Children (NSPCC) in 1889 were born. The 'discovery' of child abuse, now more commonly called child maltreatment, had begun, and it was not long before legislation against child cruelty was enacted, giving public agencies powers to protect and remove children (Parton, 2007). Before this there had been no laws protecting children from physical abuse from their parents with social norms around 'sparing the rod and spoil the child' prevalent in the private realm of the home.

The construction of **child abuse as a social problem** allowed for state intervention where considered necessary. In the UK, NSPCC inspectors worked mostly in the homes of poorer communities in cases relating to child cruelty. As Parton (2007) outlines, in doing so these communities were described, classified and assigned deviancy, and the foundations of contemporary forms of knowledge about child maltreatment were laid down. These inspectors were given the roles of advocating on behalf of children – something which is sometimes referred to in the literature as them being 'child savers' or the 'cruelty men' – with an overt focus on changing the behaviour of abusive parents and therapeutic approaches for children who had experienced maltreatment (Parton, 2007; Radford et al., 2011). During WW1, women inspectors were employed because men had gone to war, feminising this role.

From the mid-19th century, there was growing concern about such maltreatment. Widespread concern among the middle classes emerged about child cruelty carried amongst the poorer populations of the UK. A key concern was that child cruelty contributed to delinquency or potential delinquency in children who needed, therefore, to be 'saved'. As Parton (2007) outlines, the late 19th and early 20th century periods are: 'the period that provided the foundations and many of the central elements for what, until recently, has been termed child protection, and is now called 'the safeguarding of children' (Parton, 2007:10). Contemporary emphasis on **children's rights** has been formed from this background and societal changes in industrialising countries. These rights imply a degree of separation from the family that would have been unthinkable a century earlier. In other words, **what constitutes 'childhood' is historically variable**.

'Childhood' also differs across contexts. As Hart and Tyrer (2006; see also Key Thinker Box 6.1) suggest:

> Every society has concepts and practices which identify "children" as a section of the population distinct from "adults". However, the ways in which different societies and cultures imagine such distinction varies greatly. In any case, the line between "childhood" and "adulthood" is usually vague, with responsibilities and entitlements acquired at various stages and in accordance with factors that extend beyond simple chronological age.
>
> (Hart and Tyrer, 2006:6)

Hart and Tyrer (2006) go on to explain how these **variations in the notion of 'childhood'** might relate to domestic responsibilities, caregiving or agricultural labour – which are all considered to be a normal element of children's lives in some settings, but inappropriate in other settings. The conventional 'Western' view of a child being under 18 years and moving through a stage where they are being socialised towards later engagement in society as adults may not apply in such a universal way. The dominant view in post-1945 social policies in European and North American thought was that children were somehow **'human becomings'** (in the future). This contrasts with the dominant view in sociological studies of their being **'human beings'** (in the present) because of their own rights in the present and not because of their future potential as adults who can contribute to society.

As outlined earlier, international law considers a child to be under 18 years regardless of these variations in the notion of 'childhood' and a variety of views beyond a 'Western' lens. Child 'rescue' – the removal of children from unsatisfactory circumstances – is part of the family-state relationship and best interest principles of the child in many states. **The notion of 'childhood' is varied across time and context.** Childhood has been developed as a sheltered period in 'Western' countries, with the assumption that this period in a child's life requires protection. This is, of course, inconsistent to the realities and lives of many children from 'less privileged or less Westernised backgrounds' (Hart and Tyrer, 2006; see also Cairns, 1996).

Children and young people arriving into 'Western' countries, particularly if travelling alone, can be seen perceived as inconsistent to the view that children should be sheltered and protected. Notions of what constitutes a social problem can also interfere with ensuring the wellbeing of children and young people. The focus on asylum in 'Western' countries might force children and young people into legislative and/or policy frameworks that bear no relation to their lives. Accounts about children beyond such constructions and policy frameworks are often **devoid of more contextualised accounts of alternative forms of 'childhood'**. Complex backstories involving persecution, deprivation, abuse, environmental degradation, family reunion and a range of other possible circumstances driving migration often remain unexplored in these contexts.

Seeberg and Goździak (2016) suggest that: 'increasing numbers of children are growing up, not primarily in a place or a period, but within a social space that we call migrancy.' They outline how where you grow up shapes experiences, life chances, identities and personalities and that constructs around 'childhood' during a given period are important. However, for children who migrate, or children of parents who migrate, they suggest that this in itself becomes a marker. In other words, it is not only the place or time in which children grow up that shapes such 'childhoods' but also the experience of migration itself.

In relation to Vietnamese conceptions of 'childhood' and 'adulthood', Barber and Nguyen (2015) have suggested that **migration by young people can be a rite of passage,** outlining how, in Vietnam: 'migration is often tied into the transition to adulthood for Vietnamese youth through the process of life events and through the taking on of certain financial responsibilities and notably it is signalled through economic success' (Barber and Nguyen, 2015:2).

Economic **success is linked to the transition to adulthood**, with important life events such as marriage, dependent upon this success. As Barber and Nguyen outline:

> Contrary to the Western approaches to child protection and children's rights, which tend to separate economic activities from childhood, Vietnamese practices value and honour the economic contributions made by children.
>
> (2015:3)

Vietnamese children reach adulthood at 16 years of age and are often 'actively encouraged to leave their family to go and seek their futures' (Barber and Nguyen, 2015:8), often through migration.

Points for discussion – socially constructed 'childhood'

- How do you think 'childhood' is experienced across different countries and local contexts?
- Do you consider that there is an ideal version of 'childhood' that all countries should aim for?
- How is 'childhood' used as a concept by campaigning organisations?

Key Thinker Box 6.1   Jason Hart – Children Living in Situations of Political Violence and Armed Conflict and the Role of Anthropology

Jason Hart is a social anthropologist at the University of Bath. His work explores the experiences and responses to young people on the margins of society, particularly around children's participation, child rights, asylum and refugees. Much of his research has been undertaken in situations of political violence, armed conflict and displacement.

In 2006, Hart outlined the role of anthropology in the 'project of saving children' (2006:6). Detailing the work of both Margaret Mead and Eglantyne Jebb, Hart questions why Mead's aim to understand the differences and diversity of children's lives and childhood experiences has progressed more slowly than Jebb's universalising vision of childhood as a period to be enjoyed without responsibilities. In this, Hart suggests that a key challenge for anthropology is the need to question assumptions around the distinctiveness or conceptual boundaries between children and adults, childhood and adulthood.

Also in 2006, Jason Hart and Bex Tyrer explored conducting research with children in situations of armed conflict and emergency contexts beyond the medical and psychological research conducted around trauma in these settings. Suggesting that research should explore the lives of children from their own perspectives, Hart and Tyrer outline what meaningful participation in research might look like in such contexts. After outlining the meaning of 'childhood' and 'children' across cultures, a rationale for child-centred research is advanced that recognises the agency, resilience and resourcefulness of children in the face of extreme adversity. The principles of participatory research – and particular methods of conducting participatory research – are then explored, including the motivations, benefits, risks and hazards of this type of research and how to do this ethically. The selection of language-, culture- and age-appropriate tools that take account of the context within which children live are then examined, and Appendix 1 provides an extensive range of these tools, including timelines, spider diagrams, problem trees and body maps.

Hart continued writing on participation in a 2008 paper that examined how child-focussed international organisations were operationalising participation from the early 1990s onwards. Harts suggests that participatory projects seeking to achieve the transformation of children's lives often pay little attention to the political contexts in which such transformation is sought. As such, limitations of this approach are provided, focussing on power, societal change and the necessary political will to achieve these aims. This ongoing critique that local participatory efforts are disconnected to larger systems, structures and power relations is explored.

Often-used socio-ecological models that nest children within concentric circles from family through to societal relationships are outlined as being 'highly static' (2008:411) if situational and contextual aspects such as rural-urban migration, intra-state conflict and other contexts are not incorporated. Overall, Hart suggests that children may have benefitted from participating in the projects of international and intergovernmental organisations – through enhanced self-confidence, knowledge, skills and networks – but that 'more systemic changes that would positively affect the lives of all remain elusive' (2008:416) without wider societal change.

In a chapter on children and forced migration in 2014, Hart explores how understandings of children in such settings are evolving, outlining three approaches that are shaping understanding of children and forced migration – 'mental health and social work', 'legal' and 'ethnographic' research. Each of these are explored in brief, but mental health scholars explicitly focus on 'trauma' and a trauma-focussed model that pre-supposes 'that children are inherently and universally vulnerable by virtue of their age or stage in the development process' (2014:386). This approach is considered to be especially influential but, by focussing on the psycho-social needs of children, it is also able to sidestep potentially politically sensitive priorities articulated by children themselves. The legal approach relates laws and legal systems that relate to children, such as the UNCRC outlined earlier and is often undertaken to address policy and/or practice to improve the lives of children. Various categories of children are outlined in line with the legal categorisations designed to address the needs of children who have been internally displaced, are separated, or are fleeing sexual violence or forcible recruitment. Hart favours an ethnographic approach that focusses on displacement not as a cause, but rather as a context, for children's experiences. This leaves open the possibility that forced migration may have a negative impact but may also present opportunities around, for example, 'renegotiation of convention hierarchies built around age, gender or socio-economic class' (2014:389).

In 2016, Hart outlined how the age of young displaced people is a key consideration in programmatic efforts, particularly with protracted refugee situations around the globe, and many people find themselves displaced for decades. As Hart explains:

> While some have experienced flight first-had, there are also many who have been born into a setting of displacement and may themselves have become parents or even grandparents to children who inherit refugee status
>
> (2016:219).

Hart suggests that consideration of such generational and the relational dynamics of age is an area of research that is behind understandings around gender. Detailing an account of one young man in Palestine, Hart explores the role of age in the ambiguous and marginal setting of a camp for long-term refugees. Hart outlines how efforts to standardise humanitarian interventions have recently begun to take account of the chronological age of a 'child', 'adolescent' or 'youth'. What Hart asks for is that individual histories of exile be told that consider the complex and dynamic histories of Palestinian refugees in any future search for solutions.

Key references – Jason Hart

Hart, J. (2006) Saving Children: What Role for Anthropology? *Anthropology Today*, 22, 5–8.

Hart, J. (2008) Children's Participation and International Development: Attending to the Political, *International Journal of Children's Rights*, 16, 407–418.

Hart, J. (2014) Children and Forced Migration, in Fiddian-Qasmiyeh, E., Loescher, G., Long, K. and Sigona, N. (Eds.), *The Oxford Handbook of Refugee and Forced Migration Studies*, Oxford University Press, Oxford.

Hart, J. (2016) Locating Young Refugees Historically: Attending to Age Position in Humanitarianism, *European Journal of Development Research*, 26, 219–232.

Hart, J. and Tyrer, B. (2006) *Research with Children Living in Situations of Armed Conflict: Concepts, Ethics and Methods*, Working Paper No.30, Refugee Studies Centre, University of Oxford.

What do we know about 'children on the move'?

Statistics, data and evidence about children on the move are limited. In March 2020, UNICEF, IDMC, IOM, UNHCR, OECD, UNDESA, Eurostat and other supporters launched an International Data Alliance on Children on the Move. It is hoped that this collaboration will improve statistics on children across the range of reasons for migration and consequently enable better protection.

Gaps in statistics remain for children who are forcibly displaced, but of 79.5 million people, an estimated 40% were children and young people below the age of 18 years (UNHCR, 2020). This represents a slight decrease from the previous year, wherein children made up about half of the displaced population (UNHCR, 2019). Statistics produced by UNHCR for end 2018 illustrate how children under the age of 18 made up 52% (16.3 million) of cases where age-disaggregated data was available (UNHCR, 2018).

Flagged as underestimates according to UNHCR, some 27,600 unaccompanied and separated children sought asylum during 2018 which, added to an existing total of 111,000 unaccompanied and separated children, meant 138,600 children were reported to be seeking asylum globally. Based on reports from 60 and 53 countries respectively, both numbers are considered underestimates. Germany received the most asylum claims from unaccompanied and separated children, mainly from children from Afghanistan, followed by children from Somalia, Guinea, Eritrea, Syria and Iraq.

As of the end of 2019, the IDMC (2020) reports that there are **18.3 million internally displaced persons who are children** under the age of 15 years (6.6 million who are under 5 years old and 11.7 million who are 5–14 years old). According to UNICEF (2020), internally displaced children lack access to basic services in many countries around the world. This may limit or deny them the right to education, health and basic protections children are entitled to under the UNCRC. UNICEF (2020) also points to negative coping strategies during internal displacement, such as child labour, child marriage, exploitation, abuse and trafficking. Recording the prevalence of these issues is sensitive and, with IDPs often being in hard-to-reach places, also poses challenges in recording of data. UNICEF (2020) suggests that internally displaced children may be displaced multiple times or living in contexts of protracted internal displacement, again affecting the education and health needs of children. Children's ability to participate in a meaningful way – a key principle of the UNCRC – is severely compromised in these contexts.

Children may inherit statelessness when born to parents without a nationality (Boyden and Hart, 2007). Although thorough statistics on the numbers of people stateless in the world today are lacking, it has been estimated by the Institute on Statelessness and Inclusion (ISI) that there are 15 million people living without a nationality, as of end 2019 (ISI, 2020). In line with Article 7 of the UNCRC, the need for children who are stateless to have their rights protected relies on their right to registration at birth, nationality laws that address gender discrimination and understanding that children born out of recognised wedlock be legally recognised. Children of refugee parents may face particular difficulties in registering births, putting their children at risk of being 'stateless' or 'undocumented' (ISI, 2020).

Hannah Arendt's critiques around the enforceability of human rights are relevant here. Bhabha (2009; also see Key Thinker Box 6.2) has suggested that migrant children – in what she calls 'Arendt's children' – are *de facto* stateless and do not have the same 'right to have rights' as other children. In other words, children might live in the cracks of an incomplete patchwork of nationally-based legal provisions for children on the move.

Undocumented migrant children (Sigona and Hughes, 2012) include those who are not classed as unaccompanied asylum seekers or children considered trafficked. Their research considers the everyday experiences of children in the UK who might have different legal statuses and different levels of access to rights and entitlements as a result. They assert that this hidden population is to some extent uncountable, but estimated in 2010 that there were some 155,000 migrant children in the UK, of which 85,000 are UK born and the remaining 70,000 children had entered the country either as a dependent or independently, through a range of routes (Sigona and Hughes, 2012:29).

As Faulkner (2019) asserts, the trafficking of children has received extensive attention in recent years. Through research in the League of Nations archives in Geneva, Faulkner tracks the evolution of child trafficking, demonstrating parallels with the White Slavery Convention of the early 20th century. In this Faulkner teases out how a predominant focus on trafficking for the purposes of sexual exploitation is predominant in the work of the Committee on the Rights of the Child, as set up under the UNCRC. The focus on 'women and children' across both the 1921 International Convention to Suppress the Traffic in Women and Children and contemporary usage of the 2000 Protocol to Prevent, Suppress and Punish Trafficking in Persons, especially Women and Children (the Palermo Protocol – see Chapter 4) is explored. Faulkner explains how the image of a 'trafficked child' has been constructed within a 'powerful protectionist discourse' that dominates discussions around children, inadvertently stripping children of the autonomy contained within, for example, the UNCRC (Faulkner, 2019:15). Faulkner outlines how the trafficking of children omits the 'means' element of the Palermo Protocol definition and that this in itself **removes the agency of children** to make decisions about their own lives. For Faulkner, a focus on prevention of migration and 'rescue' serves as: 'a deflection from the complicity of states allowing factors that drive migration to flourish and . . . mirrored through today's response to human trafficking' (Faulkner, 2019:16).

The trafficking of children has also been explored within various national contexts (Craig, 2010). For example, Hynes (2010) explored the trafficking of children and young people into, within and out of the UK. A key finding was that this type of forced migration is **often viewed as a one-off, often nationally-bounded, 'event'** by those who have a duty to care for children and young people, but what was required was a broader sociological and international process to provide a greater understanding of the backgrounds of individual children, the human rights contexts within countries of origin and individual migration trajectories undertaken. Hynes (2015) also suggests that for identification of children as having been trafficked, there is a role for migrant and refugee community-based organisations to participate in formal referral processes.

In a recent evidence review of child sexual abuse and sexual exploitation across high-, middle- and low-income countries, it was found that there is a lack of evidence in humanitarian contexts around child sexual exploitation (Radford *et al.*, 2015a). Gaps in protection were found in contexts that were considered to be about short-term relief efforts rather than those with a focus on the longer-term needs of children and their rights to participation and protection.

As with definitions around the forced migration of adults, definitions and labels assigned to children are powerful. Children and young people also often have to contend with their being **no details of child-specific forms of**

persecution within international instruments such as the 1951 Refugee Convention. They might also have to contend with the **conflicting emphasis on participation and agency** contained within Conventions and Protocols surrounding the particular form of migration undertaken. Their **migration pathways** may be misinterpreted, or reframed, to fit within nationally based legislative and policy frameworks.

Points for discussion – 'children on the move'

- Can you think of any reason why children may need to migrate outside of the categories explained in this section?
- What happens to children who move themselves alongside other members of their family?

Key Thinker Box 6.2   Jacqueline Bhabha – *Child Migration and Human Rights in a Global Age*

Jacqueline Bhabha is a Professor of Health and Human Rights at Harvard University and Director of Research at the FXB Center for Health and Human Rights. From 1997 to 2001 Bhabha founded and directed the Human Rights Program at the University of Chicago after practising human rights law in London and at the European Court of Human Rights. Her publications focus on issues such as transnational child migration, refugee protection, children's rights and citizenship.

Bhabha and Young's (1999) early work on **child-specific persecution** as a way of advancing grants of asylum for children as independent applicants was highly influential on the development of US Asylum Child Guidelines, leading to research into 'seeking asylum alone' across the US, Australia, the UK, the Netherlands, Germany, Austria, Sweden and Norway.

Another key contribution made by Jacqueline Bhabha has been a 2009 paper engaging with Hannah Arendt's question around who has the 'right to have rights' and whether children who migrate in the contemporary world have such rights to rights. Bhabha refers to these children as **'Arendt's children'**, functionally stateless regardless of whether or not they have legal nationality. Bhabha outlines how children have, in theory, rights under international law but that the issue of enforceability (see Chapter 5) denies these in practice. Bhabha's (2011) ongoing work on child statelessness was prompted by the way in which family reunification rules and practice privilege the adult citizen when considering who has capacity to initiate family reunification.

In 2014 Bhabha published *Child Migration and Human Rights in a Global Age*, which explores rights of family life, citizenship and the contested terrain of intercountry adoption as well as consideration of children within armed conflict, children who are trafficked, the unequal battle for refugee protection experienced by children and 'survival' migration for children and adolescents. She notes early on in the book that although migration journeys undertaken by children are complex, the **backstories of children remain 'a largely untold and unanalysed story'** (2014:1). Bhabha then goes on to argue that children tend not to feature in the larger picture of migration, that migration is now often seen as a 'voluntary adult phenomenon requiring management and control' (2014:1) and that children tend only to feature as 'possessions of others' (2014:3) and occasional 'appendages to adults' (2014:2) in this picture. It is in this context that Bhabha asks whether our neglect of child migrants' rights is about an unresolved ambivalence in terms of the policy challenges its presents and protection gaps they face. However, Bhabha also argues that it is **not simply invisibility or lack of awareness** of the issues children face. Rather, 'injustices are not self-correcting once they come to light' (2014:14) due, it is argued, to this **unresolved ambivalence towards children who migrate**. Bhabha also then sets out the gulf between children's rights under international law (the UNCRC) and the lived realities of these children who find themselves in detention, denied family reunion or guardians who are able to help them navigate complex immigration or social care processes and the range of rights provided to children with citizenship.

A report in 2016 by Bhabha – 'Children on the Move: An Urgent Human Rights and Child Protection Priority' – documented protection failures of children on the move, pointing out how protection, particularly during transit, is lacking worldwide. It explores siloed legislative frameworks and the failure of law to reflect the realities of what it means for children and young people to be separated from support networks. Bhabha *et al.* outline how **legal frameworks for children on the move fall into three principal approaches – regulatory, criminalizing and protective**. The regulatory approach (most domestic and regional immigration law) relates to legislation that assumes 'children are dependents of the family unit, without autonomous agency' (2016:6). The criminalizing approach applies to both 'smuggled' and 'trafficked' children, focussing on 'penalizing and preventing exploitative child migration' in a punitive fashion, dating back to legislation on the 'white slave trade' (2016:7). For children who are trafficked, Bhabha *et al.* outline how the Palermo Protocol does not require states to treat victims of trafficking with the same long-term protection as for refugees. It is also argued that the child-trafficking lens 'dominates current policy responses to the exploitation of children on the move', leading to some unintended effects, including 'removal' and 'rescue' from exploitation without substantive engagement with drivers or root causes of vulnerability in the first instance (2016:9). The protective approach relates to the UNCRC and other international laws and guidelines that provide a core set of universally applicable human rights for the protection of children. After mapping these existing protection frameworks, Bhabha sets out a number of case studies about children in transit in Lesbos, Greece; on the Western Balkan Route via Serbia; during entry into the USA and Australia; the impacts of persistent exclusion for the Rohingya leaving Myanmar; and internal migration from Bihar to Rajasthan in India.

Jacqueline Bhabha continues to conduct research on adolescents at risk of violence, social exclusion or discrimination. Together with Mike Dottridge, Bhabha also continues to provide policy recommendations that children should be recognised first and foremost as children, regardless of their immigration status; the root causes that drive children to leave their homes should be addressed; and family unity should be respected and ensured for all children when it is in their best interests (Bhabha and Dottridge, 2016, 2017).

Key references – Jacqueline Bhabha

Bhabha, J. (2009) Arendt's Children: Do Today's Migrant Children have a Right to Have Rights? *Human Rights Quarterly*, 31(2), 410–451.

Bhabha, J. (Ed.) (2011) *Children Without a State: A Global Human Rights Challenge*, MIT Press, Cambridge, MA.

Bhabha, J. (2014) *Child Migration and Human Rights in a Global Age*, Princeton University Press, Princeton, NJ and Oxford.

Bhabha, J. and Dottridge, M. (2016) *Recommended Principles to Guide Actions Concerning Children on the Move and Other Children Affected by Migration*, United Nations Action for Cooperation against Trafficking in Persons (UN-ACT), Bangkok.

Bhabha, J. and Dottridge, M. with Hong, A. (2017) *Child Rights in the Global Compacts: Recommendations for Protecting, Promoting and Implementing the Human Rights of Children on the Move in the Proposed Global Compacts*, Initiative for Child Rights in the Global Compacts, convened by Save the Children and Terre des Hommes, view at: https://principlesforcom.jimdofree.com/who/

Bhabha, J. and Young, W. (1999) Not an Adult in Miniature: Children as Refugees, *International Journal of Refugee Law*, 11(1), 84–125.

Bhabha, J. et al. (2016) *Children on the Move: An Urgent Human Rights and Child Protection Priority*, Harvard FXB Center for Health and Human Rights, Boston.

Key Thinker Box 6.3   Mike Dottridge – *Children on the Move*

Mike Dottridge has worked in the human rights field for four decades, having worked for both Amnesty International, where he focussed on sub-Saharan Africa, and Anti-Slavery International as Director between 1996 and 2002. Much of his work is focussed on the prevention, protection and rights of adults and children in situations of exploitation, be it concerns about child labour, sexual exploitation of children, forced labour or trafficking in human beings. He has worked for various UN organisations, NGOs and private donors in the role of consultant, and much of this is based around helping organisations with institutional learning and lessons learnt.

After a decade learning about trafficked and exploited children, he became increasingly worried about the tendency of international organisations to regard all independent child migrants as victims of exploitation. In 2008 his report for Terre des Hommes – 'Kids Abroad: Ignore Them, Abuse Them or Protect Them? Lessons on how to Protect Children on the Move from being Exploited' – focussed on young people who leave home or travel abroad to seek work and also on children who are sent away from home by their parents. This report **explored initiatives which have had the effect of reducing the likelihood of children being subjected to economic or sexual exploitation**. Looking beyond the 'vulnerable situations' faced by children, techniques that have proven helpful to children on the move are examined beyond those outlined within a narrow focus on sexual abuse and child trafficking. Dottridge suggests that:

> more general methods that serve to protect children in general from abuse, or ALL young people who travel as 'separated children' have been neglected.
>
> (Dottridge, 2008:9, author's emphasis)

Thereafter the report focusses on risks faced by children and how to minimise these risks; chapters on Central America, Southeast Europe, Western Europe, West Africa, South Asia and Southeast Asia; a discussion of the commonalities of initiatives across these six regions; then techniques described across these regions to enhance the protective capacity of individual children, their families and communities. Organisations are not forgotten, with a dichotomy revealed between those that think children should be discouraged from moving or migrating altogether and those who advocate making migration less unsafe (Dottridge, 2008). This latter type of organisation is considered optimum, and recommendations around **assistance in transit**, **listening to children** and **attention to 'indigenous' practices** in the effort to protect children are made.

Dottridge has a keen interest in the methods that help young people to be safe while migrating. In a 2012 report for Terre des Hommes, Dottridge developed a handbook for organisations wanting to prevent child trafficking, exploitation and the worst forms of child labour based on two workshops in Kolkata and Bangkok. He reiterates that organisations involved in trying to prevent children from being exploited have noted the weakness that methods used are approached by form of exploitation, as if requiring their own specific prevention methods. Their conclusion was that **more effort should be made to build child protection systems which are designed to protect all children from harm, abuse and exploitation** (Dottridge, 2012:11). In this he refers to Roger Hart's Ladder of Participation to explain why listening to children on the move is important and how important it is to move beyond tokenism in these efforts.

With a foreword by François Crépeau, the former UN Special Rapporteur on the Human Rights of Migrants, Dottridge edited *Children on the Move* in 2013. This outlined the rights of all children in the context of international migration, pointing out there is **no one homogenous profile of the migrant child**. The broad concept of children 'on the move' was then defined:

> Those children moving for a variety of reasons, voluntarily or involuntarily, within or between countries, with or without their parents or other primary caregivers, and whose movement, while it may open up opportunities, might also place them at risk (or at an increased risk) of economic or sexual exploitation, abuse neglect and violence.
>
> (Introductory chapter by Dottridge, M. in Crépeau *et al.*, 2013)

This definition, which had been adopted by the Inter-Agency Working Group on Children on the Move, thereby captured not only the difficulties faced by children when changing their place of residence, but also the opportunities they may come across in doing so during their own migration projects (François Crépeau *et al.*, 2013:7).

A 2014 report looked at locally developed child protection practices concerning mobile children in West Africa. This report consolidated information available about locally developed practices to protect children leaving home to earn a living, be that before departure, while travelling or upon reaching their destination. The report concentrated on Benin, Burkina Faso, Guinea, Mali and Togo, with additional contributions from Ghana. Addressing both positive and negative aspects of children's mobility, both risks and opportunities associated with movement were explored, beyond the imposition of concepts within legal definitions such as 'child trafficking'. West African organisations involved suggested **the term *mobility* was a better descriptor than *migration* or *movement*,** allowing for an understanding of the social mobility of young people involved. Concentrating on bottom-up approaches to develop local strengths rather than top-down approaches from government level that were operationalised through community-based systems, the concept of **locally-developed child protection practices** emerged.

Related to this, thorough understanding of how children's mobility concerns religious practices drew on findings about ceremonies being significant and having protective effects before a child left home. These included 'initiation ceremonies, . . . family rituals such as weddings, naming ceremonies (baptisms) and scarification (a sign of belonging, identity recognition) provid[ing] security to the child' (Dottridge, 2014:24). These forms of identity allowed for subsequent interaction with **people who shared the same identity as a form of protection after leaving home** but are 'frequently regarded as unacceptable by law enforcement or child protection officials in the countries concerned' (Ibid., 2014:24).

In 2017, Mike Dottridge, together with Jacqueline Bhabha (see Key Thinker Box 6.2), provided **guidance on child rights within the two new Global Compacts**, putting forward goals, targets and indicators to ensure a common global approach to protecting children on the move.

By 2020, Dottridge's work on trafficked children were reflective of a disillusionment with government policies around the world and a reluctance to listen to children or take their views into account. He drew attention to numerous cases in which anti-trafficking policies backfired against the children or adults whom they were meant to benefit. The contrast between entitlements and practice were highlighted, giving consideration to the different forms of exploitation, including begging, stealing and within a range of labour sectors. This work concludes by noting that **trafficked children continue to face immense challenges in getting access to justice**.

Key references – Mike Dottridge

Bhabha, J. and Dottridge, M. with Hong, A. (2017) *Child Rights in the Global Compacts: Recommendations for Protecting, Promoting and Implementing the Human Rights of Children on the Move in the Proposed Global Compacts*, Initiative for Child Rights in the Global Compacts, convened by Save the Children and Terre des Hommes, view at: https://principlesforcom.jimdofree.com/who/

Crépeau, François *et al.* (2013) *Children on the Move*, Inter-Agency Working Group on Children on the Move and International Organization for Migration (IOM), Geneva.

Dottridge, M. (2008) *Kids Abroad: Ignore Them, Abuse Them or Protect Them? Lessons on how to Protect Children on the Move from Being Exploited*, Terre des Hommes International Federation, Geneva.

Dottridge, M. (2012) *What Can You Do to Protect Children on the Move? A Handbook to Enable Organisations to Review How they Prevent Child Trafficking and Exploitation, and Whether they Ensure that the Best Interests of the Child Guide their Activities*, Terre des Hommes International Federation, Geneva.

Dottridge, M. (2014) *Locally-Developed Child Protection Practices Concerning Mobile Children in West Africa*, Terre des Hommes and the Regional Working Group on Child Protection in West Africa, Geneva.

Dottridge, M. (2020) Trafficked Children, in Todres, J. and King, S.M. (Eds.), *The Oxford Handbook of Children's Rights Law*, Oxford University Press, Oxford.

Are children an inherently 'vulnerable' group?

Populations of children and young people who are often identified as 'vulnerable' in policy, programs, projects and practice include children who are considered displaced, unaccompanied, affected by human trafficking, somehow marginalized and/or 'at risk', including children within care systems. This notion of 'vulnerability' is often cited around the safeguarding and protection of children by state agents authorized to intervene in the lives of such children or international agencies mandated to protect displaced people. **Vulnerability is a broad and contested term**, and it is necessary to use it in context, looking at the broader situation in which it is being used, particularly around power relations that may have rendered people vulnerable.

Hart and Tyrer (2006) suggest that children living in situations of armed conflict are perceived as being 'victims' first and foremost, passively in receipt of violence by adults. This perception, they suggest, is in line with dominant notions of 'childhood' and ignores the resilience and resourcefulness shown by some children in the face of adversity. They outline how:

> In considering protection it is important to avoid the view of children as inherently vulnerable. . . . Firstly, such thinking serves to distract us from the ways in which children may manifest strength and capacities for coping with adversity. Secondly, the assumption of inherent vulnerability can blind us to the ways in which vulnerability may actually be created, not least through the practices of organization that see which as victims and, as a result, fail to engage with them as participants in their own protection. . . . Thirdly, the association of 'children' – as an entire section of the population – with vulnerability may cause us to overlook the fact that no group of children are homogenous in terms of the risk that they face. Age, gender, class, education, language, particular settings, all position children differently with respect to the risk (and opportunities) created by conflict. Discrimination and marginalization are, in themselves, sources of risk that will obviously affect certain children more than others.
>
> (Hart and Tyrer, 2006:10)

O'Connell Davidson and Farrow (2007) reiterate a number of these points in a report on **child migration and the construction of vulnerability**. In this they outline how policies introduced by national governments to manage migration have profound implications for children's rights. They suggest that policy makers have to date paid little attention to issues around children and migration and, where they have, this has been around 'child trafficking' (particularly for sexual exploitation) and 'unaccompanied' asylum-seeking and refugee children as their entry point, to the detriment of children who fall outside these categorisations (Ibid., 2007:9). They note that an over-emphasis on trafficking, out of context with broader migration patterns, runs the risk of the adoption of a crime-control rather than rights perspective, with trafficking being used by governments to develop more restrictive approaches to migration. They outline how **States play a role in constructing vulnerability of certain groups of children** through immigration regimes and that rights violations experienced by children are not inevitable consequences of migration, but rather reflect a lack of political will to protect the rights of children. They also suggest that policies emphasizing the vulnerability of the 'separated child' need to be modified and balanced by a recognition that independent child migration can lead to positive as well as negative outcomes and that children who do migrate with families are not necessarily safe from harm (Ibid., 2007:11). They call for safer routes and regular channels for children to migrate and, upon arrival, meaningful forms of participation in decision about their own futures, **recognizing children's own capacity for agency** during the migration processes.

The **absence of opportunities for children to migrate safely** is magnified within countries that have tight border controls. In the UK, the number of children who arrive alone and go missing from care within the first few hours or days has started to be explored in the literature (ECPAT UK, 2016; Setter, 2017). In 2016, ECPAT UK found that 28% of children within the study who were suspected or identified as having been trafficked went missing from local authority care at least once. Other studies have found that Vietnamese children in particular tend to go missing from local authority care (Kohli *et al.*, 2015, 2019). Arguably, tight border controls and a perception that there is a culture of disbelief towards people arriving into the UK have rendered 'vulnerable' children who have their own concept of what is safe or who can or cannot be trusted.

The focus of the UNCRC on children having the right to express their own views, to have their own opinions taken into account (Article 12) and to participate recognises the agency of a child or young person. Participation is seen as both an end in itself and as a means to realise other rights within the UNCRC (Hart and Tyrer, 2006). This includes children living in situations of armed conflict or post-conflict contexts where past discussions have tended to focus on them as 'victims' – passive recipients of the violence of adults and experiencing 'trauma' and 'damage' as a consequence (Hart and Tyrer, 2006:9).

Points for discussion – children and young people as 'victims' or 'agents'?

- Discuss how you feel about children – do you see them as passive 'victims' or resilient 'agents' of their own destinies?
- How do you think this relates to the construction of 'childhood' as a period of innocence?
- How would you feel about children in different contexts such as within an industrialised setting and within a refugee camp?

'Women and children', men and boys

The causes and consequences of forced migration are gendered, as is the protection of those displaced, including during asylum processes (Crawley *et al.*, 2018; Ezeilo, 2018; Faulkner, 2019; Fiddian-Qasmiyeh, 2014; Hynes, 2017; Indra, 1999; Kempadoo, 2015; Malkki, 1995; Pearce *et al.*, 2009). Women and children have typically been depicted as 'apolitical', 'weak', 'vulnerable', 'victims' and/or 'carers' across different contexts of displacement. As Malkki suggested in 1995, viewing photographs of refugees results in a **portrayal of women engaged in various forms of being productive, nurturing or engaged in virtuous activities** and creates an awareness of 'the perennial resonance of the woman with her child. This is not just any woman; she is composed as an almost madonnalike figure' (Ibid., 1995:11).

This embodiment of the 'refugee woman' as a pure 'victim' is highly problematic (1995:12). Attempts to engender knowledge and integrate gender into forced migration research and practice involve challenges (Indra, 1999). Indra outlines discourses around gender that are pertinent in framing, representing and revisioning forced migration studies. As Indra suggests:

> [There are] two very basic assertions drawn from contemporary feminist theory in the social sciences: that neither in talk, research, analysis, policy, nor programming can 'gender' be equated solely with women, nor solely with women's activities, beliefs, goals, or needs; and that 'gender' is instead a key *relational* dimension of human activity.
>
> (Indra, 1999:2, author's emphasis)

Indra then provides an account of development discourses relevant to gender, from the 'Women in Development' (WID) approach of the 1970s, the 'Women and Development' (WAD) approach from the late 1970s, to the 'Gender and Development' (GAD) orientation from the late 1980s and during the 1990s that drew on Amartya Sen's highly influential formulation of entitlement analysis applied to the study of famine (see Chapter 5, Key Thinker Box 5.2). Gender and forced migration (GAFM) is taken up by Fiddian-Qasmiyeh (2014), who outlines how the 'Women in Forced Migration' (WIFM) and the 'Gender and Forced Migration' (GAFM) paradigms broadly paralleled the WID and GAD discourses. Fiddian-Qasmiyeh (2014) also details the feminist critiques of the 1951 Refugee Convention, often approached and interpreted through a framework of male experiences. It is suggested that this Convention has failed to recognise women's resistance to oppression and violence, making understanding the gendered nature of forced displacement an add-on to attempts to protect refugees.

Additionally, the 1951 Refugee Convention does not address violence that occurs in the private sphere, such as domestic or sexual violence. This has led to arguments that it is discriminatory in contexts where there are effectively no public support services, or where legal frameworks do not recognise interpersonal violence.

Strategies around the prevention of violence against children, and in particular sexual abuse and sexual exploitation, tend to be approached in three ways (Radford *et al.*, 2015a, 2015b). Firstly, **approaches that are aimed at mobilisation to change social norms, attitudes and behaviour**. For example, programmes within refugee camps often seek to address interpersonal or gender-based violence, attempting to change attitudes and behaviours around these forms of violence. Secondly, **situational prevention** approaches seek to alter the environmental and situational contexts that provide opportunities for abuse. An example might be changing aid provisions to include firewood so that women no longer have to forage and collect firewood in unregulated terrain. Thirdly, prevention may be approached by attempts to **reduce risks and vulnerabilities** of children. Examples include vocational education, gender equity programmes, conditional and unconditional cash transfers. As Radford *et al.* (2015a, 2015b) found in an evidence review of sexual abuse and sexual exploitation, there are many such prevention strategies operating around the globe. In high-income countries these tend to be focussed more on child sexual abuse, whilst in low- and middle-income countries more attention has been given to child sexual exploitation, AIDS prevention and gender-based intimate partner violence (Radford *et al.*, 2015a, 2015b).

Within trafficking debates, the issue of **sexual exploitation** is hotly debated and often **uncritically conflated with 'sex work'** (Agustin, 2007; Anderson, 2013; Doezma, 2010). Agustin (2007) has argued that the label of 'trafficking' invokes a victimising discourse and does not reflect reality. She argues that the 'helpers' and moral agendas surrounding 'rescuing' those involved denies agency and makes those involved passive 'victims' (2007). Gendered perspectives of 'victims' being female and 'perpetrators' of trafficking being male are only now being slowly broken down, 20 years after the Palermo Protocol defined this crime.

People who are displaced have sometimes been considered within analytical frameworks that break down the journeys they have been through, from country of origin through to country of asylum and, in a number of cases, return to countries of origin. The experiences of women and children during *dis*placement as well as their journeys towards future *em*placement highlight how separate legal and policy frameworks make finding spaces for disclosure, recovery or restoring trust complex (Hynes, 2017).

Sexual and gender-based violence (SGBV) during conflict and/or forcible displacement **rarely incorporates displaced men and boys** into programming (Fiddian-Qasmiyeh, 2014). Male experiences of SGBV during displacement and/or human trafficking are beginning to be documented (Dolan, 2014). However, as Dolan (2014) explains, reports of sexual violence against men and boys have been found in major conflict zones including Afghanistan, Cambodia, Northern Ireland, Rwanda, South Africa and the former Yugoslavia. Many present-day conflict-affected countries do not have laws that provide protection to male victims of sexual violence, again including Afghanistan, but also Egypt, Malaysia, Myanmar, Nigeria, Sudan, South Sudan and Yemen. Dolan notes that precise evidence of prevalence is difficult to get and that 'Internalised feelings of shame, fear of stigmatization, and legal frameworks and social services that do not recognise men as victims' prevent disclosure and reporting (2014:2). Dolan also questions gendered assumptions, which have obscured sexual violence towards women and girls, masking what is happening to men and boys. Dolan questions frameworks in which a **'real man' is defined as strong, in control and invulnerable** and **women are essentialised as submissive, weak and vulnerable** (2014:2). In post-conflict settings, levels of sexual violence against males are higher than assumed or publicly admitted and, as a consequence, are rarely included in humanitarian programmes.

Another example, this time in the UK, in a report for the Children's Society, details of public enquiries into the 'internal trafficking' and 'child sexual exploitation' of girls are noted, but the need to consider how boys and young men are also affected who are often obscured from reports is noted as well (Leon and Raws, 2016):

> Once in the UK, sexual exploitation of boys is likely to be embedded within multiple forms of exploitation, which can obscure its existence from the authorities. The criminalisation of trafficked boys – for activities they have been forced to undertake as part of their exploitation – can also shift the focus of interventions away from inquiry into potential trafficking or sexual exploitation.
>
> (Leon and Raws, 2016:14)

Noting the barriers involved in disclosing sexual exploitation, Leon and Raws (2016) detail how **men and boys are reluctant to be identified as 'victims'** within trafficking discourses and may wish to avoid any action that will negate family expectations and their responsibilities towards family in the longer term.

In a systematic review of prevention and management strategies for the consequences of gender-based violence (GBV) in refugee settings, Asgary *et al.* (2013) point out the lack of evidence relating to the efficacy and effectiveness of responses to GBV. They outline how multiple panels of expert recommendations and **existing guidelines are not supported by primary data** on actual displaced populations. Rather they are largely broad, theoretical, expertise-driven and emphasise the need for good data collection but based on unpublished data (Asgary *et al.*, 2013). These are gaps in protection in humanitarian or emergency contexts that require further research and evidence.

Key concept and point for discussion – sexual and gender-based violence (SGBV)

- Who do you consider might be most affected by SGBV before, during and after conflict?
- What types of SGBV might occurring during the journey towards a safer destination?
- Who do you think men and boys might have been concentrated on less than women and girls in this respect?

Case Study 6.2 Cambodia-Thailand Border – Lifting the Sarongs of Recipients of Aid

In what would now be perceived as an extraordinary set of events along the Cambodian-Thailand border in the mid-1980s, the gender of recipients of aid became a key part of the distribution of aid leading to a 'women only' system. The layers of power within refugee camps led to a point wherein a system was introduced involving only women and girls over 8 years old or 110cm in height. These women and girls would receive enough food to feed 1,850 calories per day to 2.75 people per week. This 'women only' distribution system caused significant food shortages in many households (Reynell, 1989:74–75). This system had been brought in to prevent male combatants from receiving food aid and make it logistically easier to distribute food by halving the number of recipients. Tickets entitling women and girls to receive food were handed out during headcounts wherein families with insufficient food rations tried to pass ineligible children through the screening gates (Ibid., 1989:76). As Reynell recounts:

> At the time of the six-monthly headcounts, when ration tickets were distributed, 8-year-old girls queued up and passed by a screening gate so that their height and sex could be checked. Parents with more boys than girls often tried to disguise them by dressing them in girls' clothing and allowing them to grow their hair long. To prevent this method of getting extra rations, agency workers used to examine the children's genitals. This practice as later banned by UNBRO but, despite this, when the child was found to be male, the Khmer youths

standing by the gate would add to the child's humiliation by grabbing his genitals and laughing and jeering.

(Reynell, 1989:159)

That this system led parents to encourage children to be deceitful was, at that time, also deeply humiliating towards boys. Girls too young to be eligible for rations would be dressed up with large hats and built-up shoes and chastised if unsuccessful. Ultimately UNBRO decided to change this ration system to one of direct distribution, reducing the severe inequalities in people's access to food.

Safe spaces, advocates and guardians

Much has been learned about the provision of aid, child protection and safeguarding of children and young people since that outlined in historic Case Study 6.2, and there are now standards in place to avoid such degrading practices.

The **Sphere Standards** set out a humanitarian charter and established minimum standards in humanitarian responses (see www.sphereproject.org). The Sphere Standards began in 1997, bringing humanitarian agencies together to improve the quality of humanitarian assistance and improve accountability of humanitarian actors. The **Sphere Handbook** is the most recognised set of common principles and universal minimum standards used in humanitarian responses. It is based on two core beliefs:

*   Those affected by disaster or conflict have a right to life with dignity and, therefore, a right to assistance
*   All possible steps should be taken to alleviate human suffering arising out of disaster or conflict

Point 7 of these standards relates to the right to protection and security, in particular the safety and security of people in situations of disaster or conflict who are of particular humanitarian concern, including the protection of refugees and internally displaced persons. It outlines how the right to seek asylum or sanctuary remains vital to the protection of those facing persecution or violence, relating this to the principle of *non-refoulement* under the 1951 Refugee Convention and the 1998 Guiding Principles on Internal Displacement and related regional and national laws.

For children, the adoption of a **Safe Spaces** approach in developmental and mainly rural areas allows for the creation of safe spaces close to home where adolescents can discuss problems with their peers in small groups and build social networks away from the pressures of family and male-centred society (Radford *et al.*, 2015a, 2015b). In refugee camps, some international agencies have established **Child Friendly Spaces** to allow children space to play and interact, but also to allow space for child protection. For example, World Vision set up Child Friendly Spaces within the camps in Bangladesh for children of the Rohingya population.

Within industrialised countries, **multi-agency approaches** are fairly well established, providing children who are separated or on the move with access to national child protection processes and systems. The notion of the right to individual Guardianship is also often key to the protection of children and their best interests. The type of protection and care received from a Guardian depends upon the country in which the child has entered and also upon the legal status of the child. For example, children who are seeking asylum or have experienced trafficking may be more likely to access this type of provision. In Europe, children seeking asylum have the right to a representative under the Common European Asylum System. However, although **references to such a 'legal guardian' appear in the UNCRC**, there is no uniform approach to implementation. Where Guardianship is effective, children and young people have been found to navigate complex systems of social care, immigration and criminal justice more effectively, resulting in fairer outcomes (Kohli *et al.*, 2015). In Norway, the right of children to participate and express their own views has been taken into the asylum adjudication process through the introduction of **'child conversations'**, which allow for less formal conversations than the adult asylum interview system of many other countries within Europe (Liden and Rusten, 2007). The authors also raise the need for increased awareness of child-specific forms of persecution and a more systematic approach to the use of human rights standards in the analysis of claims (Ibid., 2007:274).

Key Thinker Box 6.4   Heaven Crawley – *When is a Child not a Child?*

Heaven Crawley is a Professor at the Centre for Trust, Peace and Social Relations at Coventry University, where she now leads a major project on South-South Migration – the Migration for Development and Equality (MIDEQ) Hub (MIDEQ) – which aims to understand relationships between migration and inequality in the context of the Global South. Prior to this, Heaven Crawley had been Head of Asylum and Migration Research at the UK Home Office, an associate director at the Institute for Public Policy Research (IPPR) and a consultant and Director for the Centre for Migration Policy Research (CMPR) at Swansea University. She has published on a wide range of asylum and immigration issues, including issues around gender and the experiences of children and young people on the move. As will be seen in the final chapter of this book, Heaven Crawley has recently focussed on the experiences of people crossing the Mediterranean during Europe's so-called 'migration crisis' and the failures of politicians, policy makers and the media to accurately reflect and respond to evidence on its causes and consequences.

Her work on children and young people relates in part to assessing the age of children, which has become a key aspect of asylum policy in the UK. Heaven Crawley's 2007 publication *When is a Child not a Child? Asylum, Age Disputes and the Process of Age Assessment* provided the first detailed, evidence-based analysis of this practice in relation to age disputes of children and young people seeking asylum in the UK. Age disputes were then arising at ports or screening units when an asylum claim was first being made, and they continue to take place today. They involved **a child trying to prove how old they are in order to access the protections available for other children**, usually through social services departments. At the time of writing in 2007, nearly half (45%) of all asylum applicants presenting as separated children were age disputed and treated as adults. A significant proportion were then subsequently assessed as being under 18 years old. These disputes had remained unresolved over time with implications for these children (Crawley, 2007).

The research found that age disputes were linked to 'prevailing cultures of cynicism and disbelief among immigration officers and some social workers' (Crawley, 2007). It also found there was an **over-reliance on physical appearance as an indicator of age**; that there were failings in procedures for appropriate referrals made by children; and that there was considerable variation in the quality of the age assessment process. It was also found that:

> There is a potential conflict of interest between the requirement of social service departments to undertake age assessments and the obligation to provide services to children in need.

For a separated child, the **implications of an incorrect age assessment** meant that social care support, access to education and other basic services were affected when (wrongly) age assessed as an adult.

In a subsequent 2009 paper, Heaven Crawley continued to explore the experiences of separated children during asylum interviews. The way these interviews were conducted led Crawley to suggest they were based around a particular conceptualisation of 'childhood' that undermines the ability of children to fully articulate their experiences and thereby secure access to protection, rights and entitlements under international and domestic laws. A particularly disturbing aspect of these findings was that **separated asylum-seeking children were significantly less likely to be granted refugee status than adults** and that children expressing political views and agency were often not being considered to be children at all.

Heaven Crawley now conducts research about global, local and social inequalities that limit human potential and opportunities to move safely, again linked to gender, age and ethnicity that affect the ability to access protection, rights and entitlements enshrined within law.

Key references – Heaven Crawley

Crawley, H. (2007) *When is a Child not a Child? Asylum, Age Disputes and the Process of Age Assessment*, Immigration Law Practitioners' Association (ILPA), London.
Crawley, H. (2009) 'No One Gives You a Chance to Say What You are Thinking': Finding Space for Children's Agency in the UK Asylum System, *Area*, 42(2), 162–169.

Further reading

Aries, P. (1973) *Centuries of Childhood*, Penguin Books, Harmondsworth.
Boyden, J. and Hart, J. (2007) The Statelessness of the World's Children, *Children and Society*, 21(4), 237–248.
D'Costa, B. (2018) Catching Dreams and Building Hopes for Children: A Research-led Policy Agenda on Migration and Displacement, *Migration Policy Practice*, VIII(2).
Dolan, C. (2014) *Into the Mainstream: Addressing Sexual Violence against Men and Boys in Conflict: A Briefing Paper*, Overseas Development Institute, London, Plan International, War Child, London and Refugee Law Project, Makerere University, Kampala.
Indra, D. (1999) *Engendering Forced Migration: Theory and Practice*, Berghahn Books, Oxford and New York.
Institute on Statelessness and Inclusion (2020) *The World's Stateless: Deprivation of Nationality*, ISI, London.
James, A. and Prout, A. (Eds.) (1997) *Constructing and Reconstructing Childhood*, Falmer Press, London.
O'Connell Davidson, J. and Farrow, C. (2007) *Child Migration and the Construction of Vulnerability*, Save the Children Sweden and University of Nottingham, Nottingham.
Parton, N. (2007) Safeguarding Children: A Socio-Historical Analysis, in Wilson, K. and James, A., *The Child Protection Handbook* (3rd ed.), Balliere Tindall Elsevier, Edinburgh, London and New York.
Passarlay, G. (2016) *The Lightless Sky: A Twelve-Year-Old Refugee's Extraordinary Journey Across Half the World*, Harper Collins, New York.
Wells, K. (2009) *Childhood in a Global Perspective*, Polity Press, Cambridge.

References

Agustin, L. M. (2007) *Sex at the Margins: Migration, Labour Markets and the Rescue Industry*, Zed Books, London and New York.
Anderson, B. (2013) *Us & Them? The Dangerous Politics of Immigration Control*, Oxford University Press, Oxford.
Aries, P. (1973) *Centuries of Childhood*, Penguin, Harmondsworth.
Asgary, R., Emery, E. and Wong, M. (2013) Systematic Review of Prevention and Management Strategies for the Consequences of Gender-Based Violence in Refugee Settings, *International Health*, 5, 85–91.

Barber, T. and Nguyen, H. (2015) *'Becoming Adult by Remaining a Minor': Reconfigurations of Adulthood and Wellbeing by Young Vietnamese Migrants in the UK*, Working Paper, Researching Young Migrants' Uncertain Futures, Oxford.

Beddoe, C. (2017) *An Independent Inquiry into the Situation of Separated and Unaccompanied Minors in Parts of Europe*, Human Trafficking Foundation, London.

Bhabha, J. and Young, W. (1999) Not an Adult in Miniature: Children as Refugees, *International Journal of Refugee Law*, 11(1), 84–125.

Bhabha, J. et al. (2016) *Children on the Move: An Urgent Human Rights and Child Protection Priority*, Harvard FXB Center for Health and Human Rights, Boston.

Cairns, E. (1996) *Children and Political Violence*, Blackwell Publishers Ltd, Oxford.

Craig, G. (Ed.) (2010) *Child Slavery Now: A Contemporary Reader*, Policy Press, Bristol.

Crawley, H., Duvell, F., Jones, K., McMahon, S. and Sigona, N. (2018) *Unravelling Europe's 'Migration Crisis': Journeys over Land and Sea*, Policy Press, Bristol.

Doezma, J. (2010) *Sex Slaves and Discourse Masters: The Construction of Trafficking*, Zed Books, London.

ECPAT UK and Missing People (2016) *Heading Back to Harm: A Study on Trafficked and Unaccompanied Children Going Missing from Care in the UK*, ECPAT UK and Missing People, London.

Ezeilo, J. (2018) Trafficking in Human Beings in the African Context, in Piotrowicz, R., Rijken, C. and Uhl, B.H. (Eds.), *Routledge Handbook of Human Trafficking*, Routledge, Abingdon, Oxfordshire and New York.

Faulkner, E. (2019) Historical Evolution of the International Legal Responses to the Trafficking of Children: A Critique, in Winterdyk, J. and Jones, J. (Eds.), *The Palgrave International Handbook of Human Trafficking*, Palgrave Macmillan, London.

Faulkner, E. and Nyamutata, C. (2020) The Decolonisation of Children's Rights and the Colonial Contours of the Convention on the Rights of the Child, *International Journal of Children's Rights*, 28, 66–88.

Fiddian-Qasmiyeh, E. (2014) Gender and Forced Migration, in Fiddian-Qasmiyeh, E., Loescher, G., Long, K. and Sigona, N. (Eds.), *The Oxford Handbook of Refugee and Forced Migration Studies*, Oxford University Press, Oxford.

François Crépeau et al. (2013) *Children on the Move*, Inter-Agency Working Group on Children on the Move and International Organization for Migration (IOM), Geneva.

Gladwell, C., Bowerman, E., Norman, B. and Dickson, S. with Ghafoor, A. (2016) *After Return: Documenting the Experiences of Young People Forcibly Removed to Afghanistan*, Refugee Support Network, London.

Henrick, H. and Horn, P. (1997) *Children, Childhood and English Society, 1880–1990*, Cambridge University Press, Cambridge.

Hynes, P. (2010) Global Points of 'Vulnerability': Understanding the Processes of the Trafficking of Children into, within and out of the UK, *International Journal of Human Rights*, 14(6), 949–967.

Hynes, P. (2015) No 'Magic Bullets': Children, Young People, Trafficking and Child Protection in the UK, *International Migration*, 53(4), 62–76.

Hynes, P. (2010) Global Points of 'Vulnerability': Understanding the Processes of the Trafficking of Children into, within and Out of the UK, *International Journal of Human Rights*, 14(6), 949–967.

Hynes, P. (2015) "No Magic Bullets": Children, Young People, Trafficking and Child Protection in the UK, *International Migration*, 53(4), 62–76.

Hynes, P. (2017) Trafficking and Gender, in Lombard, N. (Ed.), *The Routledge Handbook of Gender and Violence*, Routledge, Oxon and New York.

Internal Displacement Monitoring Centre (IDMC) (2020) *Global Report on Internal Displacement*, IDMC and Norwegian Refugee Council, Geneva.

Kempadoo, K. (2015) The Modern-Dave White (Wo)Man's Burden: Trends in Anti-Trafficking and Anti-Slavery Campaigns, *Journal of Human Trafficking*, 1(1), 8–20.

Kohli, R.K.S., Connolly, H., Stott, H., Roe, S., Prince, S., Long, J. and Gordon-Ramsay, S. (2019) *An Evaluation of Independent Child Trafficking Guardians – Early Adopter Sites: Final Report,* Research Report 111, Home Office, UK.

Kohli. R.K.S., Hynes, P., Connolly, H., Thurnham, A., Westlake, D. and D'Arcy, K. (2015), *Evaluation of Independent Child Trafficking Advocates Trial: Final Report,* Research Report 86, Home Office, UK.

Leon, L. and Raws, P. (2016) *Boys Don't Cry: Improving Identification and Disclosure of Sexual Exploitation among Boys and Young Men Trafficked to the UK,* The Children's Society, London.

Liden, H. and Rusten, H. (2007) Asylum, Participation and the Best Interests of the Child: New Lessons from Norway, *Children & Society*, 21, 273–283.

Malkki, L. (1995) *Purity and Exile: Violence, Memory and National Cosmology among Hutu Refugees in Tanzania*, University of Chicago Press, Chicago and London.

Pearce, J.J., Hynes, P. and Bovarnick, S. (2009) *Breaking the Wall of Silence: Practitioners' Responses to Trafficked Children and Young People*, NSPCC and University of Bedfordshire, London.

Radford, L., Allnock, D. and Hynes, P. (2015a) *Preventing and Responding to Child Sexual Abuse and Exploitation: Evidence Review*, UNICEF, New York.

Radford, L., Allnock, D. and Hynes, P. (2015b) *Promising Programmes to Prevent and Respond to Child Sexual Abuse and Exploitation*, UNICEF, New York.

Radford, L., Corral, S., Bradley, C., Fisher, H., Bassett, C., Howat, N. and Collishaw, S. (2011) *Child Abuse and Neglect in the UK Today*, NSPCC, London.

Reynell, J. (1989) *Political Pawns: Refugees on the Thai-Kampuchean Border*, Refugee Studies Programme, University of Oxford, Oxford.

Seeberg, M.L. and Goździak, E. (Eds.) (2016) *Contested Childhoods: Growing up in Migrancy*, IMISCOE Research Series, Springer Open, Heidelberg, Germany.

Setter, C. (2017) Unaccompanied Asylum-Seeking Children and Trafficked Children, in Shalev Green, K. and Alys, L. (Eds.), *Missing Persons: A Handbook of Research*, Routledge, London and New York.

Sigona, N. and Hughes, V. (2012) *No Way Out, No Way In: Irregular Migrant Children and Families in the UK*, Centre on Migration, Policy and Society, University of Oxford, Oxford.

UN Special Rapporteur on the sale of children, n.d., view at: https://www.ohchr.org/en/issues/children/pages/childrenindex.aspx

UNICEF (2016) *Uprooted: The Growing Crisis for Refugee and Migrant Children*, UNICEF, New York.

UNICEF (2020) *Lost at Home: The Risks and Challenges for Internally Displaced Children and the Urgent Actions Needed to Protect Them*, UNICEF, New York.

United Nations High Commission for Refugees (UNHCR) (2017) *Global Trends: Forced Displacement in 2016*, UNHCR, Geneva.

United Nations High Commission for Refugees (UNHCR) (2018) *Global Trends: Forced Displacement in 2017*, UNHCR, Geneva.

United Nations High Commission for Refugees (UNHCR) (2019) *Global Trends: Forced Displacement in 2018*, UNHCR, Geneva.

United Nations High Commission for Refugees (UNHCR) (2020) *Global Trends: Forced Displacement in 2019*, UNHCR, Geneva.

7 Understanding legislative and policy responses and ethical imperatives

Introduction

Previous chapters have explored different categories of forced migrants by looking at who is a refugee, a stateless person, an IDP, a 'victim' or 'survivor' of human trafficking and a 'child on the move'. This chapter focusses on legislative and policy responses towards these populations who live in contexts that are a mix of care, control and uncertainty. Global, regional and national policy responses in the 20th and 21st centuries to date are explored. This includes a short chronology of UNHCRs 'durable solutions' of resettlement, local integration and repatriation; policies for IDPs; legislation around people who have experienced human trafficking; and responses specific to children on the move.

Finally, consideration is given to working with and/or conducting ethically informed research with people who have experienced displacement. This chapter also includes the contributions of key thinkers on these topics and key concepts within these debates. A series of scenarios, based on working within and/or conducting research in humanitarian contexts, and ethical dilemmas for in-class discussions are provided.

20th-century responses

> The history of responses to refugees in the twentieth century has been one long series of attempts to circumvent the problem.
>
> (Harrell-Bond, 1995)

> It is the absence of burden sharing in the post-Cold War era which explains the growing acceptance of involuntary repatriation as a solution to the global refugee problem.
>
> (Chimni, 1999:1)

In these quotes, Harrell-Bond and Chimni address how responses to refugees failed to address the situation of refugees during the 20th century (see also Key Thinker Boxes 2.1 and 7.1). Chimni's quote considers the inequalities of responses to refugees, drawing on the idea that the 'burden' of assistance to refugees can be shared in an equitable way across low- and high-income countries. 'Burden sharing' as an idea has a long history within refugee studies and is a well-established term in the global refugee regime (UNHCR, 2000). The 'prejudicial connotation' of the term has been highlighted by several academics and campaigning organisations (Thielemann, 203:225). This is now increasingly referred to as 'responsibility sharing', with other terms such as 'the equal balance of efforts' or 'international solidarity obligations' beginning to impact on the way responses to refugees are debated (Thielemann, 203:225; UNHCR, 2005).

So-called burden sharing can be about sharing or shifting financial and other costs. A special edition of the *Journal of Refugee Studies* in September 2003 examined 'burden sharing' in a European context, referring to how refugee burden-sharing issues had increasingly risen to the top of the political agenda at this regional level (Thielemann, 2003). At that time, it was argued that the purpose of burden sharing was to 'institutionalise redistribution' in ways counter to how distribution would occur without intervention. According to Thielemann (2003:228–232), sharing this 'burden' could involve harmonisation of refugee and asylum legislation (sharing policy), redistribution of resources (sharing money) and/or the reallocation of asylum seekers (sharing people). This latter action was considered the most effective but also the most controversial way to share the 'burden' throughout the EU at that time.

Another important aspect of the response towards refugees has been the way in which they live has been described as living **in limbo or in liminal situations**. Within the literature of forced migration, there is considerable reference to refugees living in limbo, particularly in relation to refugees in camps (Bousquet, 1987; Hitchcox, 1990; Kunz, 1973; Malkki, 1995; Reynell, 1989; Turton, 2004). For example, Bousquet's 1987 study of Vietnamese refugees in closed camps in Hong Kong explored how refugees were living in an intermediate state where they had left their surroundings but were not yet accepted elsewhere. It described how the government of Hong Kong opposed attempts to improve camp conditions and, in doing so, retained the perception of the camp as a temporary holding centre. Malkki's seminal 1995 study also explored such liminal positions (see Key Thinker Box 2.2). This position of being **liminal and being held in temporary conditions** has been continuously replicated in responses to refugees worldwide.

Shacknove has suggested that throughout the 20th century, providing asylum has been viewed by governments as a 'worthy exception to immigration control rule' for those lacking the protection of their own governments (1993:517). However, Shacknove and others have also suggested that this space for asylum is contracting in the post-Cold War era simultaneously with States attempting to **contain refugees within their countries or regions of origin**. Containment relates to efforts to impose visa restrictions and carrier sanctions, returning refugees to their countries of first asylum, and other restrictive measures that constitute a 'non-entrée regime' (Chimni, 1998:351). Shacknove examines this preference for the **containment of forced migrants** in countries and regions of origin, outlining how an enhanced capacity for administrative control and militarisation of borders is being used to deter forced migrants, how the growth of bureaucracies with a preference for order above welfare or rights is operationalising this **deterrence** and how States are making challenges to the institution of asylum. As Shacknove outlines, this third aspect relates to the way in which:

> affluent States are curtailing asylum to the extent that doing so is administratively possible and politically acceptable to citizens . . . and linkage between development assistance and co-operation on migration issues by aid-receiving States.
>
> (1993:522)

The justification for containment thereby relates to the suggestion that 'substantially greater numbers of refugees can be aided locally than through costly asylum and resettlement policies' (Ibid., 1993:523). Such justifications, and containment methods, in the words of Shacknove: 'allow States *de facto* to circumvent the letter and spirit of the 1951 Convention and the 1967 Protocol' (Ibid., 1993:532).

To help ground and unravel these arguments, a short chronology of responses to refugees across the globe is provided in Box 7.1. This looks at the establishment of the current refugee framework post-WWII, established at the beginning of the 1950s. The set of norms established included the right to seek asylum in other States and a prohibition on refugees being sent back to countries where they would be at risk. As outlined in earlier chapters, this was to avoid the repetition of a situation in which victims from distinct populations were unable to find sanctuary elsewhere in the world and to manage future refugee movements. The chronology includes phases of use of UNHCRs 'durable solutions' of resettlement, local integration and repatriation and an emergent hierarchy of these solutions as evolved over time (see Chapter 2 for individual explanations). It also begins to outline actions for internally displaced persons (see Chapter 3).

Box 7.1　Selective Chronology of Responses to Refugees and IDPs in the 20th Century

1950　United Nations High Commissioner for Refugees (UNHCR) established

1912–1969　Nearly 50 million Europeans sought refuge abroad, and all were resettled (Chimni, 1998)

1945–1985　Resettlement promoted as a durable solution in practice, with voluntary repatriation accepted in principle as the preferred solution (Chimni, 1999)

1950 United Nations Relief and Works Agency for Palestine Refugees in the Near East (UNRWA) established as a temporary agency to provide humanitarian relief

1951 Convention relating to the Status of Refugees defines who is an individual refugee in Europe

1966 Bangkok Principles Concerning Treatment of Refugees adopted by the Asian-African Legal Consultative Committee formulated as an instrument for the protection of refugee rights

1967 Protocol relating to the Status of Refugees removes the time and geographical limitations of the 1951 Refugee Convention

1969 Convention governing the Specific Aspects of Refugee Problems in Africa adapted the definition to groups of refugees facing the realities of the developing world

1979 International Conference on Indochinese Refugees, where 71 nations met to discuss refugees from Vietnam, Laos and Cambodia and made commitments for resettlement and orderly departure from Vietnam

1984 Cartagena Declaration in South America adapted the definition to groups of refugees, including those threatened by generalized violence, foreign aggression, internal conflicts and violations of human rights

1989–1996 Conference on introducing a Comprehensive Plan of Action (CPA) in Southeast Asia, decoupling the automatic link between asylum and resettlement (Nah, 2016; Courtland Robinson, 1998)

1989–1993 An International Conference on Central American Refugees (known by the Spanish acronym, CIREFCA) held to resolve regional refugee, displaced persons and returnee issues in South America and to seek durable solutions; conceived as a follow-up to the 1984 Cartagena Declaration (Kneebone, 2016)

1985–1993 Voluntary repatriation promoted as the durable solution, emphasising the voluntary character of repatriation (Chimni, 1999)

1989 United Nations Convention on the Rights of the Child (UNCRC)

1980s/1990s Western European countries began to put restrictive policies in place which aimed to 'combat illegal immigration and abuse of the asylum system' (UNHCR, 2000:161); sometimes referred to as 'Fortress Europe', these included:

- 'Non-arrival' policies (carrier sanctions, visa requirements, fines for transport companies)
- 'Diversion' policies ('safe third countries' lists created to return asylum seekers to countries of origin)

- Increasingly restrictive application of the 1951 Convention
- Introduction of 'deterrent' measures (detention, denial of social assistance, compulsory dispersal, restricted access to employment and restrictions of family reunification)

1992　Creation of the mandate of the Representative of the UN Secretary-General on Internally Displaced Persons

1993 onwards　The notion of safe return introduced in the context of temporary protection regimes in Western Europe (Chimni, 1999)

1996 onwards　The doctrine of 'imposed return' introduced and acceptance of the reality of involuntary repatriation meaning that refugees could be sent back to 'less than optimal conditions in their home country' against their will (Chimni, 1999)

1996 onwards　Increasing use of 'temporary solutions'

1998　Guiding Principles on Internal Displacement devised

**Key Thinker Box 7.1　Bhupinder S. Chimni –
'A View from the South'**

Professor Bhupinder S. Chimni has recently retired from the position of Professor of international law at Jawaharlal Nehru University in New Delhi. During the course of his career, Professor Chimni served as a member of the Academic Advisory Committee of the Office of the UNHCR and was on the editorial board of several academic journals such as *Refugee Survey Quarterly* and the *Journal of International Law*. He has also been a Visiting Professor at the American University of Cairo, Brown and Tokyo Universities and has held Visiting Fellowships within various universities, including Cambridge, Harvard and the Max Planck Institute of Comparative and International Law. Drawn to the work of Marx and the role of class from an early stage in his career, Professor Chimni's contributions are considered seminal to refugee studies and international law relating to refugees. He has been part of a group of scholars self-identifying as the Third World Approaches to International Law (TWAIL) scholars, established to articulate a critique of contemporary international law and institutions from the perspective of the Global South, and focussing on imperialism, the role of resistance in international law and different legal regimes.

In 1991, Chimni provided a **critical perspective of voluntary repatriation** – which at that time was being increasingly promoted as the 'most desirable solution, leaving local settlement and resettlement in that lessor order of priority' (Ibid., 1991:541). Pointing out that most refugees at that time were in the developing world, and that in a post-Cold War context, non-European refugees were unwelcome. By 1993, the meaning of words and the role of UNHCR in voluntary repatriation were being explored by Chimni, including words such as 'facilitation', 'promotion', 'encouragement' and 'safe return' in contexts of voluntary repatriation and wider contexts of restrictive policies within the developed world. Chimni suggests UNHCR's involvement in facilitating voluntary repatriation might encourage return in times of continuing conflict and warned against the dangers of coerced return, resulting largely from receiving and developed States' concerns to 'solve' problems, back to 'situations from which they fled in the first place' (1993:442). The **shift to returning refugees to their countries of origin** to avoid the international community carrying (or in more recent terms, sharing) the 'burden' of refugees is also explored.

Throughout his work, Chimni develops the idea that the global refugee regime was established at the end of WWII and was complicit in the fight against the Soviet Union and its allies, with **every refugee fleeing the Soviet bloc essentially voting with their feet** against the Soviet Union (see, e.g., Chimni, 2004). The end of the Cold War meant that the initial reasons for the refugee regime also disappeared, with **refugees no longer having ideological or geopolitical value. The image of a refugee during that time was a white, male anticommunist – not those living within the 'third world'.** With the loss of the centrally planned economies of the 'second world', 'first world' capitalist countries' interventions in the 'third world', also referred to as 'non-aligned countries', created refugees. The generation of millions of refugees became a reality alongside these 'first world' interventions, with refugees from Iraq, Kosovo, Afghanistan, Libya and other countries.

In his seminal 1998 contribution on the geopolitics of refugee studies, from the perspective of the Global South, Chimni outlines how **post-1945 policy on refugees has moved from a position of neglect** in the 'third world', **to use as pawns in Cold War politics** to **containment and reliance on the solution of voluntary repatriation** to facilitate such containment policies. In this discussion, Chimni outlines how the absence of burden sharing is reflected in responses to refugees which accept involuntary repatriation as a solution. In a 1999 working paper, Chimni reiterates these points, spelling out distinct phases in the history of 'durable solutions' between 1945–1985, 1985–1993, 1993–1996 and 1996 onwards (see Box 7.1 for an enhanced chronology).

In the 1998 contribution Chimni also critiques the imperialist nature of the 'refugee studies' project, observing that its framing has become the domain of scholars in the Global North and with a postcolonial critique largely absent. This argument was taken forward in a 2009 paper that explored how Refugee Studies, or Forced Migration Studies, served the geopolitics of States but that both needed to be viewed against a backdrop of the history and relationships of colonialism and humanitarianism.

In recent work, Chimni has reflected on the contradictions of expanding globalisation against State systems that assert sovereignty and border control, within contexts of economic crisis and xenophobia, leaving political leaders unable to pursue liberal asylum policies. His most recent publications (2012, 2017) continue to argue for a historical perspective to be adopted and for the positive aspects of refugees and migration to be spoken about more frequently.

Key references – Bhupinder S. Chimni

Chimni, B.S. (1991) Perspectives on Voluntary Repatriation: A Critical Note, *International Journal of Refugee Law*, 3(3), 541–546.

Chimni, B.S. (1993) The Meaning of Words and the Role of UNHCR in Voluntary Repatriation, *International Journal of Refugee Law*, 5, 443–460.

Chimni, B.S. (1998) The Geopolitics of Refugee Studies: A View from the South, *Journal of Refugee Studies*, 11(4), 350–374.

Chimni, B.S. (1999) *From Resettlement to Involuntary Repatriation: Towards a Critical History of Durable Solutions to Refugee Problems*, New Issues in Refugee Research, Working Paper No.2, UNHCR, Geneva.

Chimni, B.S. (2004) International Institutions Today: An Imperial Global State in the Making, *European Journal of International Law*, 15, 1–39.

Chimni, B.S. (2009) The Birth of a 'Discipline': From Refugee Studies to Forced Migration Studies, *Journal of Refugee Studies*, 22(1), 11–29.

Chimni, B.S. (2017) *International Law and World Order: A Critique of Contemporary Approaches* (2nd ed.), Cambridge University Press, Cambridge.

Chimni, B.S. and Malvarappu, S. (Eds.) (2012) *International Relations: Essays for the Global South*, Pearson, New Delhi.

As can be seen from the chronology and from Chimni's work (see Key Thinker Box 7.1), 20th-century responses to refugees have included moments in time when the international community has worked together to protect refugees and seek durable solutions – notably the CPA and CIREFCA conferences in 1989 and an earlier 1979 conference in Southeast Asia to address resettlement needs of 'Indochinese' refugees and the need for countries of 'first asylum' in that context. As Nah (2016) outlines, the CPA did not imbue norms of refugee protection across Southeast Asia, with a rejection of protection norms perceived to be in 'Eurocentric' and consequently imposing **unacceptable burdens on developing states**. Both the 1979 conference and 1989 CPA occurred after the Vietnam/American War and have to be viewed within that context, with past guilt informing much of the debates around resettlement options. CIREFA has been considered to be a form of peace process and the search for regional durable solutions following the 1984 Cartagena Declaration in comparison (Kneebone, 2016).

21st-century responses

Moving into the 21st century, this chronology in relation to refugees and IDPs is continued. However, from 2000 onwards, actions, policies and legislation in relation to human trafficking are included (see Chapter 4), within a shift towards an agenda of securitisation.

Box 7.2   Selective Chronology of Responses to Refugees, IDPs and 'Victims' of Human Trafficking in the 21st Century

15 November 2000 Protocol to Prevent, Suppress and Punish Trafficking in Persons, Especially Women and Children (also known as the Palermo Protocol) adopted at UNGA – supplements the United Nations Convention against Transnational Organized Crime

    2002   The Bali Process on People Smuggling, Trafficking in Persons and Related Transnational Crime initiated at a regional conference in Bali, Indonesia, aiming to address practical issues, intelligence sharing and improved cooperation among law enforcement agencies to deter, combat and criminalise smuggling and trafficking networks

    2002   The Office of the High Commission for Human Rights adopted the Recommended Principles and Guidelines on Human Rights and Human Trafficking to promote and facilitate the integration of human rights perspectives into national, regional and international anti-trafficking laws, policies and interventions

    2003   UNHCR introduced the Framework for Durable Solutions, which aimed to achieve sharing burdens and responsibilities more equitably and redouble the search for durable solutions. Introduced through Development Assistance for Refugees (DAR), Repatriation, Reintegration, Rehabilitation and Reconstruction (4Rs) and Development through Local Integration (DLI)

    29 September 2003   Protocol to Prevent, Suppress and Punish Trafficking in Persons, Especially Women and Children notice of entry into force (also known as the Palermo Protocol)

    28 January 2004   Protocol against the Smuggling of Migrants by Land, Sea and Air adopted at UNGA – supplements the United Nations Convention against Transnational Organized Crime

2004   UN Commission on Human Rights established the mandate of the Special Rapporteur on Trafficking in Persons, especially Women and Children

2005   UNHCR introduced Convention Plus with the aim to improve refugee protection worldwide through multilateral special agreements and to mobilise support and commitments towards refugees

2006   Protocol on the Protection and Assistance to Internally Displaced Persons adopted by Member States of the International Conference on the Great Lakes (also known as the Great Lakes IDP Protocol)

2009   African Convention on Protection and Assistance for Internally Displaced Persons in Africa (also known as the Kampala Convention)

19 September 2016   New York Declaration for Refugees and Migrants adopted by 193 UN Member States recognising the need for a comprehensive approach to human mobility and enhanced cooperation at a global level

September 2016   Coinciding with the UN Summit, the Government of Canada, UNHCR and the Open Society Foundations launched a joint initiative to increase private sponsorship of refugees across the globe. The initiative builds on the resettlement of more than 275,000 private sponsored refugees since the late 1970s in Canada. The initiative had three primary objectives:

1   Contribute to enhanced responsibility-sharing by expanding the use of private sponsorship as a pathway for refugees in need of protection and solutions

2   Encourage the expansion of resettlement by building the capacity of states, civil society actors and private citizens to launch private sponsorship programs

3   Provide a vehicle that mobilizes citizens in direct support of refugees and encourages a broader political debate that is supportive of refugee protection

January 2017   Newly elected President of the US, Donald Trump, imposed a four-month suspension of all refugee admissions into the US and indefinitely banned entry to all Syrian refugees. The executive order placed a temporary 90-day ban on people from Syrian, Somalia, Iraq, Iran, Libya, Sudan and Yemen.

17 December 2018   Global Compact on Refugees (GCR) affirmed by the UN General Assembly to provide a framework for more predictable and equitable responsibility-sharing and international cooperation to find sustainable solutions to refugee situations that:

• Ease pressures on host countries
• Enhance refugee self-reliance

- Expand access to third-country solutions
- Support conditions in countries of origin for return in safety and dignity

10 December 2018   Global Compact for Safe, Orderly and Regular Migration (GCM) developed and adopted by the majority of UN Member States as a non-binding agreement to cover all dimensions of international migration in a holistic and comprehensive manner that respects States' sovereignty

Global responses to refugees since 2000 have involved initiatives from UNHCR such as the 2003 Framework for Durable Solutions, 2005 Convention Plus and more recently involvement in the 2016 New York Declarations and 2018 Global Compact on Refugees (GCR).

However, as Crisp (2016) suggested in response to treatment of Syrian refugees: 'The Syrian refugee crisis is a symptom of the disorder which currently exists in the international system' (Crisp, 2016). And:

> While European countries are now doing everything in their power to halt the arrival of Syrian and other refugees, it seems highly unlikely that they will be dissuaded from making that journey, however long, difficult, dangerous and expensive it proves to be. In that context, it is important to challenge the conclusion drawn by some European leaders, namely that human smugglers are a primary cause of the refugee movement across the Aegean and Mediterranean seas. They are not. Smugglers simply facilitate and profit from people's desire to move on.
>
> (Crisp, 2016)

Here we can starkly see the interplay between a lack of responses to refugees and reference to human smugglers which became part of the increasing securitisation agenda from the early 2000s.

In this same article, Crisp outlines how the refugee regime is 'now under threat from its founders'. This addresses the **ironic situation that the European founders of the 1951 Refugee Convention (see Chapter 2) are now those same States which are erecting fences and walls across Europe**, deploying warships in the Aegean and Mediterranean Seas and drawing up deals such as a 6 billion Euro deal for Turkey to be responsible for returning people from Greece and processing them if they arrive in Greece after a 20 March 2016 cut-off date.

In 2014, responses to refugees in Europe also included the EU deciding to end the Italian Navy's humanitarian search and rescue operation – Mare Nostrum – and replace it with a scaled down version – Operation Triton – which was primarily focussed on border enforcement rather than rescuing individuals from the sea. The end of Mare Nostrum did not, unsurprisingly, deter people from migrating in the first instance, nor did it lead to a drop in departures. It could, however, be linked to an increase in deaths at sea. During 2014, when Mare Nostrum was operational, the death rate was about 1 in 50 people; this rose to 1 in 23 in the first three-and-half months of 2015 (Amnesty International, 2015). Border control, rather than saving the lives of individuals, was reflected in maps showing areas patrolled by both operations and indications of rescues largely taking place.

During 2015 around a million people crossed the border into the EU with both humanitarian and medical needs largely left unmet. As outlined by the civil society organisation, Medecins Sans Frontieres (MSF), 2015 would be: 'remembered as the year in which Europe catastrophically failed in its responsibility to respond to the urgent needs of assistance and protection of hundreds of thousands of vulnerable people' (MSF, 2016). Increasing **deterrence and anti-immigration policies** across Europe did however create an upsurge of solidarity from ordinary citizens, with civil society and volunteers providing services to people in places and spaces neglected by governments.

During the summer of 2015, parallel narratives played out in the media of refugees in boats in the Aegean, Mediterranean and Andaman Seas. In 2015 alone, more than one million people were estimated to have crossed the Mediterranean Sea to European countries seeking refuge, with thousands dying en route (Crawley *et al.*, 2018; IOM, 2016). Tens of thousands who made it to the 'safe haven' of Europe were left facing fear of daily violence (Human Rights Watch, 2016a) with their rights and freedoms severely curtailed (Human Rights Watch, 2016b). This 'refugee crisis' in Europe took the centre stage in media and policy discourses taking material shape in new border fences and translating into increasing negative attitudes among European citizens towards non-European immigration.

Policies enacted from 2015 onwards in Europe displayed an increasingly curious range of tactics to deter people from trying to reach particular countries. For example, the Danish government placed advertisements in Lebanese newspapers telling Syrians not to come to Denmark. These advertisement detailed changes to Denmark's asylum laws that would make it a less desirable place for refugees. Denmark also created a law to seize valuables such as jewellery and cash from refugees arriving into the country. Switzerland warned refugees that they would have to hand over any property worth more than 1,000 Swiss francs (c.$980). Some states in southern Germany started seizing from refugees assets worth more than 750 Euros (c.$812). The Slovakian government said that it would refuse entry to Muslim refugees, announcing that it would take in only Christians. The Danish city of Randers made it mandatory for public institutions, including cafeterias in kindergartens and day-care centres, to have pork dishes on their menus with the idea that this might maintain a Danish identity. A number of countries began giving sexual education and etiquette classes to refugees following often unfounded reports of sexual assaults. Perhaps most bizarrely, Norway forced some refugees to cycle across the border to Russia in the dead of winter after a number of refugees used a legal loophole to enter Norway on a bike; the Norwegian government deported them back to Russia. In some cases, the refugees cycled back into the Arctic north of Russia. This 'Arctic route' has since been reviewed by Norway.

The momentum for development of the Global Compact on Refugees (GCR) and the Global Compact for Safe, Orderly and Regular Migration (GCM) was in response to the arrival of asylum seekers in Europe in 2015 with other, longer-standing issues of concern included in discussions (Ferris and Martin, 2019). This non-binding and 'aspirational' Compact now offers 'the first widely accepted, new, normative frameworks on the movement of people since the ratification of the 1951 Refugee Convention and its 1967 Protocol' (Ferris and Martin, 2019).

Beyond Europe, the response to Rohingya refugees crossing the into Bangladesh having been displaced from Myanmar is explored in the next and final chapter.

Outcomes from the development of the **non-binding GCR and GCM** remain to be seen. Ferris and Martin (2019) suggest that the **lack of a clear line between voluntary and forced migration** will create future difficulties and that two, rather than one, Compacts on global mobility will set in stone the distinctions between refugees and other migrants in terms of legislative and policy responses. With mixed migration characterising the movement of people, coordination between agencies involved is not well established in these Compacts. They go on to explain that within the current anti-migration environment, precarious and dangerous journeys undertaken that result in abuse and violence cannot be considered together as human rights abuses within a framework that has specific actions to address protection for refugees and migrants separately. They also suggest that IDPs, for example, are not best served in this framework: 'An even more glaring omission in the global compacts is the fact that internal migrants and internally displaced persons (IDPs) are virtually ignored in the two global compacts. . . . The GCM does not mention internal migrants' (Ferris and Martin, 2019:15).

Regional actions for internally displaced persons within Africa have included the 2006 Great Lakes IDP Protocol and the 2009 Kampala Convention. What happens next in terms of addressing the gap for IDPs globally remains to be seen.

Quite where people who have experienced human trafficking sit within these Compacts is also unclear as there is a largely unexplored interface between seeking asylum and human trafficking. However, under the GCM, Objective 7 – to address and reduce vulnerabilities in migration – has seen a shift from previous language on 'vulnerable migrants' to 'migrants who face situations of vulnerability' in the final drafting of this objective. This objective also details how these situations of vulnerability may arise from circumstances during travel or conditions in countries of origin, transit and destination. Objective 10 details actions to prevent, combat and eradicate trafficking in persons in the context of international migration.

Since the introduction of the 2000 Palermo Protocol two decades ago, much has been learned about the forms and different facets of human trafficking, particularly how a shift from a criminal justice to a human rights and social justice approach is necessary (UN Special Rapporteur address, 2020). This Protocol now has now been adopted by 176 States with the aim of preventing and combating human trafficking, with most States criminalising trafficking in national laws. There is now a move towards addressing the gaps – particularly around human rights – within the human trafficking agenda to the extent of creating a new international instrument to address the human rights of people who experience trafficking.

Key Concept 7.1   Deterrence Policies

Deterrence, as it relates to asylum seekers and refugees, refers to policies that attempt to discourage future arrivals by imposing difficult living conditions and a lack of opportunities for rebuilding lives within a country of asylum. As outlined within the chronology in Box 7.1, from the 1980s, Western European countries began putting restrictive policies in place which were sometimes referred to as **'Fortress Europe'**. These included non-arrival and diversion policies, an increasingly restrictive interpretation of the 1951 Refugee Convention and specific deterrence measures such as increasing use of detention, policies creating destitution through denial of social assistance, compulsory dispersal and deportation (UNHCR, 2000:161). Restricted access to employment, family reunification and health services have also become common measures used to make seeking sanctuary from persecution less appealing. As outlined in the next and final chapter, asylum seekers now face the closure of borders across Europe; increasingly dangerous sea crossings to Italy, Greece and other countries; inhumane reception conditions in a number of countries and complex asylum, social care and criminal justice processes.

   Such deterrence measures have been enacted across the globe. In the early 1990s, Australia responded to the arrival of asylum seekers with mandatory detention policies which aimed to deter subsequent arrivals. In 2001 Australia reacted to arrivals of asylum seekers by boat by introducing what became known as the **'Pacific Solution'**. The aim was to deter asylum seekers making the dangerous journey by boat, and this was operationalised by removing those intercepted to third countries for processing. This involved asylum seekers being intercepted or moved by boat by the Australian Navy and transferred to offshore processing centres on Nauru and Manus Islands in Papua New Guinea, operated by IOM. Whilst detained, access to legal advice was denied and lengthy processing times were largely left unchecked. By the time this scheme was dismantled in 2008, a total of 1,637 people had been detained. Following a brief period where a more liberal asylum policy was adopted, offshore processing for asylum seekers was reintroduced; by 2013 the Manus Island processing centre was enlarged, and Nauru processing centre reopened.

Writing from Manus Island, Kurdish journalist Behrouz Boochani's account of seeking asylum in Australia and being sent and detained on Manus Island from 2013 is now available as a book – *No Friend but the Mountains: The True Story of an Illegally Imprisoned Refugee*. Boochani spent nearly five years typing passages of this book, one text at a time, from a secret mobile phone whilst detained. Manus Island Regional Processing Centre was declared illegal by Papua New Guinea in 2016 and closed in October 2017.

As Welch and Schuster (2005) outline, detention of asylum seekers in the USA takes place in a way that is 'quietly concealed by government officials' as opposed to the 'public and loud' voices against detention in the UK (2005:398). They suggest that unnecessary detention of asylum seekers in a post-9/11 USA relates to prevailing trends in imprisonment and policies seen to be 'tough on crime' (2005:403). Currently in the USA, deterrence policies include those that Amnesty International considers to be aimed at the full dismantling of the US asylum system (Amnesty International, 2018). These policies and practices include pushbacks of asylum seekers at the US-Mexico border; well publicised family separations, including the separation of children from their parents; and, increasingly arbitrary and indefinite detention of asylum seekers (Ibid., 2018).

Pushing asylum seekers back into countries of origin at borders is a long-held practice in many nations. **When pushbacks happen, the principle of *non-refoulement* is compromised.** UNHCR has been detailing pushbacks within Southeast Asia since at least 1984, when people were pushed back into Laos from Thailand in eight separate occasions, and in 1988, when a boat with nationals from Vietnam was pushed back into international waters (Courtland Robinson, 1998:116, 182). Burmese refugees have been frequently pushed back into Myanmar following the end of the political 'buffer' and demise of the Karen National Union, which opposed the central Burmese military government along the Thailand-Burma border in the late 1990s. This is something that continues today.

Whilst there is often a common-sense perception that there is a relationship between deterrence measures and numbers of new arrivals, there is little evidence that this is actually the case. Deterrence policies developed over the past few decades have, however, increased the demand for and reliance on 'smuggling' networks, pushing people towards increasingly more precarious and dangerous routes, which can create exploitative conditions fitting definitions of human trafficking.

Working with and/or conducting ethically informed research with displaced populations

Given the policies of containment and deterrence developed in recent decades, it is essential that working with and/or conducting research with refugees is carried out ethically. The context for refugees is such that power imbalances are built into responses to refugees and asylum seekers, which can render people vulnerable and their lives precarious. The concept of 'harm' built into ethical frameworks therefore needs to be interpreted broadly to avoid reifying the indignities of systems designed to deter. Should you find yourself in a position of working and/or carrying out research with people who have been forced to migrate, it is important that your thinking and actions are informed by ethics.

Standards for humanitarian responses were set out in 1997 to improve the quality of humanitarian assistance and accountability of humanitarian actors in the field. The Humanitarian Charter and Minimum Standards in Humanitarian Response – also known as **the Sphere Standards** – have been partially outlined in the previous chapter. The Sphere Standards are the most internationally recognised set of common principles and universal minimum standards used in humanitarian responses. They set out twin core beliefs that people have a 'right to life with dignity' and a consequent 'right to assistance', plus all possible steps are taken towards alleviating human suffering following conflict or disasters.

For conducting ethically informed research with people who have experienced displacement, both standard research ethics frameworks and guidelines specifically designed around these populations are available.

For example, the Refugee Studies Centre at the University of Oxford published 'Ethical Guidelines for Good Research Practice' in the journal *Refugee Survey Quarterly* in 2007. These guidelines govern research conducted at the Refugee Studies Centre and contain provisions on good practice applicable to conduct of research on forced migration. They cover the effects of involvement and consequences of working with individuals and groups among whom fieldwork is conducted (research participants or 'subjects'); colleagues within the discipline; collaborating researchers, funders, employers and gatekeepers; their own or host governments and other interested groups within the wider society in which research is conducted.

It is clear from the Preamble of these guidelines that competing duties, obligations and conflicts of interest can result in the need to make choices between values and between the interests of different individuals and groups. Because ethical and legal dilemmas can occur at all stages of research (see Figure 7.1)– be this in the selection of topic, area of population, choice of sponsor, source of funding, negotiation of access, during fieldwork, during interpretation and analysis phases, publication of findings and disposal of data – following such guidelines is essential. The guidelines suggest:

> Researchers have a responsibility to anticipate problems and insofar as is possible to resolve them without harming the research participants or the scholarly community. They should do their utmost to ensure that they leave a research field in a state which permits future access by other researchers. As scholars committed to the pursuit of knowledge and the public disclosure of findings, they should strive to maintain integrity in the conduct of their research.
>
> (Refugee Studies Centre, 2007:1)

In respect of each set of relationships during research, these guidelines address specific ethical issues as outlined in Key Concept Box 7.2, for consideration at each stage of the research process, as per Figure 7.1.

* Identifying topic, developing the research question, identifying a theoretical perspective/worldview

* Work/organisational context

* Research design

* Development of techniques and tools

* Gaining access

* Data collection

* Data analysis

* Writing-up

* Sharing of findings

* Disposal of data

Figure 7.1 Ethics and the Research Process

Key Concept 7.2   Ethical Guidelines for Good Research Practice

- **Relations with and responsibilities towards research participants**, which relates to personal and moral relationships, trust and reciprocity and recognition of power differentials between the researcher and researched. Principles relate to:

  1   Protecting research participants and honouring trust
  2   Anticipating harms
  3   Avoiding undue intrusion
  4   Negotiating informed consent
  5   Rights to confidentiality and anonymity
  6   Fair return for assistance
  7   Participants' intellectual property rights
  8   Participants' involvement in research

- **Relations with and responsibilities towards sponsors, funders and employers** to ensure that obligations to research participants and colleagues are clear. Principles relate to:

  1   Clarifying roles, rights and obligations
  2   Obligations to sponsors, funders and employers
  3   Negotiating 'research space'
  4   Relations with gatekeepers

- **Relations with, and responsibilities towards, colleagues and the discipline**, recognising that scholars derive their status and certain privileges of access by virtue of their personal standing but also by virtue of their professional citizenship. Principles relate to:

  1   Individual responsibility
  2   Conflicts of interest and consideration for colleagues
  3   Sharing research materials
  4   Collaborative and team research
  5   Responsibilities towards research students and field assistants

- **Relations with own and host governments**, with researchers being honest and candid in their relationships with governments. Principles relate to:

  1   Conditions of access
  2   Cross-national research
  3   Open research
  4   Legal and administrative constraints

> • **Responsibilities to the wider society**, with researchers depending upon the confidence of the public and research that does not attempt to exaggerate the accuracy of their findings. Principles relate to:
>
> 1 Widening the scope of social research
> 2 Considering conflicting interests
> 3 Maintaining professional and scholarly integrity

In November 2018, the International Association for the Study of Forced Migration (IASFM, 2018) also produced a three-page **IASFM Code of Ethics: Critical Reflections on Research Ethics in Situations of Forced Migration** freely available at: http://iasfm.org/wp-content/uploads/2018/11/IASFM-Research-Code-of-Ethics-2018.pdf

This code of ethics recognises that:

> Research with people in situations of forced migration poses particular ethical challenges because of unequal power relations, legal precariousness, extreme poverty, violence, the criminalization of migration, politicized research contexts, the policy relevance of our research and/or dependence on government and non-governmental services and funding.
>
> (IASFM, 2018:1)

Recognising that Research Ethics Boards (REBs) may not be aware of key issues relating to forced migration, or that these REBs may not be available in all countries, this code of ethics draws on: 'indigenous research methodologies [that] incorporate a broad, engaged and critical notion of ethics that recognizes power differentiations and the agency of the participants within exploitive research histories' (IASFM, 2018:1).

The code sets out principles that are considered the starting point for 'respectful research' that is active and engages critically with ethical issues in research. Definitions of *research*, *gatekeepers* and the term *people in situations of forced migration* are provided, the latter including refugees, asylum seekers, people who are trafficked and IDPs. Key ethical principles are outlined, including:

• Voluntary, informed consent
• Confidentiality and privacy
• A 'Do no harm' principle
• Autonomy of people in situations of forced migration to make their own decisions about their lives and participation in research
• Equity and the need to mitigate intersecting and unequal power relations in research

- Recognition of diversity of experiences of forced migration and culturally specific research ethics
- Competence and approaches adapted to cultural contexts
- Partnerships to inform the research process

In relation to human trafficking, Zimmerman and Watts (2003) (see Key Thinker Box 4.5) was the co-author of the World Health Organization's *WHO Ethical and Safety Recommendations for Interviewing Trafficked Women*. In this, ten **Guiding Principles** for ethical and safe conducting of interviews with women who had been trafficked were elaborated:

1 Do no harm
2 Know your subject and assess the risks
3 Prepare referral information but do not make promises that you cannot fulfil
4 Adequately select and prepare interpreters and co-workers
5 Ensure anonymity and confidentiality
6 Get informed consent
7 Listen to and respect each woman's assessment of her situation and risk to her safety
8 Do not re-traumatise a woman
9 Be prepared for emergency intervention
10 Put information collected to good use

These Guiding Principles can be found at: www.who.int/mip/2003/other_documents/en/Ethical_Safety-GWH.pdf

Whilst these principles were designed for interviewing adult women, when interviewing anyone who has been trafficked, these principles should act as a minimum standard when conducting research. Interviews with people who have experienced human trafficking can take place during or after their experiences, and ensuring no harm is created through research is vital.

Some scenarios for considering ethical research

To begin to think about conducting research ethically with people in situations of forced migration, the following scenarios can be considered and discussed with others:

Scenario 1: Barbara Harrell-Bond conducted fieldwork in Sierra Leone in the late 1950s, investigating the experiences of 754 people with professional qualifications in the country. These people were often closely connected through kinship and most knew one another. Despite her attempts to conceal identities, she found some readers could identify almost everyone in her first report and could provide other details such as their political affiliations, spouse's ethnic background, educational qualifications and other, more intimate, details (Harrell-Bond, 1976, cited in Israel and Hay, 2006).

Points for discussion – participants' rights to confidentiality, anonymity and privacy

- How could you avoid revealing people's identities?
- What identifying features would you have to anonymise?
- What would you do if someone was able to identify people in the report?

Scenario 2: You have just arrived at a border between two different countries where there are hundreds of refugees arriving on foot after having walked for days out of their country. They are exhausted and in need, first and foremost, of medical care and support. Your job is to collect their 'testimonies' of what has happened to them before they began their journeys.

Points for discussion – anticipating harms and the 'Do no harm' principle

- What do you do?
- Do you go ahead and begin the collection of 'testimonies'?
- How might you avoid 'doing harm' to these people?
- Would carrying out your job to collect 'testimonies' involve undue intrusion?

Scenario 3: You are carrying out research about the use of child soldiers in government and opposition armies. One of the opposition armies has offered you the opportunity to stay in their camp for a week to interview child soldiers they have 'rescued' from government forces. However, when you get there after travelling along dirt tracks for 8 hours, you realise that their opposition army also recruits child soldiers.

Points for discussion – contravention of ethical principles

- What do you do?
- Do you go ahead and interview the child soldiers they have arranged for you to speak to?
- Do you ask to also speak to the other child soldiers in their army?
- What are the ethical implications of interviewing combatants rather than civilians during such a conflict?
- What if they say no – would your research be biased?
- What ethical principles might you be contravening if you went ahead?

Scenario 4: You are working in a refugee camp with a local translator so that you can interview people for a research report that will be published for the world to see and may even be used within United Nations discussions. As you begin the interviews, about 200 people arrive saying that their village has been burned down, people have been killed and several women have been raped. When talking about this, your translator realises one of the women she knows has been left behind, and there are reports she has been raped and killed.

Points for discussion – the balance between benefit and harm in research

- What do you do?
- Do you carry on with the interviews once your translator stops being upset?
- What harms and what benefits would carrying on involve?

Scenario 5: You are working with an organisation that works with people who have experienced human trafficking or other forms of exploitation. One of the people you interviewed for your research disclosed to you that they had experienced sexual violence in the past, when they were a child. They told you several details. However, they then asked you never to tell anyone because in their community speaking about this is taboo and, if people knew, there would be a stigma attached to that person and their family.

Points for discussion – limits to confidentiality

- What do you do?
- Do you tell anyone?
- What are the child protection implications of not telling someone?
- What are the implications of breaching confidentiality?
- Would your response need to be different for an adult or a child?

Beyond 'Do no harm' in research with people in situations of forced migration

In recent years the principle of 'Do no harm' – sometimes referred to as the principle of beneficence – has been questioned in refugee research (Mackenzie *et al.*, 2007; Hugman *et al.*, 2011). Mackenzie *et al.* (2007) argued that researchers should seek ways to **move beyond harm minimisation** to recognising an obligation to design and conduct research that brings about reciprocal benefits for refugees and refugee communities. To do this, Mackenzie *et al.* (2007) outline how the standard practice of gaining informed consent is often inadequate in research in refugee settings because this does not allow for an ongoing relationship to be established that is based on mutual respect and trust. Instead they propose an **iterative model of the consent process** that enables the establishment of ethical relationships between the researchers and participants that respond to the needs, concerns and values of participants. This constitutes a shift in research ethics – with participants shifting from being subjects *of* research to participants *in* research and 'from harm minimization to reciprocal benefit' (Ibid. 2007:311).

In longitudinal research with people who have experienced human trafficking in Cambodia, a key finding has been that deep trust between participants and a research team has led to richer and more authentic interviews over a decade (Chab Dai Coalition, 2018). It was found that retention of participants was largely due to their trusting that their identities would be kept confidential, their stories mattered and they were valued as individuals throughout the research (Chab Dai Coalition, 2014).

Further reading

Amnesty International (2015) *Europe's Sinking Shame: The Failure to Save Refugees and Migrants at Sea*, Amnesty International, London.

Castles, S. (2004) Why Migration Policies Fail, *Ethnic and Racial Studies*, 27(2), 205–227.

Courtland Robinson, W. (1998) *Terms of Refuge: The Indochinese Exodus and the International Response*, Zed Books, London.

Crisp, J. (2016) *The Syrian Refugee Emergency: Implications for State Security and the International Humanitarian System*, Middle East Institute, viewed on 26 March 2020 at: www.mei.edu/content/map/syrian-refugee-emergency-implications-state-security-and-international-humanitarian-system

Ferris, E.E. and Martin, S.F. (2019) The Global Compacts on Refugees and for Safe, Orderly and Regular Migration: Introduction to the Special Issue, *International Migration*, 57(6), 5–18.

Fortify Rights (2015) *United Nations: Establish Independent Investigation into Genocide in Myanmar*, viewed on 7 July 2020 at: www.fortifyrights.org/publication-20151029.html

Hugman, R., Pittaway, E. and Bartolomei, L. (2011) When 'Do No Harm' Is Not Enough: The Ethics of Research with Refugees and Other Vulnerable Groups, *The British Journal of Social Work*, 41(7), 1271–1287.

International Association for the Study of Forced Migration (IASFM) (2018) *IASFM Code of Ethics: Critical Reflections on Research Ethics in Situations of Forced Migration*, IASFM, Canada.

Mackenzie, C., McDowell, C. and Pittaway, E. (2007) Beyond 'Do No Harm': The Challenge of Constructing Ethical Relationships in Refugee Research, *Journal of Refugee Studies*, 20(2), 299–319.

Medecins Sans Frontieres (2016) *Obstacle Course to Europe: A Policy-Made Humanitarian Crisis at EU Borders*, MSF, Brussels.

Refugee Studies Centre (2007) Ethical Guidelines for Good Research Practice, *Refugee Survey Quarterly*, 26(3), 162–172.

Shacknove, A. (1993) From Asylum to Containment, *International Journal of Refugee Law*, 5(4), 516–533.

Thielemann, E.R. (2003) Between Interests and Norms: Explaining Burden-Sharing in the European Union, *Journal of Refugee Studies*, 16(3), Oxford.

Zimmerman, C. and Watts, C. (2003) *WHO Ethical and Safety Recommendations for Interviewing Trafficked Women*, World Health Organisation and London School of Hygiene and Tropical Medicine, Geneva and London.

References

Amnesty International (2018) *USA: 'You Don't Have Any Rights Here': Illegal Pushbacks, Arbitrary Detention and Ill-treatment of Asylum-Seekers in the United States*, Amnesty International, London.

Bousquet, G. (1987) Living in a State of Limbo: A Case Study of Vietnamese Refugees in Hong Kong Camps, in Morgan, S. and Colson, E. (Eds.), *People in Upheaval*, Centre for Migration Studies, New York.

Chab Dai Coalition (2014) *Reflection on Methodology*, Chab Dai Coalition, Cambodia.

Chab Dai Coalition (2018) *Top 10 Findings . . . So Far . . . : Butterfly Longitudinal Research*, Chab Dai Coalition, Cambodia.

Chimni, B.S. (1999) *From Resettlement to Involuntary Repatriation: Towards a Critical History of Durable Solutions to Refugee Problems*, Working Paper No.2, UNHCR, Geneva.

Courtland Robinson, W. (1998) *Terms of Refuge: The Indochinese Exodus and the International Response*, Zed Books, London.

Crawley, H., Duvell, F., Jones, K., McMahon, S. and Sigona, N. (2018) *Unravelling Europe's 'Migration Crisis': Journeys Over Land and Sea*, Policy Press, Bristol.

Harrell-Bond, B. (1976) Studying Elites: Some Special Problems, in Rynkiewich, M.A. and Spradley, J.P. (Eds), *Ethics and Anthropology: Dilemmas in Fieldwork*, John Wiley, New York.

Harrell-Bond, B.E. (1995) *Refugees and the International System: The Evolution of Solutions*, Queen Elizabeth House, Oxford.

Hitchcox, L. (1990) *Vietnamese Refugees in Southeast Asian Camps*, MacMillan Press, London.

Human Rights Watch (2016a) *Greece: Refugee 'Hotspots': Unsafe, Unsanitary*, viewed on 7 July 2020 at: www.hrw.org/news/2016/05/19/greece-refugee-hotspots-unsafe-unsanitary.

Human Rights Watch (2016b) *Austria: Drastic, Unjustified Measures against Asylum Seekers*, viewed on 7 July 2020 at: www.hrw.org/news/2016/04/27/austria-drastic-unjustified-measures-against-asylum-seekers

International Organization for Migration (IOM) (2016) *Assessing the Risks of Migration Along The Central and Eastern Mediterranean Routes: Iraq and Nigeria as Cast Study Countries*, IOM, Geneva.

Israel, M. and Hay, I. (2006) *Research Ethics for Social Scientists: Between Ethical Conduct and Regulatory Compliance*, Sage Publications Ltd., London.

Kneebone, S. (2016) Comparative Regional Protection Framework for Refugees: Norms and Norm Entrepreneurs, *International Journal of Human Rights*, 20(2), 153–172.

Kunz, E.F. (Summer 1973) The Refugee in Flight: Kinetic Models and Forms of Displacement, *International Migration Review*, 7(2), 125–146.

Malkki, L. (1995) *Purity and Exile*, The University of Chicago Press, Chicago.

Nah, A.M. (2016) Networks and Norm Entrepreneurship amongst Local Civil Society Actors: Advancing Refugee Protection in the Asia Pacific Region, *International Journal of Human Rights*, 20(2), 223–240.

Reynell, J. (1989) *Political Pawns: Refugees on the Thai-Kampuchean Border*, Refugee Studies Programme, University of Oxford, Oxford.

Turton, D. (2004) *The Meaning of Place in a World of Movement: Lessons from Long-Term Field Research in Southern Ethiopia*, Working Paper No. 18, Refugee Studies Centre, University of Oxford, Oxford.

UNHCR (2000) *The State of the World's Refugees*, United Nations High Commissioner for Refugees, Geneva.

UNHCR (2005, January) *Speech at the 9th International Association for the Study of Forced Migration Biennial Conference*, Latin America Representative of UNHCR, San Paulo, Brazil.

Welch, M. and Schuster, L. (2005) Detention of Asylum Seekers in the UK and USA: Deciphering Noisy and Quiet Constructions, *Punishment & Society*, 7(4), 397–417.

8 Contemporary issues, the refugee 'crisis' and proposed 'solutions'

Introduction

This book has been written during a global pandemic when the 'age of migration' (Castles *et al.*, 2014) outlined at the beginning of this book has been questioned, social distancing in places such as camps in Greece and Bangladesh has been impossible, the death of George Floyd and the subsequent Black Lives Matters movement have seen statues of colonists and slavers fall, and new questions are being asked about the lives of those seeking asylum or being forced to migrate across the globe.

This chapter introduces and addresses just some of the contemporary situations for the forcibly displaced, arbitrarily drawn from those occurring during the past five years. However, as will be seen in cases such as the Rohingya from Burma, it is always vital to look at the historic backdrop to these situations that are today being described as refugee or migration 'crisis' situations. A discussion around the 'migration crisis' following refugees and migrants crossing the Mediterranean and Aegean Seas reinforces the idea that viewing the historic backdrop and backstories involved is essential to understanding migration but also appropriate policy responses, protection and assistance. Some recent ideas to find solutions for the forcibly displaced are outlined, and some speculatory comments are made on the impact of the COVID-19 global pandemic and how the study of forced migration might engage further in issues of race and racism. Suggested further reading then completes this book.

The Rohingya from Myanmar

The Rohingya from Rakhine State in Myanmar are considered to be amongst the most persecuted minorities in the world. This Muslim group who lives in a majority Buddhist country, has experienced discrimination and persecution for decades. This has included arbitrary arrest, detention, extortion, severe limitations on marriage and freedom of movement and a range of other human rights violations, not least deprivation of their Myanmar citizenship (Ibrahim, 2016).

This **deprivation of citizenship** has occurred over time, from being described as *Rohingya* in the 1961 Census, to the 1974 Constitution, which removed the status of Rohingya and insisted on identity cards describing them as 'Foreigners', again reinforced in the 1982 Burmese Citizenship Law. As a direct result of their statelessness, the Rohinyga now face the denial of basic human rights. It has been argued by de Chickera (2018) that the statelessness of the Rohingya has not been adequately factored into the responses to the Rohingya situation. As de Chickera suggests:

> There are many reasons why this is so, and many seen and unseen consequences. It reflects a wider lack of capacity among humanitarian and other actors to identify statelessness, recognise how it relates to their work and respond accordingly. It also reflects a lack of serious engagement – by all influential players – with the most important, structural and root causes of the crisis. Inevitably, this has contributed to the cyclical denial of identity, persecution, displacement, lack of protection and repatriation that has plagued the Rohingya since the 1970s.
>
> (de Chickera, 2018:7)

Rohingya refugees have fled Myanmar before. In 1978, some 290,000 people fled Myanmar, followed by a repatriation of some 180,000 people. Between 1991 and 1992, 260,000 people fled the country, again followed by a repatriation of around 200,000 people. As Crisp recounts, the repatriations in the 1970s and 1990s involved 'large numbers of Rohingya refugees [who] were [sic] returned to Myanmar in a manner that was premature, involuntary and unsafe' (2018:13).

From 2012 onwards the decades of persecution took on a new and intensified form, with violence and segregation escalating (Green *et al.*, 2015:99). International advocacy organisations had been describing the situation for the Rohingya as a process of 'slow-burning genocide' over the past 35 years (Zarni and Cowley, 2014), the final stages of 'a genocidal process' (Green *et al.*, 2015:99), and 'genocide' (Fortify Rights, 2015, 2016, 2017, 2018). During 2015, media reports drew attention to Rohingya refugees having crossed the Andaman Sea and having nowhere to disembark as Southeast Asian countries denied asylum. Media outlets also reported graves found in jungle camps in southern Thailand bordering Malaysia, describing how 'smugglers' and/or 'traffickers' were exploiting and holding people in camps for months while ransoms were demanded from their families inside Myanmar.

Thereafter, consistent reports have indicated that **since violence in Rakhine State in August 2017, more than 670,000 Rohingya have crossed into Bangladesh**, joining existing Rohingya communities and a total of some 900,000 people, one of the largest concentrations of refugees in the world. This violence by the Myanmar security forces against the Rohingya, replicated the killings, rapes, torture, enforced disappearances, destruction of property and looting of villages seen in other ethnic States across the country. Attacks against the civilian population were considered to have been systematic and coordinated, intended to drive the Rohingya population out of Myanmar. For example, an attack on the village of Tula Toli on 30 August 2017 saw hundreds of men separated from women and children, rounded up along a riverbank and executed in front of their families. Many women and children were killed or raped, and the village was looted and burned to the ground. As Human Rights Watch (2017) demonstrates with satellite images, whole villages were destroyed in Rakhine State during this violence.

Refugee camps in Bangladesh are spread over an area in Cox's Bazar and, since their arrival, overcrowding, health issues, and cyclone and monsoon preparedness have been key considerations. People remain in precarious situations, almost completely reliant on humanitarian assistance. Discussions around hosting Rohingya on an uninhabited and muddy Bay of Bengal island called Bhasan Char have been ongoing, seen as a temporary arrangement to ease congestion in the Cox's Bazar camps. Beyond Bangladesh, other Rohingya refugees have tried sea routes to Thailand, Malaysia and other Southeast Asian countries. There are also an estimated 40,000 Rohingya living in India. However, refugee camps close to Delhi in India were burned down in April 2018. Discussions about repatriation to Myanmar have also been ongoing in Bangladesh with commentators suggesting that this is premature and, like the repatriations of the 1970s and 1990s, likely to be unsafe, involuntary and undignified given that repressive laws and policies are yet to be dismantled within Myanmar.

A report by the All-Party Parliamentary Group on the Rights of the Rohingya have called for a 'whole-of-society-approach' to longer-term investment in Cox's Bazar in order to deliver 'triple wins' for host communities and Rohingya whilst at the same time advancing Bangladesh's development ambitions and encouraging progress towards the SDGs by supporting the 'left-behind communities in Cox's Bazar' (APPG, 2019:5). This report also challenges the culture of impunity within Myanmar, the 'overwhelming evidence collated . . . that the crimes committed against the Rohingya by the Myanmar military amount to crimes against humanity – and possibly genocide' and the need for referral to the International Criminal Court without further delay (APPG, 2019:6). In 2019 Gambia took Myanmar to the International Court of Justice (ICJ) alleging the crime of Genocide against the Rohingya. Myanmar was represented by the Nobel Peace Prize Laureate, Aung San Suu Kyi, who defended the military's actions.

Points for discussion – the Rohingya

- Why do you consider that repatriation became a key narrative of the Rohingya situation so quickly after people arrived into Bangladesh?
- Why do you think this 'durable solution' was the key focus and not local integration or resettlement options?
- How would it be possible for the Rohingya to return to Myanmar in a safe, voluntary and dignified way?
- What laws and policies would have to be dismantled before the Rohingya returned to Myanmar?

- What support might the international community give to Bangladesh to support progress towards the SDGs, and how does this relate to the Rohingya population in Cox's Bazar?

The Mediterranean 'migration crisis'

During 2015 over one million people crossed the Mediterranean to Europe, and this movement of people very quickly became referred to as Europe's 'migration crisis' (Crawley *et al.*, 2018; Crawley *et al.*, 2016; IOM, 2016; MSF, 2015). At least 3,770 people were thought to have died in the sea whilst trying to make this journey during this same year, and in the previous year, 2014, that number was 3,379 people (IOM, 2016). Although this 'migration crisis' was represented as something new and/or seen as uncontrolled and unregulated movement, the movement of people across the Mediterranean to Europe has taken place since the 1990s (Crawley *et al.*, 2018). However, as MSF commented, 2015: 'will be remembered as the year in which Europe catastrophically failed in its responsibility to respond to the urgent needs of assistance and protection of hundreds of thousands of vulnerable people' (MSF, 2015:4).

MSF (2015) and other commentators also pointed out how **this 'crisis' was met by volunteers and ordinary citizens in the vacuum left behind by State and NGO assistance programmes**. MSF also outlined how this was less a crisis of migration and more a crisis of policy that failed to recognise the need for safe and legal routes, policy that was expensive, disjointed and inconsistent (Crawley *et al.*, 2018). As Crawley *et al.* (2018) suggest, this also failed to recognise historic events and processes leading up to 2015. In 2008 there had been a global financial crisis that had triggered European austerity policies. The Arab Spring of 2011; the Greek debt crisis; wars in Syria, Iraq and Libya; a security crisis related to the rise of terrorism; and humanitarian emergencies/ crisis across Turkey, Jordan, Lebanon, along the Balkan route and in countries of first arrival such as Greece and Italy were all factors in the emergence of this so-called migration crisis (Crawley *et al.*, 2018).

Additionally, the backstories of those arriving – the causes and dynamics involved in their decisions to make such journeys and the fragmented nature of these journeys – were largely lost in Europe's 'migration crisis'. This untold story failed to distinguish the different characteristics of those making the journey as well as distinct routes via Italy and Greece and their differing responses. As Crawley *et al.* (2018) outline, Italy had experience of refugees and migrants arriving by sea, at least since 1991 when a boat – the *Vlora* – with thousands of people from Albania arrived in Apulia. Italy had also put in place a set of measures since 2011, following the Arab Spring, with search and rescue systems in place and a system for disembarkation. Greece, having had more limited arrivals by sea, was less prepared for the sea arrivals, leading to chaotic scenes and inadequate humanitarian responses which remain in place on the island of Lesvos to date.

Routes taken to Italy (the Central Mediterranean route) and Greece (the Eastern Mediterranean route) were composed of people with differing characteristics (Crawley *et al.*, 2018). Those arriving in Italy came from diverse countries of origin such as Eritrea, Nigeria, Somalia and Sudan and only around 3% from Syria – having crossed by boat mainly from Libya. Their routes prior to this were diverse with North, West and East African routes converging in Libya. Those arriving in Greece mainly came from three countries – Syria, Afghanistan and Iraq – having mainly travelled through Turkey from neighbouring countries or taken routes via the Middle East or North Africa. The oversimplification of the use of 'smugglers' and 'smuggling networks' has been the focus of attention by European governments, although considered a necessity (however violent and abusive) by those making these journeys (Crawley *et al.*, 2018).

Europe's response to people arriving across the Mediterranean, whilst small in comparison to other contexts of displacement, was based upon 'a series of flawed assumptions about the dynamics of migration across the Mediterranean' and little understanding of the complexities or factors that led people to leave in the first instance (Crawley *et al.*, 2018:129). That the EU was slow to respond, failed to share responsibility for arrivals in a principled or pragmatic way and was based on preventing or discouraging people from making the journeys became apparent during subsequent years (Crawley *et al.*, 2018; see also Chapter 7 on containment strategies and deterrence policies).

Closing borders, building fences and reinforcing border controls led in time to an agreement between the EU and Turkey in March 2016, wherein new arrivals from Greece were returned to Turkey in exchange for resettlement of Syrian nationals from Turkey to the EU, established on the basis of Turkey being a 'safe third country' to process such systems (Crawley *et al.*, 2018). Another agreement, between the EU and the Libyan coast guard to return people intercepted in the Mediterranean to Libya has led to use of detention, migrants being sold as slaves within Libya, extortion, torture, rapes and deaths of those attempting this journey.

Points for discussion – the 'migration crisis' and the EU

- Why do you consider that this movement of people was represented as a 'crisis'?
- Why do you think that this has not been the case in other humanitarian contexts that may have been larger in scale?
- What 'durable solutions' have been emphasised within the EU?
- How does this reflect on Europe's creation of the 1951 Refugee Convention and its associated Protocol immediately following WWII?
- What impact will this so-called crisis have on the future of protection of refugees and the principle of asylum within the EU and across the globe?
- What role do you think 'smugglers' and 'traffickers' had within this movement of people?

Human smuggling and human trafficking

Growing interest in the routes people take to Europe since 2015 has, as noted by Crawley *et al.* (2018), seen media attention on the numbers of people crossing the Mediterranean. During this period the terms **human smuggling and** *human trafficking* **became almost interchangeable**, despite their distinct basis in international and domestic law and policy. With borders closing or becoming more impenetrable, fences being erected, and further deterrence policies being introduced, people's reliance on agents, brokers or facilitators necessarily increased. Alongside these 'smugglers', the use of abuse, violence, extortion and/or exploitation has become increasingly apparent within literature on human trafficking (see Chapter 4).

In recent research on human trafficking from Vietnam, Albania and Nigeria to the UK, 'vulnerability' to trafficking was found to be influenced by a constellation of overlapping and interconnected factors which cut across individual, household and family, community and structural levels, varying from country to country (Hynes *et al.*, 2019). Journeys to the UK were found to often begin with rational decision-making, hope, promises of employment and accommodation but were sometimes based on unreliable information about costs, length, dangers, legal requirements, alternatives, or conditions en route and at destination. The desire, aspiration and hope to have a safer future were key aspects of this. Once journeys had begun, they often became progressively precarious, with individuals facing new, rapidly changing 'vulnerabilities'. These included violence, extortion, abuse, exploitation, lack of food or water and, sometimes, death. Journeys from Vietnam, for example, were found to be particularly dangerous with widespread violence, abuse and exploitation in multiple locations and over extended periods of time.

This research found routes to the UK were often very **fragmented, long and complicated, sometimes undertaken in stages and taking months or years** to complete (Hynes *et al.*, 2019). The journey from France to the UK was recounted as being particularly problematic and fraught with dangers with interviewees recounting journeys clinging onto the chassis of lorries or travelling in poorly ventilated containers or refrigerated lorries. This part often took the longest time to complete with interviewees recounting how travel from Lens, Dunkirk or from an informal camp in Calais referred to as 'the Jungle' was perceived to be the most dangerous stage of their journeys after waiting weeks or months to embark (Hynes *et al.*, 2019).

Part of the ongoing debate concerns whether categorisations and labels constructed by policy makers or agencies with mandates to protect people who meet particular criteria are useful when thinking about (forced) migration. The terms *human trafficking*, *victims of trafficking*, *potential victims of trafficking* and *survivor of trafficking* are no exception and require vigorous interpretation.

Points for discussion – smuggling and trafficking of human beings

- Why do you think human trafficking has been approached from a criminal justice and organised crime perspective rather than a human rights perspective?
- How are policies surrounding migration related to human trafficking?
- What might be the impact of being labelled a 'victim' or 'survivor' of human trafficking?

The quest for solutions – *Refuge*, *Refugia*, island nations and rights–based approaches

In recent years the failure of the refugee system to protect people forced to migrate and/or seek asylum has been a key topic of debate. A recent book, *Refuge: Transforming a Broken Refugee System*, by Betts and Collier (2017) argued that the world had, until recently, largely ignored the plight of refugees but that the 2015 'crisis' in the Mediterranean meant that, for the first time, refugees moving 'spontaneously' in large numbers from the poorer to the richest regions of the world had woken up the world to their plight, particularly those displaced within and from Syria. The authors suggested that, for the first time in its history, Europe was receiving a 'mass influx of refugees from outside of the European region' (Ibid., 2017:2). In April 2015, 700 people died crossing to Lampedusa, part of the autonomous region of Sicily, Italy, which saw the media proclaiming a 'global refugee crisis'. Betts and Collier refer to this as a 'European crisis' and a 'crisis of politics rather than a crisis of numbers' that led to a 'muddled and incoherent' response to the 'rickety boats manned by gangs whose core business was migrant-smuggling' (Ibid., 2017:2).

Against this backdrop, Betts and Collier set out to answer a key question – what, in the 21st century, should the world do about refugees? To answer this question, *Refuge* looked at why the refugee system was not working and what needed to be done to build a system that works.

To do this they examined what is referred to as the 'broken system' of refugee protection, outlining how the two main roles of UNHCR – to provide protection to refugees and to find solutions to their plight – are not being met by existing 'durable solutions'. Instead they suggest that **in the 21st century, new ideas are required, ideas that 'harness the remarkable opportunities of globalization'** (Ibid., 2017:9), find ways of allowing refugees to work, enable these jobs through the internet and engage with new actors including the private sector, civil society, diaspora organisations and refugee-led community organisations (Ibid., 2017:10). Their argument that there needs to be a paradigm shift away from a focus on 'vulnerabilities' and towards the 'capabilities' of refugees is important but not new, having been a key thread for example of the work of Barbara Harrell-Bond from the 1980s onwards (see Key Thinker Box 2.1).

What is new is the presentation of **global capitalism coming to the rescue of the refugee system through the creation of Special Economic Zones (SEZs)** which offer tax breaks and reduced regulation to richer countries. This idea gained traction in Jordan and Lebanon in 2015, and a pilot – the 'Jordan Compact' – was subsequently designed. This involved Jordan receiving around $2 billion in assistance and investment in exchange for offering up to 200,000 work permits to Syrians for use in SEZs where refugees would be employed alongside nationals (Ibid., 2017:173–176). Acknowledging that SEZs have had a bad reputation in the past due to their being associated with exploitative low wage labour, the authors suggest adaptation to ensure respect for (undefined) human rights and that ethical practices are upheld (Ibid., 2017:183).

Unsurprisingly, there have been **multiple critiques of the idea of utilizing refugees as merely economic resources** from whom global business can make a profit (Crawley, 2017; Newby and Gibbons, 2017; White, 2017). The reputation of SEZs alluded to by the authors has been elaborated upon, with commentators outlining how hiring workers who are easily exploited and can be paid below prevailing minimum wages. Others have focussed on the way SEZs could be another way of managing and containing migrant labour so as to prevent people entering into other countries, including those within the EU.

Both content and style have been broadly critiqued as being overly simplistic and superficial in their presentation of facts and subsequent analysis (Newby and Gibbons, 2017; White, 2017). For an extensive thread over Twitter critiquing this book, see Benjamin Thomas White's live-tweets: @rain_later.

Since 2015, two Oxford University Professors – Robin Cohen and Nicholas Van Hear – have been engaging in public debate about the problem and situations of 'mass displacement', exploring radical proposals and conceiving new ideas themselves (Cohen and Van Hear, 2017:494). They point out that the end of identity conflicts fed by ethnic, nationalistic and religious loyalties is not in sight, there is little confidence in the three 'durable solutions' on offer for refugees and that those who support tolerant attitudes towards refugees and asylum seekers and who respect rights are 'under fierce attack from right-wing and populist forces' (Ibid., 2017:494–495). As such they consider it unrealistic, in fact naïve, to continue to rely on the 1951 Refugee Convention and its 1967 Protocol, **proposing instead a transnational policy – Refugia** – to move towards peace, security, employment and contentment for those who are displaced.

The proposal involves a form of 'transnational citizenship', defined by having been displaced and based around 'refugees highly limited integration into existing, legally recognized, nation-states' (Ibid., 2017:495). It is not therefore territorially based and is not a new nation-state or single legally defined zone. The proposal is that 'Refugia' would be a 'transnational or cross-national entity, a set of connections . . . between different sites developed through initiatives mainly taken by refugees and displaced people themselves' (Ibid., 2017:497). This, the authors suggest, is based on 'pragmatic utopianism', with **'Refugians' (the citizens of Refugia)** holding dual affinities to Refugia and States which license their territories and the ability to move between different parts of Refugia, paying taxes to both Refugia and the nation-state. Van Hear's previous and influential work on diaspora communities has informed this proposal, with the suggestion that 'Refugia already exists in a fragmentary and highly imperfect form' where refugees have links with more fortunate kin and friends within their diaspora communities (Ibid., 2017:498).

In an article for *The Independent* newspaper in the UK (28 July 2018), Crawley outlines concerns about the way academics are attempting to solve the 'refugee crisis', citing the idea of Refugia', Special Economic Zones and other ideas which have included 'Europe in Africa' and the 'Refugee

Nation', both based on territorial solutions. **Europe in Africa** was a proposal for a new city-state to be built on an artificial island on the shallow Tunisian Plateau between the Exclusive Economic Zone of Tunisia and Italy, as a secure place for people who have to flee their own country and want to reach Europe. The seabed on which the island would be erected, and its surrounding territorial waters, would be rented for 99 years from Tunisia and Italy by the European Union. The **Refugee Nation** proposal was about the creation of a State for the millions of stateless people around the world. Other proposals involving **creation of refugee islands** by wealthy benefactors have not yet yielded solutions.

Crawley considers Refugia to be based on flawed conceptual underpinnings and assumptions about what it means to be a refugee, pointing out that refugees are not a homogenous group, coming from different backgrounds, with different nationalities, languages, religions and cultures. Simply coming together on the basis of having been displaced and tasked with organizing and governing themselves is not, in the eyes of Crawley, feasible. The idea of Refugia also lets States who may have ratified international Conventions 'off the hook' and ignores examples around the world where communities have mobilized support for refugees and, in doing so, have improved community relations. Crawley also outlines how **ideas to solve the 'crisis' tend to be skewed towards the Global North**, often leading to 'out of sight and out of mind' solutions based on maintenance of the status quo, which do not challenge global inequalities.

Perhaps more concretely, and relating to migration more broadly than solely forced migrants, the former UN Special Rapporteur on the Human Rights of Migrants – Professor François Crépeau – proposed **eight goals to transform the way States manage migration** in a 2017 article for *Refugees Deeply* and other publications (2015, 2017). In this he suggests that the language deployed about migration is problematic but that **the 'migration crisis' is policy-driven**. Migration itself is a natural part of human existence; it is not a crime or a problem and has the potential to remedy many social ills. The eight goals highlighted are:

- Goal 1: Offer regular, safe, accessible and affordable mobility solutions to all migrants, regardless of status or skill level
- Goal 2: Protect the labour and human rights of all migrant workers, regardless of status and circumstances
- Goal 3: Ensure respect for human rights at border controls – including return, readmission and post-return monitoring – and establish accountability mechanisms
- Goal 4: End the use of detention as a border-management and deterrence tool against migrants
- Goal 5: Provide effective access to justice for all migrants
- Goal 6: Ensure easy access for all migrants to basic services, including education and health

- Goal 7: Protect all migrants from all forms of discrimination and violence, including racism, xenophobia, sexual and gender-based violence, and hate speech
- Goal 8: Increase the collection and analysis of disaggregated data on migration and mobility

With respect to refugees from Syria, Professor Crépeau discussed how the option of resettlement could work:

> We should collectively offer to resettle one million Syrians over the next five years. For a country like the UK, this would probably be around 14,000 Syrians a year for five years. For Canada, it would mean less than 9,000 a year for five years – a drop in the bucket. For Australia, it would probably be less than 5,000 per year for five years. We can manage that.

Drawing on historic examples in an article for *The Guardian* in the UK, Professor Crépeau suggested that:

> We should do for the Syrians what we did 30 years ago for the Indo-Chinese, and that's a comprehensive plan of action where all global north countries – and that includes Europe, Canada, the US, Australia and New Zealand and probably other countries – offer a great number of Syrians an option so that they would line up in Istanbul, Amman and Beirut for a meaningful chance to resettle, instead of paying thousands of euros only to die with their children in the Mediterranean.

This idea to increase resettlement options for Syrian refugees has run alongside other recent policy suggestions to:

- Restore the Mediterranean search and rescue operation to at least its 2014 level
- Work on equitable responsibility-sharing across the EU
- Improve family reunification schemes
- Ensure greater recognition of the drivers of migration in refugee-generating countries (conflict, human rights violations, protracted socio-economic hardship)
- Provide safe and orderly mechanisms for asylum seekers to reach EU
- Develop fairer Refugee Status Determination processes
- Stop conflating 'traffickers'/'trafficking' with 'smugglers'/'smuggling' in debate
- Address the root causes of forced displacement

As Crawley *et al.* (2018) outline, there is a **need for a new and rights-based approach** to migration in Europe. This needs to address the drivers of migration, provide access to protection and rights where needed, create safe and legal

Figure 8.1 Refugee Shelter

entry routes to avoid recourse to routes that involve exploitation and/or human suffering and, importantly, consider moving beyond the current politics of containment that have contributed to the failure of migration policies to date.

Whether this quest for solutions offers some hope on the horizon for those who have experienced forced displacement remains to be seen. However, it is unlikely that any real solutions will be found until there is engagement and a willingness to listen to refugees themselves and engage with the realities of their lives (Hynes and Loughna, 2005; see also Figure 8.1). Some movement towards this in the form of a **Global Refugee-led Network (GRN)** of 650 people, many of whom are refugees, stateless, asylum seekers or people who have experienced human trafficking, provides some hope that this may be in motion.

Points for discussion – the quest for solutions

- What key principles do you think should be involved in any quest for solutions for the world's displaced?
- How might these work in practice?
- Who would be involved?
- What logistical challenges would you anticipate?

Today's 'children on the move'

As outlined in Chapter 6, there are children on the move who have been displaced as a result of conflict or natural disasters, are stateless, have experienced trafficking or are migrating for better life opportunities (Bhabha, 2011, 2014, 2016; Boyden and Hart, 2007; D'Costa and Toczydlowska, 2017; D'Costa, 2018; Hart, 2006; O'Connell Davidson and Farrow, 2007; Seeberg and Goździak, 2016). There is a variety of reasons why children migrate, voluntarily or involuntarily, with or without parents or primary caregivers.

The umbrella definition of 'children on the move' covers a multitude of categories into which children have – sometimes unhelpfully – been divided. There is no single piece of legislation that systematically addresses the issue of children on the move in the world today (Bhabha *et al.*, 2016). The 1989 United Nations Convention on the Rights of the Child (UNCRC) is the most comprehensive compilation of legal standards for the protection of children, defining children as being below the age of 18 years.

D'Costa and Toczydlowska (2017) outline how, within migration pathways, there is a need to **explicitly recognize the rights of children**, not as migrants or as refugees, but **as children first**. They outline how analysis of child migration reveals a lack of understanding about children's mobility. They point to specific Articles of the UNCRC but also specific goals and targets of the SDGs as ways to address such migration. Their research also indicates how existing European migration assistance **systems, laws, policies and practices are not always child-friendly,** how publications around unaccompanied and separated children can **overlook accompanied, undocumented and/or missing children** and that there is **insufficient understanding of the situation of children who are returned to their country of origin** or to a third country (D'Costa and Toczydlowska, 2017:2). They call for children in migration pathways to be respected and their voices heard. This is something taken up by Bhabha (2018), who discusses **the imperative to enable safe, regular and legal migration for children and young people**, including through expanded educational opportunities.

Bhabha (2011) has also studied child statelessness, prompted by the reflection that family reunification rules and practice privilege adult citizens when considering who has the capacity to initiate reunification. This led Bhabha to question whether children are really considered 'citizens' at all – and what that citizenship brings to them. This brought a consideration of different types of child statelessness – *de jure* (such as children from the Rohingya population), *de facto* (such as undocumented children who cannot turn to a government for protection) and *effective* (children without birth registration who cannot prove the citizenship they have).

As Reale (2008) has outlined, children on the move can be particularly vulnerable to exploitation and abuse, **but movement can be positive for children** when it occurs in safe conditions. There is a need for policy-makers and practitioners to understand the reasons why children are moving, their specific needs and the role of children's decision-making and experiences. Mann (2001) has outlined the networks of support and care issues for separated children, highlighting how the **role of the family is conceived differently in different communities**, that child fostering is a widespread childcare practice in many parts of the world and that the way children are raised and socialized differs enormously across contexts and regions.

It is clear that child protection principles are often subsumed within immigration rules (Pearce *et al.*, 2013), and various studies and examples of documentation have focused on how children and young people are being detailed or deported across the globe. For example, in the US children were separated from their parents at the US-Mexico border by the Department of Homeland Security in 2018 under a policy of 'zero-tolerance' against 'illegal immigration' by the Trump administration. Australia's immigration detention system on Nauru recently received considerable attention as a result of leaked documentation published from inside Nauru detention centre. These documents included more than 2,000 incident reports written by guards, caseworkers and teachers on the remote Pacific island. They detailed events such as self-harm, sexual assaults, child abuse, hunger strikes, assaults and injuries and harm experiences as a result of prolonged detention in Australia's offshore detention camps. These **Australian 'Nauru Files'** can be viewed in an interactive database at: www.theguardian.com/australia-news/ng-interactive/2016/aug/10/the-nauru-files-the-lives-of-asylum-seekers-in-detention-detailed-in-a-unique-database-interactive

For an example of literature on the deportation of children, Gladwell *et al.* (2016) documented the experiences of 25 young people forcibly removed to Afghanistan from the UK (from the 2,018 care leavers forcibly removed from the UK between 2007 and 2016). They found that, without exception, the young people had experienced a range of difficulties on return. These included contact with families, with only 12 of the 25 young people being able to live with their families on return. A **fear of stigma or discrimination** had created a barrier to building friendships, leaving them isolated. Insecurity was a very real part of their lives upon return, with 12 young people having **first-hand experiences of being caught up in bomb blasts or suicide attacks**. Three young people had been threatened or targeted as a result of issues connected to their original claims for asylum, and 7 had been **targeted because of their status as a returnee** to Afghanistan. Continuing their education on return had proved impossible for most, as had finding employment. Many had left Afghanistan again to find a future for themselves.

Points for discussion – children on the move

- What are the key areas of concern for children on the move?

COVID-19

It is too early to understand the full scale of impacts of COVID-19 on people who are forced to migrate. However, with the onset of a global pandemic in 2020, the impossibilities of regular handwashing, social distancing and sanitation in camps were quickly noted across different contexts such as Bangladesh and on the Greek island of Lesbos. The pandemic has also affected other areas of life for refugees. For example, for the Rohingya in Cox's Bazar, Bangladesh, women have been affected by food shortages and an increase in domestic violence, with children witnessing abuse in confined accommodation. This has emphasized how 'home' is not necessarily a safe place for all under any conditions. Lockdowns in India have affected employment and seen price rises of essential commodities. During the pandemic, asylum seekers in shared and often temporary accommodations have experienced being forced to live with strangers. The pandemic has also highlighted the absence of social protection for populations most vulnerable to insecurity, and there is some evidence beginning to emerge that extending social protection policies would be beneficial.

New terms are emerging such as ***forced immobility*** to describe lockdown conditions and such barriers to migration during the pandemic. It is also likely that remittances will be affected, given the enforced lockdown of members of diaspora communities. Although generalisations at this early stage may be unhelpful, there is a danger that migration and responses to those forced to migrate will be even more tightly controlled, with COVID-19 as another reason cited for closing borders. If so, people forced to move may take increasingly dangerous, difficult, invisible and perhaps exploitative journeys to reach safety.

It is also a time to reflect on what positive actions may have emerged out of this pandemic. When NGO staff and volunteers were unable to continue aid distribution and communications during the pandemic, community-based and self-organised groups have emerged in places to cater for the needs of families.

Points for discussion – COVID-19

- What do you think will be the impact of COVID-19 on refugees, asylum seekers, internally displaced persons, stateless people and people who have experienced trafficking?

Race, racism and Black Lives Matter

Since the death of George Floyd and the subsequent Black Lives Matters movement, statues of colonists and slavers have been taken down or fallen during protests. Commentators discussing refugees and IDPs have pointed out the **colonial and paternalistic nature of responses** in the past (Harrell-Bond, 1986). However, this is an area of study that has been especially **slow to engage with the work of decolonising** in terms of both content and methodologies involved (Mayblin and Turner, 2020). Unequal power relations and uneven distribution of resources relating to the study of forced migration are part of this challenge. The contested nature of language, terminology and labelling of forced migrants is often central to analysis in these areas (Zetter, 2007), as outlined in Chapter 2. Mayblin and Turner (2020) have turned towards understanding colonial and imperialistic links in migration studies, critiquing and analysing colonial logics that continue to shape the dynamics of migration and suggesting that use of postcolonial and decolonial scholarship offers a vital way forward. In a body of work, Paula Banerjee explores population movements during colonial periods and calls on forced migration scholars to decolonise a system of knowledge historically informed by colonial assumptions (Banerjee and Samaddar (2019).

Within studies on human trafficking, questions are beginning to be asked about what it looks like to be called a 'victim' or 'survivor' of human trafficking. The term **modern slavery has become part of the terminology with little consideration of its relationship with colonial pasts**. Race and racism are often overlooked in human trafficking debates but, from work in countries with a colonial past, 'race' can play a critical role in the construction of exploitation. The Beyond Trafficking and Slavery (BTS) webpage of Open-Democracy regularly features articles that challenge anti-trafficking structures and focus on structures of exploitation created under European colonisers (see www.opendemocracy.net/en/beyond-trafficking-and-slavery/). This lack of engagement relates to how knowledge is produced in relation to human trafficking. For example, in a recent study of human trafficking from Viet Nam, Albania and Nigeria, it was found that there are a significant lack of studies exploring the lived experiences and perspectives of those who have themselves experienced human trafficking and that there is a need for research into human trafficking within source countries and development of an Indigenous evidence-base (Brodie *et al.*, 2018; Hynes *et al.*, 2019).

As outlined in Key Thinker Box 1.2, Anthony Richmond's seminal 1994 text – *Global Apartheid* – examined globalisation in relation to migration, 'racial conflict' and 'ethnic nationalism'. This text and others that provide historic and nuanced accounts of the 'root causes' and underlying dynamics of migration that involves involuntary movement help to unravel the structures and inequalities of colonialism. Providing an alternative history, from the voices of those who have themselves experienced displacement, may be one way to work towards a comprehensive and historical understanding of forced migration. A movement towards understanding 'race' and racism in this field is long overdue.

Concluding remarks

It remains to be seen whether the new global frameworks for migration contained within the GCR and GCM will provide an opportunity to realise a better, more responsible and comprehensive international response to forced and/or voluntary migration across the globe. Thus far these frameworks have received mixed reviews with commentators suggesting there are missed opportunities and shortcomings in these Compacts, particularly around the lack of protection for IDPs. The gaps and weaknesses of the GCR and GCM will be explored in the coming years and, over time, many of the conceptual concerns and limitations will be revealed, requiring further examination and research. Part of this is likely to involve a discussion about the implications of climate change on forced migration and the often misused description of 'climate refugees' (Zetter, 2014, 2017). What is clear is that there are multiple examples of forced displacement and protracted displacement around the globe, including children and young people who await viable, safe, dignified and voluntary solutions and this quest for solutions will continue.

Further reading

Banerjee, P. and Samaddar, R. (2019) Why Critical Forced Migration Studies Has to Be Post-Colonial by Nature, in A. Bloch and G. Dona (Eds.), *Forced Migration: Current Issues and Debates*, Routledge, London and New York.

Bhabha, J. (Ed.) (2011) *Children Without a State: A Global Human Rights Challenge*, MIT Press, Cambridge, MA.

Bhabha, J. (2018) *Can We Solve the Migration Crisis?* Polity Press, London.

Cohen, R. and Van Hear, N. (2017) Visions of Refugia: Territorial and Transnational Solutions to Mass Displacement, *Planning Theory & Practice*, 18(3), 494–504.

Crawley, H. (2017) Migration: Refugee Economics, *Nature*, 544, 26–27.

Crawley, H. (2018, 28 July) Why We Need to Protect Refugees from the 'Big Ideas' Designed to Save Them, *The Independent*, view at: www.independent.co.uk/voices/refugee-immigration-europe-migrants-refugia-self-governance-a8467891.html

Crawley, H., Duvelle, F., Jones, K., McMahon, S. and Sigona, N. (2018) *Unravelling Europe's 'Migration Crisis'*, Policy Press, Bristol.

Crawley, H., Duvelle, F., Sigona, N., McMahon, N. and Jones, K. (2016) *Unpacking a Rapidly Changing Scenario: Migration Flows, Routes and Trajectories across the Mediterranean*, Research Brief No.1, Unravelling the Mediterranean Migration Crisis (MEDMIG) Research Brief No.1, view at: www.medmig.info/

de Chickera, A. (2018, October) Statelessness and Identity in the Rohingya Refugee Crisis, in Rohingya Refugees in Bangladesh: The Humanitarian Response, *Humanitarian Exchange*, (73).

Ibrahim, A. (2016) *The Rohingyas: Inside Myanmar's Hidden Genocide*, C. Hurst & Co., London.

IOM (2016) *Mixed Migration: Flows in the Mediterranean and Beyond: Compilation of Available Data and Information 2015*, IOM, Geneva.

References

All Party Parliamentary Group on the Rights of the Rohingya (2019) *'A New Shape of Catastrophe': Two Years on from the 2017 Rohingya Crisis*, All Party Parliamentary Group on the Rights of the Rohingya, London.

Betts, A. and Collier, P. (2017) *Refuge: Transforming a Broken Refugee System*, Penguin Random House UK, Milton Keynes.

Bhabha, J. (2014) *Child Migration and Human Rights in a Global Age*, Princeton University Press, Princeton and Oxford.

Bhabha, J. *et al.* (2016) *Children on the Move: An Urgent Human Rights and Child Protection Priority*, Harvard FXB Center for Health and Human Rights, Boston.

Boyden, J. and Hart, J. (2007) The Statelessness of the World's Children, *Children & Society*, 21, 237–248.

Brodie, I., Spring, D., Hynes, P., Burland, P., Dew, J., Gani-Yusuf, L., Tran, H.T., Lenja, V. and Thurnham, A. (2018) *'Vulnerability' to Human Trafficking: A Study of Viet Nam, Albania, Nigeria and the UK*, University of Bedfordshire and International Organization for Migration (IOM), London.

Castles, S., de Haas, H. and Miller, M. (2014) *The Age of Migration: International Population Movements in the Modern World* (5th ed.), Guildford Press, New York.

Crépeau, F. (2015, April 22) UN's Francois Crepeau on the Refugee Crisis: 'Instead of Resisting Migration, Let's Organise it', *The Guardian*, view at: www.theguardian.com/world/2015/apr/22/uns-francois-crepeau-on-the-refugee-crisis-instead-of-resisting-migration-lets-organise-it?CMP=share_btn_tw

Crisp, J. (2018, October) 'Primitive People': The Untold Story of UNHCR's Historical Engagement with Rohingya Refugees, *Humanitarian Exchange*, (73).

D'Costa, B. (2018) Catching Dreams and Building Hopes for Children: A Research-led Policy Agenda on Migration and Displacement, *Migration Policy Practice*, VIII(2).

D'Costa, B. and Toczydlowska, E. (2017) *'Not Refugee Children, Not Migrant Children, Children First': Lack of a Systematic and Integrated Approach*, Innocenti Research Brief No.15, UNICEF.

Fortify Rights (2015) *United Nations: Establish Independent Investigation into Genocide in Myanmar*, Fortify Rights, Thailand, view at: www.fortifyrights.org/publication-20151029.html

Fortify Rights (2016) *"Everywhere is Trouble": An Update on the Situation of Rohingya Refugees in Thailand, Malaysia and Indonesia*, Fortify Rights and Burmese Rohingya Organization UK, Fortify Rights, US, Switzerland and Southeast Asia.

Fortify Rights (2017) *"They Tried to Kill Us All": Atrocity Crimes against Rohingya Muslims in Rakhine State, Myanmar*, Fortify Rights, United States Holocaust Memorial Museum and Simon-Skjodt Center for the Prevention of Genocide, Fortify Rights, US, Switzerland and Southeast Asia.

Fortify Rights (2018) *"They Gave Them Long Swords": Preparations for Genocide and Crimes Against Humanity Against Rohingya Muslims in Rakhine State, Myanmar*, Fortify Rights US, Switzerland and Southeast Asia.

Gladwell, C., Bowerman, E., Norman, B. and Dickson, S. with Ghafoor, A. (2016) *After Return: Documenting the Experiences of Young People Forcibly Removed to Afghanistan*, Refugee Support Network, London.

Green, P., MacManus, T. and de la Cour Venning, A. (2015) *Countdown to Annihilation: Genocide in Myanmar*, Economic and Social Research Council (ESRC), International State Crime Initiative, Queen Mary University of London (QMUL), London.

Harrell-Bond, B. (1986) *Imposing Aid: Emergency Assistance to Refugees*, Oxford University Press, Oxford.

Hart, J. (2006) Saving Children: What Role for Anthropology? *Anthropology Today*, 22, 5–8.

Human Rights Watch (2017) *Burma: Methodical Massacre at Rohingya Village*, Human Rights Watch, New York.

Hynes, P., Burland, P., Thurnham, A., Dew, J., Gani-Yusuf, L., Lenja, V. and Hong Thi Tran with Olatunde, A. and Gaxha, A. (2019) *'Between Two Fires': Understanding Vulnerabilities and the Support Needs of People from Albania, Viet Nam and Nigeria Who Have Experienced Human Trafficking into the UK*, University of Bedfordshire and International Organization for Migration (IOM), London.

Hynes, P. and Loughna, S. (2005, January) *Did Anybody Ask the Refugee? Rethinking Durable Solutions*, at 9th International Conference of the International Association for the Study of Forced Migration (IASFM), Sao Paulo, Brazil.

Mann, G. (2001) *Networks of Support: A Literature Review of Care Issues for Separated Children*, Save the Children, Sweden and Refugee Studies Centre, Oxford.

Mayblin, L. and Turner, J. (2020) *Migration Studies and Colonialism*, Polity Press, Cambridge.

Medecines Sans Frontieres (MSF) (2015) *Obstacle Course to Europe: A Policy-Made Humanitarian Crisis at EU Borders*, MSF, Belgium.

Newby, T. and Gibbons, R. (2017) *'Refuge: Transforming a Broken System' – But Into What?* CARE Insights, view at: https://insights.careinternational.org.uk/development-blog/refuge-transforming-a-broken-refugee-system-but-into-what

O'Connell Davidson, J. and Farrow, C. (2007) *Child Migration and the Construction of Vulnerability*, Save the Children, Sweden.

Pearce, J.J., Hynes, P. and Bovarnick, S. (2013) *Trafficked Young People: Breaking the Wall of Silence*, Routledge, London.

Reale, D. (2008) *Away From Home: Protecting and Supporting Children on the Move*, Save the Children, London.

Seeberg, M.L. and Goździak, E. (2016) *Contested Childhoods: Growing up in Migrancy*, IMIS-COE Research Series, Springer International Publishing, Heidelberg, Germany.

White, B.J. (2017) Refuge and History: A Critical Reading of a Polemic, *Migration and Society: Advances in Research*, 2, 107–118.

Zarni, M. and Cowley, A. (2014) The Slow-Burning Genocide of Myanmar's Rohingya, *Washington International Law Journal*, 23(3), 683–754.

Zetter, R. (2007) More Labels, Fewer Refugees: Remaking the Refugee Label in an Era of Globalization, *Journal of Refugee Studies*, 20(2), 172–192.

Zetter, R. (2014) The Environment-Mobility Nexus: Reconceptualising the Links between Environmental Stress, Mobility and Power, in E. Fiddian-Qasmiyeh, G. Loescher, K. Long and N. Sigona (Eds.), *The Oxford Handbook of Refugee and Forced Migration Studies*, Oxford University Press, Oxford.

Zetter, R. (2017) Why They Are Not Refugees – Climate Change, Environmental Degradation and Population Displacement, *Siirtolaisuus-Migration Quarterly*, 44(1), 23–28.

Index

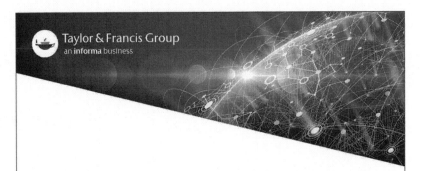